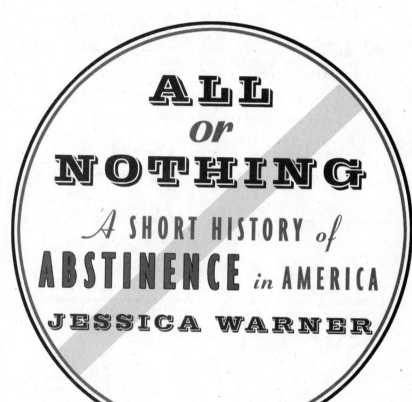

ALL
or
NOTHING

A SHORT HISTORY of
ABSTINENCE in AMERICA

JESSICA WARNER

EMBLEM

McClelland & Stewart

Cloth edition published 2008
Emblem edition published 2010

Emblem is an imprint of McClelland & Stewart Ltd.
Emblem and colophon are registered trademarks
of McClelland & Stewart Ltd.

Library of Congress Control Number: 2009935319

Library and Archives Canada Cataloguing in Publication

Warner, Jessica
All or nothing : a short history of abstinence in America / Jessica Warner.

Previously published under title: The day George Bush stopped drinking.
ISBN 978-0-7710-8854-4

1. Temperance – United States – History. 2. United States – Moral
conditions. 3. Social problems – United States – History. 4. United States –
Social conditions.
I. Warner, Jessica. Day George Bush stopped drinking. II. Title.

HN57.W278 2010   178'.10973   C2009-905031-5

We acknowledge the financial support of the Government of Canada
through the Book Publishing Industry Development Program and that
of the Government of Ontario through the Ontario Media Development
Corporation's Ontario Book Initiative. We further acknowledge the
support of the Canada Council for the Arts and the Ontario Arts Council
for our publishing program.

Cover images: Engaged couple © Kamphi; wine bottles © Irochka; wine
glasses © Rzymu; meat © Andrea Go; beer and cocktails © Migutas; marijuana © Robodread; pig © Artur Nawrocki; cigarette © Jiri Moucka; kissing
couple © Jim Mills, all Dreamstime.com; cow © Brailescu Cristian;
background texture © Maugli, both Shutterstock.com
Cover design: Kelly Hill

Typeset in Goudy by M&S, Toronto
Printed and bound in Canada

This book is printed on processed chlorine-free paper that is 100% recycled,
ancient-forest friendly (40% post-consumer waste).

ANCIENT FOREST
FRIENDLY

McClelland & Stewart Ltd.
75 Sherbourne Street
Toronto, Ontario
M5A 2P9
www.mcclelland.com

I   2   3   4   5   14   13   12   11   10

To Roberto Sabatino Lopez.
Belatedly

CONTENTS

PREFACE

Seventy, it won't make it,

Eighty, God won't take it,

Ninety, that's close,

Ninety-nine and a half is almost,

But get your hundred,

Ninety-nine and a half won't do.

"Ninety-Nine and a Half,"

as recorded by Dorothy Love Coates

and the Original Gospel Harmonettes, circa 1950

In 1986, on his fortieth birthday, George W. Bush suddenly stopped drinking. He refused to go into the reasons behind his decision, other than to allude to boyish pranks and glancing brushes with the law. What he did not mention was that he had been arrested on at least two occasions – for disorderly conduct in 1966, and for driving under the influence of alcohol in 1976.[1] Whether he was genuinely alcoholic was less clear. Bush himself has always resisted that label, saying only that he was "addicted" to alcohol. "I wasn't a knee-walking drunk," he told a group of teenagers in 2007. "I had too much to drink one night, and the next day I didn't have any."[2]

The truth was that Bush's decision had little to do with his drinking. It came just as he was starting to identify himself as an evangelical Christian, and as his commitment to evangelicalism has grown, so has his commitment to abstinence as a solution to a wide range of problems – to drug abuse, to teenage pregnancies, to the AIDS epidemic in sub-Saharan Africa. As governor of Texas, he liked to tell teenagers to avoid all sexual activity until they had entered into a "biblical marriage relationship." As a presidential candidate in 1999 and 2000, he talked endlessly about sexual morality. "I have been faithful to my wife," he would say when the subject of then president Bill Clinton's sexual transgressions came up. (When reporters pressed him on the subject and asked whether he himself had been chaste until marriage, he became evasive, saying only, "I think the thing that baby boomers have to say is not, 'Did we make mistakes?' but 'Have we learned from our mistakes and are we willing to share the wisdom?'")[3] As president of the United States, he would preside over a vast increase in federal funding for abstinence-only sex education, with expenditures peaking at US$176 million in 2007.

My goal in writing this book is to explore why abstinence is so important to evangelicals like George W. Bush. The implications would be minimal if abstinence were a private virtue and nothing more. But as Bush's example makes all too clear, the tendency in American history has been for abstinence to spill over into the public sphere. Temperance began as a voluntary movement and ended with Prohibition. The sexual purity movement of the late nineteenth and early twentieth centuries led to legislation that made it illegal to transport females across state lines for "immoral purposes" (the Mann Act). The New Virginity, an evangelical movement spearheaded by the Southern Baptist Convention, has shaded into the use of federal tax dollars to pressure public schools into teaching abstinence-only sex education.

Americans have sworn off so many different things at so many different times that a strictly chronological history runs the risk of becoming cluttered and unwieldy. I have opted instead to focus on the concept at crucial junctures in its development, from its origins in eighteenth-century England to its migration, in the late nineteenth and early twentieth centuries, to the American South. Each chapter examines the concept from a different angle, but all return to the same point: America's commitment to abstinence is a function of that country's commitment to an idiosyncratic and especially demanding strain of evangelical Protestantism. As the contours of that creed have changed, so has the face of abstinence. From its high point in the 1830s, the concept has become progressively narrower, shorn first of its social radicalism, next of its all-encompassing asceticism, and last of its post-millennial idealism. The one thing that has not changed is the faith strict evangelicals place in abstinence. More than half are teetotallers. Few use illicit drugs.[8] Almost all continue to believe in premarital chastity.

The doctrine that guides their actions has gone by any number of names over the years – Christian perfection, sanctification, holiness, the second blessing. Its core teaching, that the Christian can conquer sin, is an article of faith among evangelical Protestants. Where they have differed is in how they define sin. The trend has been for that definition to contract over time, and with it, the number of things Americans are willing to give up. The ends abstinence serves have also undergone a startling transformation. Once the handmaiden of feminists such as Susan B. Anthony and abolitionists such as William Lloyd Garrison, abstinence today is primarily associated with conservative evangelicals, with people like James Dobson, Tim LaHaye, and, of course, George W. Bush.

Susan B. Anthony, the greatest of America's suffragists, began her career as a temperance organizer in 1852. Like so many other feminists of her generation, Anthony was also a big believer in sexual purity, writing, in 1875, that "Fathers should be most particular about the men who visit their daughters, and, to further this reform, pure women not only must refuse to meet intimately and to marry impure men, but, finding themselves deceived in their husband, they must refuse to continue in the marriage relation with them." From the Library of Congress Prints and Photographs Division.

The challenge for the historian is twofold: first, to explain why the concept has migrated from one end of the political spectrum to the other, becoming, in the process, a protest against change rather than a force for it; second, to give abstinence its due place in the history of ideas. Abstinence, of course, is not like any other idea. It admits of no gradations, no competing schools of thought, no changes over time – in short, it has none of the features historians look for when they write about ideas. What can be studied are the ends this particular idea has served, and that is why this is as much a book about abstinence as it is an essay on evangelicals and how they see the world.

The question of whether abstinence is good, bad, or indifferent I leave to the reader. But I am convinced that no purpose is served by dismissing the concept out of hand. To do this is to write America's history as H.L. Mencken might have, as a series of unfortunate exchanges between yokels and sophisticates. It also misreads the way ideas work. Ideas that are merely disagreeable, that confer no benefit whatsoever, tend to have short histories and few followers.[9] If abstinence were one of those ideas, if it were a pointless exercise in Grundyism, it would never have gained the ascendancy it has over the American imagination.

THE LOGIC OF ABSTINENCE

We wish every family a part
To understand the healing art,
Without so many forms and rules
Coined and packaged by the schools.

Samuel Thomson (1769–1843)[1]

Ideas that persist over time, that have mass appeal, that transcend the barriers of race, class, and ideology, are usually taken seriously by intellectuals. Not so for abstinence in America. Its attractions are obvious to the millions who believe in it. But to the millions who do not, the very word conjures up everything Blue America dislikes about Red America – its intense religiosity, its rejection of the sexual revolution, its refusal to be more like Europe. The assumption is that abstinence is a joyless exercise in self-denial, one that could appeal only to the most crabbed and intolerant of religious conservatives.

Two facts stand in the way of this easy interpretation. The first is that the religious right does not have a monopoly on abstinence. In the case of America, the association between social conservatism and abstinence is in fact recent, dating from the early decades of the twentieth century. The second is that radicals of all stripes, some religious and some not, have always been drawn to abstinence.[2] Lenin despaired for the young comrade who "reels and staggers from one love affair to the next. That won't do for the political struggle, for the revolution. . . . The revolution demands concentration, increase of forces."[3] Gandhi preached teetotalism and practised sexual abstinence.[4] The radical feminist Andrea Dworkin was forever singing the praises of virginity, describing it as "an active element of a self-determined integrity, an existential independence, affirmed in choice and faith from minute to minute; not a retreat from life but an active engagement with it; dangerous and confrontational because it repudiate[s] rather than endorse[s] male power over women."[5] For Frederick Douglass (1818–1895), the escaped slave turned abolitionist, "It is the sober, thinking slave who is dangerous." "When a slave is drunk, the slaveholder has no fear that he will plan an insurrection, no fear that he will escape to the north."[6] Malcolm X would make the same points in his famous autobiography (1964). Why should African Americans give up pork, tobacco, alcohol, and drugs? Why should they refrain from dancing, gambling, going out on dates, attending movies and sporting events, and taking long vacations? Because the "white man *wants* the black man to stay immoral, unclean and ignorant. As long as we stay in these conditions we will keep on begging him and he will control us."[7]

These examples, of course, do nothing to dispel abstinence's reputation as a rigid and doctrinaire virtue. But if that were the whole story, abstinence would have only the smallest of followings. It would be preached by people with extreme views and practised by people with extreme habits, by the relatively small proportion of the population that is addicted to alcohol or drugs or both. In fact, just the opposite is true. Most people who abstain do so not because they have to or because they harbour radical views, but because the practice makes sense to them on several levels.

This raises an obvious question: why would a reasonable person with no particular vices choose abstinence over moderation? What, in other words, makes abstinence a rational choice for so many people? The first characteristic that recommends abstinence is its optimistic individualism. Abstainers do not look to society to fix their problems: they look to themselves. It is the flip side of this equation that is so seductive: if individuals can set themselves right, everything else will fall into place.[8] Alcoholics Anonymous pays homage to this principle in step four of its twelve-step program. This is the crucial juncture where the recovering alcoholic looks inward and makes a "searching and fearless moral inventory." There is only one way forward, and that is to stop blaming "conditions" and instead accept the "need to change ourselves to meet conditions."[9]

The second thing that recommends abstinence is its disarming simplicity. Where other ideas are hedged with elaborate theories and a multitude of exceptions, abstinence offers but one dictum: if you consistently avoid a particular activity, you will consistently avoid the risks associated with that activity. William Andrus Alcott (1798–1859), the most prolific of America's self-help writers, explained the logic in a succession of staccato sentences: "Take not the first step. Nay, indulge not for an instant, the *thought* of a first step. Here you are safe. Every where else is danger. Take one step, and the next is more easy; the temptation harder to resist."[10] But even this is needlessly elaborate. The underlying logic is so simple that it can be summed up in just one sentence – "Just say no," "There is but one positively sure method of preventing conception – one within the reach of all, and which has no bad effects afterward, and that is *to refrain from the sexual act*," "In relation to tea, coffee, tobacco, and alcoholic drinks, the only safe course is to touch not, taste not, handle not," "Abstinence works every time when it comes to making sure somebody may not have an unwanted child or someone picks up a sexually transmitted disease."[11] On a scarcely more elaborate note there is the old temperance song "Never Begin!":

> In going downhill on a slippery track,
> The going is easy, the task getting back;
> But you'll not have a tumble, a slip, nor a stop,
> Nor toil from below, if you stay at the top.
>
> So from drinking, swearing, and every sin,
> You are safe and secure if you never begin;
> Then never begin! Never begin!
> You cannot be a drunkard unless you begin.[12]

Yet another attraction of abstinence is its capacity to redefine pleasure in more exalted terms. This quality is not immediately obvious to the many people who believe (wrongly, in my opinion) that abstinence and pleasure are polar opposites. One can only laugh at the forced jocularity of so many temperance meetings, at earnest teetotallers toasting one another with cold water or hot coffee, or, in the case of one prohibitionist, with "empty glasses or with none."[13] Harriet Beecher

Stowe (1811–1896), herself a passionate believer in temperance, attended one such event in Edinburgh. Her host was forced to improvise: "If it had been in the old times of Scottish hospitality, he said, he should have proposed a *bumper* three times three; but as that could not be done in a temperance meeting, he proposed three cheers, in which he led off with a hearty good will."[14] A certain defensiveness can also be detected in the words of the Reverend Thomas De Witt Talmage (1832–1902), as quoted in the *National Temperance Orator* for 1874: "I don't believe there is a man here who has taken anything stronger than Hyson tea or Old Dominion coffee; and have you ever seen a merrier group?"[15]

Seen from this perspective, abstinence is a sacrifice and nothing more. True abstainers know better. They go without something in order to create a void for something else to fill. They deny one pleasure in order to make room for one that is bigger and better, be it worldly success, a heavenly reward, or simply the satisfaction that comes from self-mastery. More often than not, people give up something tangible and short term for something ineffable and long term. Fulton J. Sheen (1895–1979), an American Catholic theologian, put it best:

> Our Lord never asked us to give up anything; He asked us to exchange. . . . When someone is in love with God, he finds that there are some things he can get along without (his own pleasure), and something else he cannot get along without, namely, the peace of soul that comes from obeying God's Will. So he exchanges one for the other, surrenders the lesser good to gain a Kingdom.[16]

John Harvey Kellogg (1852–1943), an infinitely less subtle
thinker than Sheen, was nonetheless able to grasp the essential
paradox of abstinence: that it is only superficially about renunciation.[17] Like Sheen, he spoke about trading up. Here he is, five
hundred pages into *Plain Facts for Young and Old* (1877), rhap-
sodizing over the benefits of celibacy: "There would be less
sensual enjoyment, but more elevated joy. There would be less
animal love, but more spiritual communion; less grossness, more
purity; less development of the animal, and a more fruitful soil
for the culture of virtue, holiness, and all the Christian graces."[18]
Judith Beckett, in a lesbian relationship but celibate for eight
years, would agree: "I've discovered and had the energy to
develop my literary and artistic gifts, my capabilities as a nurse,
and my spirituality. I've found self-worth."[19]

What the abstainer acquires, in short, is a new identity, one
that sets him or her apart from those who have yet to make the
same sacrifices. This particular feature helps account for why
powerless groups repeatedly have made abstinence a part of their
collective identity.[20] Irish nationalists shamed the English by
giving up whisky.[21] Nineteenth-century African Americans
embraced temperance not because they had any particular problems with alcohol but because they hoped to "show the public
now that we are trying to promote one another's interest for the
elevation of ourselves and the rising generation."[22]

A closely related benefit of abstinence is the sense of com-
munity it confers on those who make it a pillar of their lifestyle.
This was true even in the nineteenth century, when many
Americans joined temperance societies for the same reason they
went to church: to enjoy the company of like-minded people.[23]
"*Welcome to our meeting . . . ,*" the temperance choirs sang,

Welcome to our festive meeting.
Welcome to our happy throng;
To beguile the moments fleeting,
Loud we raise our cheerful song.
Welcome! Welcome! Welcome! Welcome!
Welcome to our happy throng.[24]

The twelve-step meetings that have become such a feature of modern American life fulfill a similar function. Narcotics Anonymous bills itself "not only [as] a great recovery fellowship," but also as an "organization where we can make new friends."[25] "You will make lifelong friends," Alcoholics Anonymous promises. "You will be bound to them with new and wonderful ties, for you will escape disaster together and you will commence shoulder to shoulder your common journey." "I found my tribe, the social architecture that fulfills my every need for camaraderie and conviviality," writes one member. "Now there is a sense of belonging, of being wanted and needed and loved," writes another.[26]

The decision to abstain may be rational, but this does not make it logical. From the perspective of formal logic, it may even be the wrong choice. The basic premise, that if something is problematic on some occasions then it is problematic on all occasions, is based on the weakest of foundations – inductive reasoning – while the argument that is most commonly mustered in support of prohibiting problematic behaviours, the so-called gateway theory, is a classic example of a post hoc fallacy (the mistaken notion that if *a* preceded *b*, then *a* caused *b*). "The age of first pornography consumption is young, and the age of the average rapist is ever

This print, distributed by the Anti-Saloon League and dubbed The Easy Road and its End, *pays tribute to the idea that moderation inevitably leads to uncontrollable excess. The signposts along the slippery slope read "A Glass of Wine is Not a Sin," "Moderation," "Take a Little for your Stomach's Sake," "You Can Stop when you Please," "Go Slow and there is No Danger," and, at the edge of the precipice, "Stop Here." One is reminded of how Alcoholics Anonymous defines the "real alcoholic" in its famous "Big Book": "He may start off as a moderate drinker; he may or may not become a continuous hard drinker; but at some stage of his drinking career he begins to lose all control of his liquor consumption, once he starts to drink."*

younger," "every drunkard began by moderation," "of one hundred men who use tobacco, ninety-five use strong drink," "She begins with the smoking of 'tea' – marijuana – and from there she moves to the 'white drugs' – heroin usually," and so on.[27] But to judge abstinence by the rules of formal logic is to miss its power. What abstinence offers is the same thing religious belief offers: certitude. And it is this quality, more than any other, that has made abstinence the natural ally of religion.

ONE

THE EVANGELICAL PREMISE

How can I learn to rule myself,
To be the child I should,
Honest and brave, nor ever tire
Of trying to be good?

Louisa May Alcott (1832–1888)[1]

America was not always a nation of abstainers. There was a time, in the colonial era and the decades immediately after the Revolution, when Americans were no more enamoured of abstinence than their contemporaries across the Atlantic. The one form of abstinence that was widely preached, premarital chastity, was unremarkable, for it was also widely preached throughout Europe. The idea that people should also give up all their other vices – their liquor, tobacco, and favourite foods – had no more standing in the New World than it did in the Old, and if colonial authorities were troubled by the taverns and what went on in them, so were their colleagues in Europe.[2]

In the early nineteenth century, in scattered hamlets in New England and upstate New York, one suddenly starts to find people questioning habits they had previously taken for granted.

The first casualty was hard liquor, but once the process was set in motion, other vices started to come under scrutiny – hard cider, beer and wine, tobacco, bacon, pickles, pies, coffee, and more. It was not this scrutiny that was remarkable – the truth was that Americans *did* drink, eat, and smoke to excess – but rather the conclusion they reached: that the only safe way to handle their vices was to give them up for good.

Something changed in the early nineteenth century – but what? The first thing that stands out is that America was becoming less European at this time, and, by extension, more democratic and more suspicious of its elites. This transformation, in turn, was the result of two populist revolts, one political, the other religious. The political revolt, which ended the hegemony of New England's Federalist elites, began in the opening years of the nineteenth century, with the presidency of Thomas Jefferson (1801–1809). In the 1820s, a new and more bumptious figure emerged as the champion of America's populists: a war hero by the name of Andrew Jackson. In 1828, Jackson was elected president, ushering in a renewed and even more vigorous attack on America's

Andrew Jackson, on horseback with another horse in tow, arriving at the White House in 1829.

Jackson packed his cabinet with "plain businessmen," insisting that "The duties of all public offices are, or at least admit of being made, so plain and simple that men of intelligence may readily qualify themselves for their performance . . ." From the Library of Congress Prints and Photographs Division.

A camp meeting, circa 1829.

Camp meetings were one of the most distinctive features of the Second Great Awakening. In these revivals, people from far-flung settlements would come together, for days at a time, to be harangued by itinerating preachers intent on effecting as many conversions as possible. The meeting Frances Trollope attended was held on the "verge of an unbroken forest, where a space of about twenty acres appeared to have been partially cleared for the purpose. Tents of different sizes were pitched very near together in a circle round the cleared space." The ensuing spectacle appalled her: "But how," she wrote in 1832, "am I to describe the sounds that proceeded from this strange mass of human beings? I know no words which can convey an idea of it. Hysterical sobbings, convulsive groans, shrieks and screams the most appalling, burst forth on all sides." From the Library of Congress Prints and Photographs Division.

elites. The second revolt, a series of religious revivals known as the Second Great Awakening, began earlier, in the late 1790s, and likewise ended earlier, in or around 1830.[3] This religious revolt was to prove the deeper of the two, for it transformed American Protestantism, stripping it of the last vestiges of elitism and leaving in its place a faith that was as energetic as it was egalitarian. Two religious establishments, both already weak-ened, fell before it: Anglicanism in the South and Calvinism in the North.

Up to this point, abstinence had occupied a dubious position in Protestant theology. Luther and Calvin actually insisted on only one type of abstinence – celibacy until marriage – and while both spoke highly of fasting, they were otherwise critical of the mortifications they associated with the old Church.[4] This criti-cism, however, was only partially rooted in a desire to reform religious practice. It was also rooted in a profound pessimism about human agency. If man was powerless to overcome the dead hand of sin, then abstinence was an empty gesture, one that could neither sway God nor bring the sinner closer to Him. The one thing man could do was to exercise moderation. This is the word that repeats whenever Luther and Calvin talk about alcohol, sexual pleasure, and food. All are God's good gifts, to be enjoyed within bounds, but to be enjoyed nonetheless.[5]

The Protestantism that embraces abstinence rejects the fatal-ism of Luther and Calvin.[6] It goes by the name of *evangelical*, and the groundwork for this new and more expansive form of Protestantism was laid in the seventeenth century, when Calvin's doctrine of predestination came under sustained attack from the followers of the Dutch theologian Jacobus Arminius. In the eigh-teenth century, that attack was taken up by John Wesley, the English theologian and preacher whose followers came to be known as the Methodists. With Wesley, the modern evangelical movement was born.

A definition is in order, especially as many of the people who use the term *evangelical* have no idea what it actually means. Evangelicalism has as many variants as it has denominations, so many that it is impossible to provide a simple definition.[7] But for all their differences, these denominations have four characteristics in common. The first is the importance they attach to conversion experiences. In these the burden of sin is lifted and the believer is born again. In one the "Lord did, then and there, forgive my sins and give me religion," in another the "heart of stone was taken away, and a heart of love and tenderness assumed its place," and in yet another the "burden of sin and guilt and the fear of hell vanished from my mind, as perceptibly as a hundred pounds' weight falling from a man's shoulder."[8] The second characteristic evangelical denominations share is the expectation that their members actively express their faith, through deeds as well as words. The third is Biblical literalism, and the fourth is the conviction that Christ atoned for man's sins.[9] It is this last assumption that is crucial, for in it lies the assurance that each individual can, with enough striving, overcome the dead hand of sin.

Evangelicalism offers salvation, and to that extent it is infinitely optimistic. But where the Calvinist can never be sure whether she is saved, the evangelical is beset by an altogether different kind of anxiety: the fear that once saved, he or she might stumble and sin, and in so doing, cease to be saved.

Wesley resolved this conundrum by committing the faithful to a program of endless works. To be a Methodist was to pursue something that could be grasped but never held, to wake up each day and fight sin anew, to heed what the Anglican evangelical George William Russell (1853–1919) called a "perpetual call to seriousness."[10] And because Wesley set the bar so high – the goal was, quite literally, Christian perfection – the battle had to be waged on all fronts at once.

Wesley was exceptionally well read in Catholic theology, and in holding out the carrot of perfection he was in fact reviving a doctrine that went back to the earliest days of the Church.[11] There were, however, two important differences. The first was that the old Church had never seriously expected everyone to achieve perfection. At the top of the pyramid were the saints who had achieved holiness, and below them, the holy orders who actively sought it through prayer and mortifications. The vast majority of the faithful, the laity, might be exhorted to follow the example of the saints, but in the end they were always held to lesser standards. The second difference was that the select few who managed to achieve holiness almost invariably had done so by repudiating the world. Virgins chose death over marriage, anchorites dressed in rags, mystics starved themselves. Wesley's saints were made of coarser stuff. Everyone – not just the virtuosi of the old Church – had the potential to achieve holiness, and they could do so in the world as they found it. Wesley's saints were ordinary people living and working in a social world. Their workaday virtues – thrift, self-control, a quiet and unostentatious piety – were useful to themselves and beneficial to society.

Wesley's pronounced enthusiasm for celibacy (he himself did not marry until the age of forty-eight) suggests that he was more of a purist than he let on.[12] But he was even more of a realist, and as the head of a movement that had an enormous following among the working poor, his first priority was to avoid even the appearance of radicalism.[13] In 1742, when his activities were still regarded with considerable suspicion, he addressed the question everyone was asking: exactly what distinguished Methodists from everyone else? What Wesley said, in effect, was that his followers did not differ in the externals. They did not say outlandish things or reject the pleasures everybody else took for granted. They were not Puritans; still less were they fanatics and ascetics:

> as to all opinions which do not strike at the root of Christianity we "think and let think". . . . Nor do we desire to be distinguished, by *actions, customs,* or *usages* of an *indifferent* nature. Our religion does not lie in doing what God has not enjoined, or abstaining from what he hath not forbidden. It does not lie in the form of our apparel, in the posture of our body, or the covering of our heads; nor yet in abstaining from marriage, nor from meats and drinks, which are all good if received with thanksgiving.[14]

Abstinence, in other words, was emphatically not part of Methodism in its original form. Wesley himself banned only two substances – distilled spirits and tobacco – and in both instances he was merely following the lead of earlier churchmen.[15] Wesley did not furnish his successors with a list of things from which to abstain: he unwittingly furnished them with a rationale in the form of Christian perfection.

Wesley was vehemently opposed to American independence, and this was one of the reasons why the Methodists attracted few converts in that country during his lifetime. It was only after American Methodists had established their own Church, the Methodist Episcopal Church, that they embarked upon a period of explosive growth. Before the Revolution, American Methodists had numbered perhaps 3,000; by 1820 that number had increased to roughly 250,000, by 1830 to twice that number, by 1843, to nearly a million.[16]

One of the secrets behind the Methodists' success in America was their use of lay preachers (the famous circuit riders) to carry

"Crazy" Lorenzo Dow (1777–1834), a native of Coventry, Connecticut, was typical of the self-taught preachers who carried the message of the Second Great Awakening deep into America's backwoods. He was tireless, conducting five hundred to eight hundred camp meetings in just one year. On one of his wilderness circuits, in 1803, he "frequently saw wild game, among which were deer and turkeys. The Indians frequently came to our camp, and while we had our evening devotion, they would be solemn and mute . . ." When Dow attempted to stage American-style camp meetings in Britain, the Methodist establishment turfed him out, explaining that revivals that were "allowable in America" were "highly improper in England, and likely to be productive of considerable mischief." From the Library of Congress Prints and Photographs Division.

the gospel into the backwoods. This was in many ways making a virtue of necessity (seminarians would be in short supply in America well into the nineteenth century), but it was also a nod to the populism that was even then upending American politics.[17] Seminarians were a favourite target of the populists, but so were all other educated professionals – lawyers, bankers, and, as Dr. Daniel Drake (1785–1852) reminded a group of Ohio medical students in 1821, physicians. They were no better than anyone else, he told them: "Hitherto the philosophers have formed a distinct *caste* from the people, and like kinds have been supposed to possess a divine right of superiority. But this delusion should be dispelled, is indeed fast disappearing, and the distinction between scientific and the unscientific dissolved."[18]

The further the circuit riders pushed the Protestant command to be guided by scripture alone, the more they struggled to find the right words, the more credibility those words assumed. "Larnin' isn't religion," one lay preacher was quoted as saying, "and edication don't give a man the power of the Spirit. It is grace and gifts that furnish the real live coals from the altar. Saint Peter was a fisherman – do you think he ever went to Yale College?"[19] Peter Cartwright (1785–1872), a self-taught circuit rider, boasted that it was the "illiterate Methodist preachers" who had "set the world on fire." He worried that "colleges, universities, seminaries, and academies" that sprang up after the Second Great Awakening would be the denomination's undoing. He recalled how much better things had been when he was just getting started, how "many of us traveling preachers" had "little or no education, no books, and no time to read or study them if we could have had them. We had no colleges, nor even a respectable common school, within hundreds of miles of us." The Baptists were no better. By one count, dating from 1828, three-quarters of all Baptist preachers in Kentucky could not tell a noun from a verb. Some could barely read, and a few were completely illiterate.[20]

This deep mistrust of learning enters the story for another reason: it paved the way for a new type of relationship with God.

With ministers pushed to one side and learning to the other, nothing stood in the way of making that relationship as personal – and as intensely emotional – as possible. And that, more than any one doctrine, is the hallmark of evangelical Protestantism.[21] Peter Cartwright's epiphany had come when he was just sixteen. It was then, "feeling wretched beyond expression," that he "heard a voice from heaven, saying, 'Peter, look at me.'"[22] From that day forward Cartwright found himself in the most arduous relationship imaginable, one that resembled nothing so much as a sustained and difficult courtship. The demands were endless. How did Phoebe Palmer (1807–1874), the great female revivalist, define her relationship with God? "You would *every* moment be looking to Jesus and *trusting* in him to *save* you from sin. O! with what carefulness would you every moment be watching against sin."[23] What did being a Methodist mean to the Reverend Hiram Mattison? It meant entering into a covenant that lasted "not for a few years, but for life."[24] "Why are we not more holy? Why do we not live in eternity? Walk with God all the day long?" – these were the questions that vexed the Methodist Episcopal Church in 1872.[25]

Abstinence grew out of this lopsided relationship because always there was the need to be on one's best behaviour, to cast aside any acquaintances and diversions that threatened to derail the believer's unblinking focus on God.[26] Horace Bushnell (1802–1876), one of the most liberal theologians of his day, believed he was stating the obvious when he wrote, in 1861, that "One must be a very inobservant person not to have noticed that all his finest and most God-ward aspirations are smothered under any load of excess, or over-indulgence." How, he asked, "is the child going to be drawn by the beauty of God, and the sacred pleasures of God's friendship, when thinking always of the dainties he has had, or is again to have?"[27] Lyman Beecher (1775–1863), the great figure of the early American temperance movement, hated how drunkenness led to the "extinction of all the finer feelings and amiable dispositions of the soul; and if there have ever seemed to be religious affections, of these also."[28] Frances Willard (1839–1898), the charismatic president of the Woman's Christian Temperance Union, was adamant: "We cannot transmit the light of the truth unless we are under the power of that holy habit – sobriety."[29]

The evangelicals' wish to be on the closest possible terms with God would drive them on to ever greater displays of virtue. This by itself was not new. The old Church had always had its saints, martyrs, and virtuosi. But it did not, once it became established, hold everyone to the same exacting standards (Saint Simeon the Stylite was welcome to stand on his pillar – which he did for thirty-six years, until his death in AD 459 – but this was never held up as an example for ordinary men and women to follow).

Democracy's great contribution was to raise the bar of virtue for everyone.[30] Aristocrats as well as paupers, men as well as women, all were to be held to the high standards of the broad middle, to a code that favoured ants over grasshoppers, tortoises over hares, the long term over the short term. The very thought filled Harriet Beecher Stowe with pride. There she was in England, in 1854, the possessor of a truth her English counterparts were only beginning to grasp: that the "educated, the refined, the noble, must needs be saved by the same Savior and the same gospel with the ignorant and debased working classes."[31] The same pride can be detected in one of Ralph Waldo Emerson's more jejune remarks to Charles Dickens and Thomas Carlyle. They were talking about prostitution when Emerson suddenly blurted out, "Young men of good standing and good education with us go virgins to their nuptial beds, as truly as their brides."[32]

This redefinition of one's relationship to God came just as the doctrine of Christian perfection was itself being revived and reworked by American theologians. What was distinctive about the American variant was its sheer scope. Not only did it hold *all* human actions up to scrutiny, it also extended the doctrine's writ into the political arena, something Wesley, always the arch Tory, had gone out of his way to avoid.

The first hint of a new interpretation dates from 1824, when Timothy Merritt (1775–1845), a Methodist minister from Connecticut and one of the founding members of the American Temperance Society, published a layman's guide to Christian perfection: *The Christian's Manual*. At first glance, Merritt's little book simply repeats everything Wesley and his designated successor, John Fletcher (1729–1785), had to say on the subject. Only at the very end does Merritt set off in a radically different direction. There, in the appendix, are eighteen "Helps to a Growth in Grace," the contribution of an unnamed "female correspondent." None of these is especially remarkable – except for number fifteen: "Resolve that none of our happiness shall consist in eating and drinking," it starts, "or in any of the pleasures of sense." Merritt's friend offered a simple rule of thumb: use only those things that "may fit us for the better service of God," a stricture that necessarily excluded more than it included.[33]

It was advice that suffered by being too brief, so brief – and so poorly placed – that it was easily overlooked. Would-be perfectionists faced yet another obstacle: a lack of interest on the part of the Methodist establishment. Christian perfection is rarely mentioned in the Church's documents from the early nineteenth century, and then only in passing.[34] The doctrine was given short shrift for a very good reason: to dwell on it, to take it to its logical conclusion, was to force the Church to take an unequivocal stand against slavery.

When that issue was finally forced, in 1844, the Southern remnant of the Church seceded to form the Methodist Episcopal Church, South. This left Northern Methodists free to turn their attention to Christian perfection, and this they did with a vengeance, spurred on by the publication, in 1843, of Phoebe Palmer's best-selling *Way of Holiness*. At the same time, Northern Methodists became increasingly vocal about temperance, an issue that had, up to now, been a low priority for them.[35] A significant step forward was taken in 1848, when, after years of temporizing, they finally endorsed Wesley's original ban on distilled spirits.[36] Even so, the Northern Church proceeded cautiously, pushing the idea of total abstinence but without making this a condition of membership.[37]

The Methodists' slowness to embrace Christian perfection created a vacuum that was filled by two evangelical Presbyterians, both with strong ties to the abolitionists. The first was Charles Grandison Finney (1792–1875) and the second was Asa Mahan (1799–1889). Both had grown up in the epicentre of the Second Great Awakening, in the so-called "Burned-Over District" that extended from central New York State to Lake Ontario.[38] Finney was self-taught, while Mahan happened to be a graduate of the Andover Theological Seminary, that crucible of the early temperance movement.[39] In 1835, both men were recruited to teach at Oberlin, an experimental college underwritten by the abolitionists Theodore Weld and Arthur Tappan. Oberlin was

The Meeting House, Tappan Square (named in honour of the abolitionist Arthur Tappan), and the Oberlin Institute Buildings as they appeared in 1846.
Courtesy of the Oberlin College Archive.

extraordinary. It admitted women.[40] It banned the use of alcohol, tobacco, coffee, tea, and condiments.[41] In 1837, at the insistence of Finney and Mahan, it started admitting African Americans. And in 1838, at Finney's urging, it tried (unsuccessfully) to get the student body to stop eating meat.[42]

Finney and Mahan clearly had been pondering the merits of perfection long before they started preaching and writing about it in the late 1830s. Finney, who was best known as a revivalist, was discouraged that so few of the conversions he effected actually lasted. He was sure that something more was needed – something to keep his audiences from backsliding. Mahan, who had less experience in the pulpit, worried more generally about a fall-off in religious enthusiasm.[43] His own faith was also at low ebb, shaken by the deaths of two of his children.[44]

The master revivalist Charles Grandison Finney, from a daguerreotype taken in England in 1850.

Thanks to Finney, the rough-and-tumble camp meetings of the Second Great Awakening were transformed into genteel revivals that could – and did – appeal to the urban middle classes. "My preaching was logical instead of dogmatic," *he boasted in his memoirs,* "and therefore met the wants of the people." Courtesy of the Oberlin College Archive.

The official story, one Finney and Mahan both tell, is that they first seriously considered the implications of perfectability in 1836. The trigger was a question asked by a student during a revival on the Oberlin campus. It was this: "When we look to Christ for sanctification what degree of sanctification may we expect from him? May we look to him to be sanctified wholly, or not?"[45] Finney and Mahan were both flummoxed and excited by the question. For two years they mulled it over, praying, consulting each other, and clarifying their thinking by composing sermons on the subject. In 1839, they were sufficiently sure of their answer to publish it, Finney in the *Oberlin Evangelist*, Mahan in the *Scripture Doctrine of Christian Perfection*. What they said, in brief, was that sanctification should be *entire*, touching every possible area of the Christian's life. It was the flip side of this equation that lent itself to abstinence in its most radical form: anything that stood in the way of sanctification, anything that was even remotely inconsistent with it, should be avoided at all costs. For Mahan, entire sanctification meant offering up "our bodies, with all our physical powers and propensities" to God, a catch-all that included "food, drink, and dress."[46] Mahan's dietary theories followed from this premise (he was a great believer in eating only the simplest and most natural of foods); so, too, did his commitment to teetotalism.[47]

Finney went even further, reducing the entire doctrine to an unerring rule.[48] Where Wesley had hedged his definition of Christian perfection with caveats ("Our religion does not lie in doing what God has not enjoined, or abstaining from what he

The Americans' tendency to adapt Wesley to their own needs and circumstances is wonderfully captured in this mid-nineteenth-century print by Currier & Ives. Here Wesley is shown preaching on his father's grave, and though the scene is supposed to be set in 1742, one of the onlookers is wearing a stovepipe hat, while another is wearing a bowler. From the Library of Congress Prints and Photographs Division.

hath not forbidden"), Finney spoke loftily of "total abstinence from sin," of the "subjugation of all our appetites and passions to the will of God." Where Wesley had proscribed only distilled spirits and tobacco, Finney, like Merritt's female correspondent, proscribed "all things that are pernicious." Finney could not leave it at that. He went on to provide an exhaustive list of taboos: narcotics, alcohol, tobacco, tea, coffee – in short, all "innutritious stimulants."[49] If the goal, the "entire sanctification of the body," was extreme, so was the most visible means of achieving it: abstinence from anything the body did not need and the soul could not use.

The Oberlin definition of Christian perfection was so exacting – and so thoroughgoing – that anyone who took it seriously was obliged to do as Finney and Mahan did and embark on a multitude of reforms, personal as well as social.[50] Edward Beecher (1803–1895), the third of Lyman's thirteen children, talked excitedly about extending the "influence of the Christian system into all departments of life," of exposing "all institutions, usages, and principles, civil or religious," to a "rigid and fiery scrutiny."[51] William Lloyd Garrison's (1805–1879) goal, explicitly stated, was "universal reform."[52] Before abolitionism there had been temperance, and after it there would be more causes still – civil rights, women's rights, sexual purity.[53] Ralph Waldo Emerson's circle, with its "numberless projects of social reform," provides still more examples: "One man renounces the use of animal food; & another of coin; & another of domestic hired service; & another of the state."[54] "Do everything," Frances Willard exhorted the members of the Woman's Christian Temperance Union.[55] An admirer explained the rationale: "With her great

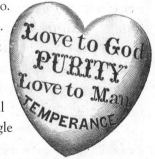

heart she saw that all reforms were but fragments of one reform, the Christianizing of society."[56]

Who among them could abstain from just one vice? To do that, to give up alcohol without also giving up tobacco and everything else that was even remotely suspect, was to stop well short of the entire sanctification of the body. Larkin Baker Coles (1803–1856), the physician whose writings would have a profound influence on the Seventh-Day Adventists, put it best: "Men who quit their cups, and still hold on upon their chewing and smoking, are only about half reformed."

The other danger in half-measures was that they left the gateways to vice wide open. In Coles's stark words, "Licentiousness in eating and drinking prepares the way for licentiousness in other things."[57] The underlying logic, that one vice begets another, was an old one.[58] What was new was the willingness of so many people to act on it. This was brought home when the American Temperance Society conducted a survey in 1835. What that survey showed was that many of the society's members had given up much more than alcohol. Some had given up tobacco. Others had given up coffee and tea. Still others had stopped eating meat and spicy foods. A heroic few, like Joseph Speed, a doctor in Tompkins County, New York, had given up all of these things. He described a struggle worthy of Saint Anthony:

I determined to take a new start in the path of reformation, and successively gave up the use of strong
high-seasoned food of every description – my
tobacco, yes, my tobacco, the idol of my life, which
I had used for nearly fifty years, and without which
life seemed a burden; yes; that dear, soothing com-
forter of my life – that vile, filthy, health-destroying
weed, had to go; and, not very long after, my tea and
my coffee. Yes, my much loved coffee, had to go, too;
but much as I loved it, our separation produced a
pang, but trifling compared to the loss of my dear,
abominable, filthy tobacco.[59]

Amasa Walker, Henry Wright, and John Ball, all from
Boston, volunteered that they had given up tobacco. And it had
been fifteen or twenty years since Edward Hitchcock (1793–
1864), a professor at Amherst College and author of *Dyspepsy
Forestalled & Resisted* (1830), had tasted tea or coffee. All
claimed, perhaps a little too defensively, that they had never felt
better. Speed was emphatic. He had *health*. He never had a cold,
scarcely "knew what an ache or a pain is." His appetite was
"*always* good." He had lost "all desire for any thing, but the plain
nourishing food on which I live." In short, he felt as if he had
"gone back many years of my life."[60]

Nineteenth-century perfectionists had an almost morbid fear of
leisure, and that fear is writ large in the fripperies they proscribed
– drinking, masturbating, copulating for purposes other than
procreation, dancing, overeating, reading novels, using tobacco
in any form.[61] Each idle moment was a truce in the ongoing war

against sin, an opportunity for the enemy to steal a march on the unwary and open the floodgates to perdition. There was

> No room for mirth or trifling here,
> For worldly hope, or worldly fear,
> If life so soon is gone.[62]

The self-help literature was full of advice on how to fill every moment of the day with purposeful activity – in the morning "you must bound out of bed instantaneously, as soon as you have the least consciousness of your situation," you must plan what to discuss at the breakfast table so as to render "even these ordinary occasions of daily life subservient to the intellectual and moral well-being of all who partake it," you must sleep no more than seven hours a day, and so on. In short, it was essential to have a plan for everything, "to mark off so many hours for particular purposes."[63]

That was the ideal. Few lived up to it. But many tried. Frances Willard tried every day of her life. Her lapses were few and always painful. "Rose at *nine* o'clock this morning, (!)," reads her diary entry for June 10, 1860.[64] Her ideal day was one that started early, at "seven to half-past (I wish it were earlier)" – and ended early, "anywhere from half-past seven to half-past nine." Always there was work to do, always at a set time: the eight hours between breakfast and tea.[65] Lady Isabella Somerset (1851–1921), the president of the British Women's Temperance Association, was in awe of her American counterpart's "capacity for work, untiring and unremitting." "Save when sleeping, I have never seen her idle," she wrote upon Willard's death in 1898. Even when walking, Willard's "hand was always busy making notes, or her brain planning, thinking, devising some new method to help forward the welfare of all the various enterprises with which she was connected."[66] Willard was not the only person driven by exigencies of her own making. "I have thought that some rules for the regulation of my time, and the distribution of my duties, might be helpful," Phoebe Palmer wrote in her journal. She came up with a plan: "I will endeavor to rise at four: spend from four to six in reading the Scriptures, and other devotional exercises: half an hour for closet duties at midday." She would try (she could make no promises) to "get an hour to spend with God at the close of the day."[67]

Others, whether intentionally or not, kept leisure at bay by filling their hours with work. The phenomenon never ceased to amaze European travellers, but none more than Michel Chevalier (1806–1879), the French engineer who visited America in the mid-1830s. Uncommon industriousness greeted him wherever he went:

> From the moment he gets up, the American is at his work, and he is absorbed in it till the hour of sleep. He never permits pleasure to distract him; public affairs alone have the right to take him for a few moments. Even mealtime is not for him a period of relaxation when he might rest his weary brain in an intimate and restful environment. It is only a disagreeable interruption of business, an interruption which he accepts because it is inevitable, but which he cuts short as much as possible. In the evening, if no political meeting requires his attendance, if he does not go to discuss some question of public interest, or to a religious meeting, he sits at home, thoughtful and absorbed in his meditations,

whether on the transactions of the day or the projects of tomorrow.[68]

The picture is unduly grim. That Americans were constantly
being told to fill their days with uplifting activities suggests that
many were doing just the opposite. And there was the occasional
rebel, like Clarence Cook (1828–1900), author of the enor-
mously popular *The House Beautiful: Essays on Beds and Tables,
Stools and Candlesticks* (1878). Cook seems to have relished the
role of leisure's brave champion. His men are pictured smoking
and drinking, this at a time when both activities were under
relentless attack, and at one point, some two hundred pages into
the book, he makes gentle fun of the "doctrine of early rising for
its own sake." But even this goes too far. He feels he must qualify
his remarks. He never has and never will "advocate a wild license
in the matter of lying a-bed, or getting up when you please."[69]

Whether ordinary Americans were guilty of lolling in bed,
of sitting around and doing nothing at all, is ultimately beside
the point. What matters is whether these stolen moments were
also moments of doubt, darkened by the thought that "Life is not
ours to waste it as we will."[70] Certainly they were moments of
doubt for Frances Willard, and, as it turns out, for Clarence Cook
as well. As long as that doubt was planted in enough people's
minds, the places most associated with leisure – the taverns and
saloons, the theatres and dance halls, even the clubs where
respectable gentlemen met to drink and smoke and socialize –
would be easy targets for each passing reformer.

All of this would have been academic had the average American
been too poor to overindulge. In that case abstinence would

have remained what it was in most of nineteenth-century Europe: a solution in search of a problem. But already by 1826, the year America celebrated its jubilee, its white male citizens were drinking more liquor, eating more food, and consuming more tobacco than all but a handful of Europeans.[71]

The cumulative impression is that of a citizenry spiralling out of control. From 1790 to 1830, per capita consumption of absolute alcohol grew with each passing decade, reaching 7.1 U.S. gallons in 1810 and hovering at that level for the next twenty years.[72] This amounted to just over five standard drinks (one drink calculated at 13.6 grams of absolute alcohol) a day for everyone age fifteen or older. What makes the figure especially alarming is that it is based on the entire adult population, including the two groups that drank almost nothing at all: women and slaves.[73] Nor does it include all the liquor that was distilled and drunk without ever being taxed and counted.

That hard liquor was the beverage of choice – whisky in those areas where grain was plentiful but too costly to transport whole; rum, brandy, and gin on the coasts and in the houses and haunts of the well-to-do – merely compounded the problem.[74] Peter Cartwright recalled how "drinking drams, in family and social circles, was considered harmless and allowable," how "if a man would not have it in his family, his harvest, his house-raisings, log-rollings, weddings, and so on, he was considered parsimonious and unsociable."[75] James Finley (1781–1856), a Methodist preacher whose peregrinations took him into the backwoods of Ohio, reported that "A house could not be raised, a field of wheat cut down, nor could there be a log rolling, a husking, a quilting, a wedding, or a funeral without the aid of alcohol."[76] Everywhere Frances Trollope (1780–1863) went in Virginia's Blue Ridge Mountains she found whisky, its "hideous

The MORNING DRAM.

effects . . . visible on the countenance of every man you meet."[77] Thomas Trotter (1760–1832), the Scottish physician and early temperance crusader, had it on good authority that the average "labouring man in an American town" drank eight gills (one quart) of cheap rum a day, two before breakfast, three before dinner, and three more by day's end.[78]

Nineteenth-century Americans were also enormous consumers of tobacco. By one estimate, dating from 1851, for every ounce of tobacco a Frenchman smoked, an American smoked, snuffed, or chewed eight. The English ratio (one to three) was closer, but still a distant second.[79] The complaints were endless. Frederick Marryat (1792–1848), a former naval officer and presumably no stranger to vice, was horrified to find chaw sold alongside gentlemen's shirts, collars, gloves, and silk handkerchiefs.[80] Charles Dickens was disgusted to find gobs of the stuff in the United States Capitol, in courthouses, at the breakfast table, and on steamboats.[81] Larkin Baker Coles could never forget the time he shook a hand moist with black spittle.[82] Frances Willard was once so overwhelmed by the smoke on a train that she was forced to take refuge in its caboose.[83]

But it was how much the Americans ate, more even than how much they drank, smoked, snuffed, and chewed, that made the biggest impression on European tourists.[84] The first thing they noticed upon setting foot in America was how tall the men were – two inches taller, on average, than their European counterparts. There was a simple reason for this: the American diet was exceptionally high in animal protein, with each person eating, on average, 178 pounds of meat a year between 1830 and 1839.[85] The second thing European tourists noticed – and almost always complained about – was the presence of meat at every meal, "ham and beef-steaks . . . morning, noon, and night."[86] William Cobbett (1763–1835) was given an earful when he asked a farmer's wife how much her family ate over the course of a year:

> I saw *fourteen* fat hogs, weighing about *twenty score a piece*, which were to come *into the house* the next Monday; for here they slaughter them *all in one day*. This led me to ask, "Why, in God's name, what do you eat in a year?" The Bill of fare was this, for the present year: about *this same quantity of hog-meat; four beeves;* and *forty-six fat sheep!* Besides the *sucking pigs* (of which we had then one on the table), besides *lambs*, and besides the produce of *seventy hen fowls*, not to mention good parcels of *geese, ducks* and *turkeys*, but, not to forget a garden of three quarters of an acre and *the butter of ten cows*, not one ounce of which is ever sold![87]

How many Americans died of surfeit, from the diseases associated with drinking too much liquor, eating too much rich food, and smoking, snuffing, and chewing too much tobacco remains a

The GROG SHOP.

matter of conjecture. Contemporaries offered wild guesses. "Our average of American life is evidently not one-half of what it ought to be."[88] "It is highly probable, not less than 4,000 people die annually, from the use of ardent spirits."[89] Alcohol caused "30 to 50 thousand individuals, above the age of twenty, [to] die prematurely" every year.[90] "Downright gluttony" killed 100,000 a year, and so on.[91] Whatever the actual numbers, they had to have been high.

The people who wanted Americans to give up liquor, tobacco, and their favourite foods were clearly acting out of a genuine sense of urgency.[92] The solution they proposed was extreme, but so, too, were the habits of most American men. As grave as the problem was, however, it took the spark of the Second Great Awakening to make healthy habits a matter of conscience. What the revivalists did, in a way that no physician ever could, was to bring home to average Americans just how far their habits fell short of Christian perfection. Who among them could give a satisfactory answer to the questions Wesley once had asked – "Do you not *eat* more plentifully or more delicately than you did ten or twenty years ago? Do you not use more *drink*, or drink of a more *costly* kind, than you did then?"[93] And who could look Charles Grandison Finney in the eye when he asked whether a "glutton, who is stupefied two or three times a day with his food, [could] be entirely consecrated, either body or soul, to God?"[94]

In its report for 1834 the American Temperance Society had stumbled on a basic truth, one that seemed to define the age. The editors' excitement, their delight in being at the vanguard of a new way of solving old problems, is palpable. "It is," they wrote, "becoming more and more common, if a man wishes to have good

TREE of INTEMPERANCE

The Tree of Intemperance, *a print dating from 1855, pays homage to two interlock-ing ideas: that a multitude of vices springs from just one source, and that once that source is cut off, all of its attendant vices will simply disappear. Acting on this principle, a youth is about to take an axe to the tree of intemperance, aiming not for its branches, but for its very roots.* From the Library of Congress Prints and Photographs Division.

done, to do it himself . . . and to do it *now*." They congratulated themselves on living in a democracy where "The feeblest and most obscure do not now despair of exerting influence that shall be felt by all people, to all ages." But most of all, they congratu-lated themselves on their refusal to meet evil halfway. No longer were men willing to chip off twigs and lop off branches, not when they could go to the root. They had learned they could not "stop the stream without drying up the fountain," that it was impossi-ble to "remove the effects" without first removing the cause.[95]

Their impatience to "have good done" had a European pedigree, stretching back to Wesley and his doctrine of Christian perfection, and, more recently, to the Romantic revolt against Enlightenment caution. But these two factors by themselves did not usher in abstinence. Both were present in Britain, and yet abstinence attracted a much smaller following in that country. When these same factors took root in American soil, with no classes and intellectual traditions capable of opposing them, the results were stunning. It was a perfect match – on one side a virtue that was as intellectually accessible as it was democratic, on the other, a people who were determined to think and do for themselves.

In their passion to think for themselves, American evangelicals had wandered far from the tenets of the Reformation, so far so that it often seemed they were at risk of lapsing back into the more comfortable certitudes of Catholicism. Not that they were reconciled to the growing number of Catholics in their midst. On the contrary.[96] An Ursuline convent in Charlestown, Massachusetts, was burned to the ground in 1834.[97] A year later Lyman Beecher accused the Catholic powers of Europe of undermining American sovereignty by "flooding the nation suddenly with emigrants."[98] And it was at about this time that Harriet Martineau (1802–1876) was "seriously told, by several persons in the south and west, that the Catholics of America were employed by the Pope, in league with the Emperor of Austria and the Irish, to explode the Union."[99] But evangelical Protestantism, no less than Catholicism, was a religion in which salvation and striving went hand in hand. In both the formula tended in the same direction, to extreme striving, to abstinence in the face of sin.[100] There was, however, a crucial difference. In America, abstinence was to lose its elitist trappings and become the virtue of the many.

TWO

HOW MODERATION BECAME A VICE

Le mieux est l'ennemi du bien.

Voltaire, *La Bégueule* (1772)

The supreme duty of the hour is to convince the moderate drinker that he is doing himself harm.

Frances Willard[1]

Temperance was the first and most successful of America's abstinence movements. Its early history has been told several times over, and I do not propose to retell it here.[2] The crusade against drink was many things – a way for women to enter the political arena, a thinly veiled protest against immigrants, a necessary step on the road to industrialization, and, of course, a response to an actual problem. But it is also a case study in how difficult it is to defend moderation once that principle comes under sustained attack. In the case of the American temperance movement, over the course of a few short years, moderation went from being a virtue to a vice. When the American Temperance Society was launched in 1826, its members were prepared to tolerate the occasional light drink; ten years later, when that society was relaunched as the American Temperance Union, they were not. This about-face raises a troubling question: why were the movement's moderates so easily – and so thoroughly – routed?

What the radicals were really attacking was a vestige of Reformation Protestantism. For the original Protestants, for the Lutherans as well as the Calvinists, alcohol was one of God's good gifts, and from this it followed that it was not a sin to drink. Sin occurred only when the drinker exceeded the bounds of moderation and drank too much. This notion underwent a subtle modification in the eighteenth century as cheap distilled spirits started to become more widely available. For the first time, in Britain as well as America, one begins to find a curious distinction between good drinks and bad drinks. Beer, ale, and cider, the traditional drinks of England's working poor, fell into the first category, while distilled spirits, the beverage that had wreaked so much havoc in the slums of eighteenth-century London, fell into the second category. But even then the goal was not to get people to stop drinking: it was to make them drink the right kinds of beverages.

One of the last people to categorize drinks in this fashion was Benjamin Rush (1746–1813), the Philadelphia physician who is commonly (and incorrectly) regarded as the founding father of the American temperance movement.[3] To cast Rush in this role is to misread him and his most famous pamphlet, *An Inquiry into the Effects of Ardent Spirits upon the Human Body and Mind* (1784). Rush, who had spent several years studying medicine in Edinburgh, was merely repeating what his British colleagues had already said: that distilled spirits were in a class of their own.[4] His quarrel did not extend to beer (it made men work harder). Nor did extend to wine (it had no ill effects whatsoever on the French peasants who drank it in "large

Benjamin Rush.

When this print was made, in 1802, Rush was at the height of his career, serving as a professor at the University of Pennsylvania while collecting a second income as the treasurer of the U.S. Mint. From the Library of Congress Prints and Photographs Division.

quantities"). Rush even allowed the use of spirits *in extremis*, "for in such cases, they produce their effects too soon, to create an habitual desire for them."[5]

Rush's pamphlet had no immediate impact on American drinking habits, and in the years following its publication, per capita consumption, as measured in U.S. gallons of absolute alcohol, actually increased, from 5.8 in 1790, the first year for which such statistics are available, to 6.8 in 1805.[6] The anecdotal evidence points in the same direction. When the Methodists met in 1790, they struck down an earlier injunction against selling spirits.[7] When they compiled their *Doctrines and Discipline* for the year 1798, they condemned drunkenness but not drinking. At the same time, they urged members to limit their use of distilled spirits to "cases of necessity."[8] When the students of Yale College organized a secret Moral Society in 1797, pledging themselves to refrain from swearing and gambling, not a word was said about giving up drink.[9]

The first inklings of a change of heart date from the early nineteenth century. That change started modestly enough, with small groups of individuals coming together to curtail their

drinking. The first temperance society that can be independ-
ently corroborated, an informal gathering of ministers at the
Andover Theological Seminary, dates from 1810.[10] These men
were the movement's first tacticians, and in 1826 four of them,
Leonard Woods (1774–1854), Justin Edwards (1787–1853),
Ebenezer Porter (1772–1834), and Stuart Moses (1780–1852),
would help launch the American Temperance Society.

But there is supposed to have been an even earlier group,
dating from 1808: the Temperance Society of Moreau and
Northumberland in New York State. This group, however, is men-
tioned in only one source, Lebbeus Armstrong's (1775–1860)
Temperance Reformation (1853). The location is plausible enough.
Moreau happened to be on the easternmost edge of the "Burned-
Over District," a region already famous for its religious revivals.
The timing is also plausible, for 1808 was a particularly busy year
for the revivalists. These facts, however, must be weighed against
Armstrong's motives in writing the book. Certainly he is the
central character in the drama, the person who can take nearly all
the credit for starting America's first temperance society. His other
literary creations – *Masonry Proved to Be a Work of Darkness*
(1830), *William Morgan, Abducted and Murdered by Masons*
(1831), *Signs of the Times . . . a Vindication of Capitol Punishment
for Wilful Murder* (1849), and the like – would also suggest that
Armstrong was no stranger to hyperbole.

Armstrong's account of the Moreau experiment starts with
Billy Clark, the local doctor. One moment Clark is reading
Benjamin Rush's pamphlet; the next moment he is beset with a
terrible thought: "*We shall all become a community of drunkards in
this town unless something is done to arrest the progress of intemperance!*" Clark immediately seeks out the town's one other savant,
who is of course Armstrong, and together they start America's

first temperance society. According to Armstrong, the forty-odd members of the Moreau society agreed to abstain from "all kinds of *distilled* liquors, unless required by medical authority, and also retrenchment of wine," which meant drinking it only under a doctor's orders (presumably Clark's) or at public banquets. Each member, in his capacity as an employer and paterfamilias, was expected to refrain from serving his dependents spirits. That the members were not entirely in earnest is suggested by the society's schedule of fines for backsliders: twenty-five cents for each lapse, and fifty for each lapse resulting in drunkenness.

If Armstrong is to be believed, the Moreau experiment attracted attention from the very start, resulting in a "diversity of opinions relative to its effects upon the conduct of its adherents." Most of these opinions were dismissive, as even Armstrong had to concede. Some regarded the society as an infringement on their liberties. Others, less serious-minded, simply laughed at it.[11] But there was at least one imitator, a group in the nearby town of Greenfield.[12]

This reliance on voluntary societies to promote temperance was in part dictated by necessity – in the absence of an effective government, nineteenth-century Americans *had* to organize if they wanted to get things done – but it was also a tribute to just how well those organizations worked. Alexis de Tocqueville, who visited America in 1830, was in awe. He hardly knew where to begin. There were so many associations, so many people volunteering their time and money, so many worthy causes and projects:

> Americans of all ages, all conditions, all minds constantly unite. Not only do they have commercial and industrial associations in which all take part, but they also have a thousand other kinds: religious,

moral, grave, futile, very general and very particular,
immense and very small; Americans use associations
to give fêtes, to found seminaries, to build inns, to
raise churches, to distribute books, to send mission-
aries to the antipodes; in this manner they create
hospitals, prisons, schools.[13]

By then, too, there were several voluntary associations operat-
ing on a national level. The first of these, the American Bible
Society, dates from 1816. This was followed by the American
Sunday School Union in 1817, the American Tract Society in
1825, and the American Home Missionary Society in 1826.

That same year the first national temperance organization,
the American Temperance Society, was founded in Boston.[14] Its
role in coordinating and magnifying the efforts of local temperance societies need not be belaboured. But its real contribution
lay elsewhere: with the emergence of a national entity, the
American temperance movement began to speak with one
voice. This made the temperance movement a force to be reck-
oned with, but it would also come at the price of eliminating all
competing solutions, including, most notably, those favoured by
the movement's moderate wing.

The steps taken were so small, the logic binding one to the
next so seemingly reasonable, that when the last step was reached
(teetotalism) any remaining moderates would find themselves
outflanked and without a viable counter-argument. The process
was also marked by an extraordinary degree of pragmatism. For
nearly ten years, from 1826 to 1835, the American Temperance
Society proceeded with the utmost caution, proscribing hard
liquor and nothing else. But its emphasis was new. Where Rush
had warmly recommended fermented beverages as a wholesome

alternative to hard liquor, the leadership of the American Temperance Society merely begrudged them. This, combined with the society's insistence on absolute abstinence from distilled spirits, helped set the stage for broadening the ban to all forms of alcohol in the mid-1830s. Lyman Beecher, writing years after the fact, explained the underlying logic: "We did not say a word then about wine because we thought it was best, in this sudden onset, to attack that which was most prevalent and deadly, and that it was as much as would be safe to take hold of one such dragon by the horns without tackling another; but in ourselves we resolved to inhibit wine, and in our families we generally did."[15]

The evolution of the early temperance movement, its gradual whittling down of what, where, and when people might drink, can be traced through Lyman Beecher's early career. A Yale graduate and a New England Congregationalist with pronounced Federalist sympathies, Beecher was typical of the men who took charge of the temperance movement in its formative years.

In 1803, when Beecher was just getting his start as a minister in the Long Island town of East Hampton, he developed an interest in William Wilberforce's Society for the Suppression of Vice. Wilberforce's definition of vice was broad, but it was also selective, effectively singling out the amusements of the working poor.[16] Cockfighting, bear-baiting, bawdy houses – these were the sorts of things Wilberforce's society went after. Why Beecher thought that this model was the right one for East Hampton is unclear. Earlier attempts to start English-style vice societies in America had ended in failure, and even in Puritan New England they had failed to catch on. Introduced in 1702, they were gone by 1714, with nothing to show for the proponents' efforts.[17]

Lyman Beecher with nine of his eleven surviving children, circa 1859.

Bottom row (l to r): Isabella Beecher Hooker, Catharine E. Beecher, Lyman Beecher, Mary Beecher Perkins, Harriet Beecher Stowe. Top row (l to r): Thomas K. Beecher, William H. Beecher, Edward Beecher, Charles Beecher, Henry Ward Beecher. Courtesy of the Harriet Beecher Stowe Center.

The real attraction for Beecher was Wilberforce's premise: that Christians had a positive *duty* to prevent other people from sinning. Besides, Beecher had one enormous advantage over Wilberforce: he was living in a country where everything was still possible. Just because other nations had "never yet resisted the influence of sin," was it "to be inferred that they never will?" Not in America, where there was less vice to begin with, "less opposition to encounter," and "nothing but our own sloth and indifference" standing in the way.[18]

At this point Beecher was no more troubled by drunkenness than he was by any other vice. His epiphany came in 1808, the same year Lebbeus Armstrong and Billy Clark are supposed to have started the Moreau temperance society. A remnant of the Montauk native tribe, now reduced to begging, still lived on the outskirts of East Hampton. The townspeople took terrible advantage of them. But the worst offender was a local "grog-seller," himself a notorious drunkard. The incident "burned and burned in my mind," Beecher recorded years later, "and I swore a deep oath to God that it shouldn't be so."*

He made a study of the subject. He read Rush's pamphlet. He composed sermons against intemperance, waiting for the right occasion to deliver them. (That occasion would not offer itself for fifteen years.) Two years later, he is to be found in Litchfield, Connecticut, at the head of a new congregation. He took another oath after witnessing still more drunkenness, this time among his fellow ministers. Never again would he attend an ordination where they smoke, drank, and "told their stories."[19] Now that he was back in Connecticut (he was from New Haven) he was close to the epicentre of the nascent temperance movement. Massachusetts had taken the lead in 1811, when the General Association of its Congregational Churches had urged its members to take up the cause of temperance.[20] This led to the creation, one year later, of the Massachusetts Society for the Suppression of Intemperance.[21] Not to be outdone, Connecticut's Congregationalists set up their own committee in 1811, charging its three members to come up with practical remedies. When a year later they reported back that nothing could be done, Beecher exploded: "The blood started through my heart when I heard this, and I rose instanter, and moved that a committee of three should

* Beecher, now in his senectitude, had a ghost writer: his daughter Harriet.

be appointed immediately, to report at this meeting the ways and means of arresting the tide of intemperance."

He was a man on a mission. The following day he presented his report, "the most important paper that ever I wrote." He was full of helpful ideas – that ministers stop drinking hard liquor at their meetings, that laymen stop serving it at their social functions, that employers stop dispensing it to their employees, that parents stop drinking it in their homes. But worse even than drunkenness was the quintessentially Calvinist fatalism that said nothing could be done about it.[22] Flushed with evangelical optimism, he exhorted his "brethren in the ministry, the members of our churches, and the persons who lament and desire to check the progress of this evil, that they neither express nor indulge the melancholy apprehension that nothing can be done on this subject; a prediction eminently calculated to paralyze exertion, and become the disastrous cause of its own fulfillment."

In 1825, the same year Timothy Merritt published his guide to Christian perfection, Beecher felt that at last the time had come to deliver the sermons he had put aside in 1808. Years later he would remember how they "took hold of the whole congregation," how "Sabbath after Sabbath the interest grew, and became the most absorbing thing ever heard of before."[23] They caused an even bigger sensation when they were published the following year under the title *Six Sermons on the Nature, Occasions, Signs, Evils, and Remedy of Intemperance.*

The tone is glum, reflecting how little had been accomplished in the seventeen years since he first spoke out against intemperance. He despaired of the voluntary associations that he had, up to now, been promoting. Their results were too fleeting, too local – "for though, in a single town, or state, they may effect a temporary reformation, it requires an effort to make them universal, and to keep up their energy." He despaired too of "self-government." It was all well and fine, laudable even, but it could only "limit the evil." All the "efforts of the pulpit and the press" – these, too, were futile without "something more radical, efficient, and permanent."

What that something might be, Beecher was not yet willing to say. But the implication was clear. The time was fast approaching for stronger measures, measures to protect the temperate few from the intemperate many. Everyone knew who he meant: the Jacksonian rabble, men "of intemperate habits and desperate fortunes," men with "no right in the soil, and no capital at stake, and no moral principle."[24]

Events were clearly moving in tandem, for in 1826, the year Beecher published his *Six Sermons*, the American Temperance Society also publicly committed itself to abstinence. But the new rule applied only to distilled spirits, leaving the question of other alcoholic beverages for another day. That same year, William Collier (1771–1843), a Boston minister, started a temperance weekly, the *National Philanthropist*, with the motto "*Temperate drinking is the downhill road to intemperance.*" Reverend Calvin Chapin (1763–1851) of Westfield, Connecticut, was even then writing a series of articles for the *Connecticut Observer*, all to the effect that "*Entire abstinence from ardent spirits is the only certain preventive of intemperance.*"[25]

Justin Edwards, one of the original members of the Andover temperance society, had long since reached the same conclusion. Like Beecher, he was a Congregationalist minister with strong evangelical leanings. Also like Beecher, he was one of the movement's stars, having made his mark in 1825 with the publication of *The Well-Conducted Farm*. Its hero, the respectable Mr. B-, owns a large farm in Massachusetts. Mr. B- has money, enough to lend to less successful farmers and to hire field hands. One day he decides to break with custom and stop serving his hands hard liquor. But he is a fair man, and so he increases each worker's wages by a dollar a month. The following year he imposes a new condition of employment: now his men must "abstain entirely, and at all times, from the use of ardent spirits." One year later, he finds himself living in a Federalist utopia. He is wealthier than ever, and his workers are docile, respectable, and God-fearing:

> Before, numbers used to spend a great portion of their wages in scenes of amusement and dissipation. Now, they have no inclination to frequent such scenes. The consequence is, they lay up more money. They are, also, more serious in their deportment, spend more of their leisure time in useful reading, much oftener peruse the Scriptures, and attend public worship; and they are more attentive to all the means of grace.[26]

Once abstinence had been established as the rule for one intoxicant, it was but a short step from there to establishing it as the rule for all intoxicants. Edward Hitchcock, Amherst's tireless temperance crusader, was already saying as much by 1830. There was "no other stopping place, that will not leave them, with a narrow and slippery foot hold, upon the side of a precipice." He himself was already calling on the undergraduates he taught to give up wine, and while it was as yet "extremely injudicious, and even quixotic, for any Temperance Society to

Edward Hitchcock, a professor of geology at Amherst College and its president from 1845 to 1854.

An early convert to temperance and the virtues of a simple diet, he encouraged undergraduates to join his anti-poisons society and to sign a pledge to abstain from hard liquor, wine, opium, and tobacco. Temperance pledges were inscribed on the college's diplomas. Courtesy of the Amherst College Archives.

require total abstinence" from beer and cider as well, as a private citizen he thought it "highly expedient and desirable, for every young man, for every scholar especially, to refrain from them entirely."[27] Hitchcock was not alone. The same year he was hectoring Amherst's undergraduates, Justin Edwards was going from church to church, calling on his listeners "to join a society on the plan of entire abstinence."[28] In 1831, the Philadelphia physicians who edited the *Journal of Health* went out on a limb and denounced the use of fermented beverages.[29] Emboldened, the Pennsylvania Society for Discouraging the Use of Ardent Spirits came out against all intoxicating drinks, entrusting a failed minister, Sylvester Graham (1794–1851), to spread its new message. Then there were all the members of the American Temperance Society who had already gone above and beyond the call of duty, forswearing not just hard liquor, but all of its weaker sisters. Or so they boasted when the society queried them on the subject in 1835. Colonel Guy Begelow of Colchester, Connecticut, had

A somewhat romanticized portrait of Sylvester Graham,
appearing in the *Harper's New Monthly Magazine* in 1880.

Contemporary descriptions were less flattering. Graham's hometown newspaper, the
Northampton Gazette, *described his speaking style as "rather fantastical for the*
pulpit. He makes great use of the screw-auger gesture boring into the left palm with his
right forefinger, and from his upward and expansive heavings with both arms, we should
judge he would make an excellent fugler for a band of lunar boy-bats, just learning to
expand their leathern wings, and go through the flying drill." From the Library of
Congress Prints and Photographs Division.

given up spirits back in 1814, twelve years before the society had
forced the issue. In 1824, Begelow gave up wine, refusing to
drink it even at his own wedding. In 1834, he gave up his last
remaining indulgence: hard cider. The Reverend Henry Wright
of Boston had drunk nothing but water for the past seven or
eight years. Elisha Taylor of Schenectady, New York, had given

up spirits fifteen years ago, and wine and beer "about seven years ago, not because I then thought they would, or did hurt me, but because I saw they impaired my influence as a friend and advocate of the cause of temperance. For the same reason, two years since I quit the use of cider, and all alcoholic drinks."[30] But for sheer virtuosity, Eleazer Parmly outdid them all. "For two years past" (he wrote in 1835),

> I have abstained from the use of all the diffusible stimulants, using no animal food, either flesh, fish, or fowl; nor any alcoholic or vinous spirits; no form of ale, beer, or porter; no cider, tea, or coffee; but using milk and water as my only liquid aliment, and feeding sparingly, or rather, moderately, upon farinaceous food, vegetables, and fruit, seasoned with unmelted butter, slightly boiled eggs, and sugar or molasses; with no condiment but common salt.[31]

The American temperance movement was at first reluctant to go through the door it had opened. As late as 1829 a member of the Massachusetts Society for the Suppression of Intemperance could still think that a group in the Berkshires was "carrying the thing too far" by proscribing wine. He took some persuading. He was relieved to find that they did not completely object to wine – as long as it was "used in moderation." But what won him over was their appeal to fairness. Why, they asked, should the poor be asked to give up their rum while the rich were allowed to keep their wine?[32]

By the mid-1830s, the hard-liners were sufficiently emboldened – and sufficiently numerous – to impose their views on a succession of state temperance conventions, in New Hampshire,

Massachusetts, and New York. In 1836, they carried the day at
the National Temperance Convention in Saratoga. The
American Temperance Society, now formally committed to a
plank of teetotalism, was reborn as the American Temperance
Union, and the movement's two venerables, Lyman Beecher and
Justin Edwards, signalled their approval by signing the new teetotal pledge.

The ease with which the radicals prevailed suggests that not
one but several factors favoured the acceptance of complete abstinence in the mid-1830s. The most obvious was the passing of the
old guard. In 1836, Lyman Beecher was sixty-one. And while
Justin Edwards was considerably younger (he was just forty-nine),

A Member of the Temperance Society, 1833 or 1834.

*This print pokes fun at the hypocrisy of abstaining from nothing more than distilled
spirits, a rule that leaves this temperance gourmand free to drink as much wine – and
eat as much food – as he pleases.* Courtesy of the American Antiquarian Society.

he took the occasion of the National Temperance Convention to announce his retirement, confident that the rising generation was more than equal to the task he was relinquishing.

They were. The literature is replete with youthful conver-sion experiences – Lorenzo Dow at fourteen, Peter Cartwright at sixteen, Frances Willard at twenty – each a confirmation of Timothy Merritt's claim that a "much larger proportion of youth experience religion, than of those in old age, or even in middle age; and it is a fact that a much larger proportion experience sanctification."[33] It was precisely in this youthful cohort, in the mechanics' and young men's temperance organizations in partic-ular, that teetotalism found its most committed following. Chief among them was New York City's Apprentices' Temperance Society, which embraced teetotalism in 1833. Other groups, in New Haven, Harrisburg, Albany, Worcester, and elsewhere, quickly followed suit.[34]

Teetotalism was also given a boost by the early temperance movement's success in reducing the demand for hard liquor. Between 1810 and 1840, per capita consumption of spirits, as meas-ured in absolute alcohol, declined from 2.1 U.S. gallons to 1.4. The consumption of fermented beverages declined during the same period, from 1.6 U.S. gallons of absolute alcohol to just 0.4. But the sheer quantities of beer consumed nearly doubled, from 0.6 U.S. gallons to 1.3, while wine consumption also rose, albeit more modestly (from 0.2 U.S. gallons to 0.3).[35] This shift in con-sumption, trifling though it was, had a good many people in the temperance camp convinced that they had substituted one problem for another.[36]

The movement's successes, moreover, were unevenly dis-tributed. Middle-class men were drinking less, but that still left large numbers of men, most of them working class, who were

Four children wake up on Christmas morning, only to find that their stockings are empty.

From "Christmas Morning in the Drunkard's Home," in The Curse of Drink: or Stories of Hell's Commerce (1909).

drinking as much as ever. They are the stock characters of the temperance weepies, always in headlong flight from the women in their lives. Their wives may plead with them, but in the end it is their daughters who drag them back into the world of worka-day respectability:

> For Susie, my darling, my wee six-year-old,
> Though fainting with hunger and shivering with cold,
> There on the bare floor, asked God to bless *me*!
> And she said, "Don't cry mamma! He will; for you see
> I *believe* what I ask for!" Then sobered, I crept
> Away from the house; and that night when I slept,
> Next my heart lay the PLEDGE![37]

Susie's determination, impressive though it is, pales beside that of little Mary Morgan, the tragic heroine of *Ten Nights in a Bar-Room, and What I Saw There* (1854). The author, Timothy Shay Arthur (1809–1885), published more than two hundred

themselves.[39] Wittingly or not, this change in priorities also played into the hands of the radicals, for only one strategy seemed to work with actual drunkards, and that was what one Baltimore newspaper called "swearing off," or giving up all intoxicating drinks.[40] "Swearing off," however, placed moderate drinkers in a bind: how could they set a good example if they themselves continued to drink? As one temperance tract put it, "If I take a little, others who follow my example, being weaker or not so careful as myself, may be led to drunkenness; but if I entirely abstain, I set an example which is safe for everybody to follow."[41] No longer was abstinence incumbent only on those who needed it most (Beecher's original formula): it was now incumbent also on those who needed it the least.

One is left to wonder how many moderates were won over by this argument, and how many instead simply dropped out of the temperance movement.[42] As in Britain, moderates and teetotallers at first tried to coexist, only to find that this was both logically and temperamentally impossible. In society after society the two groups went their separate ways. This happened to the Maine State Temperance Society in February 1837. After a "warm and protracted debate" the society was dissolved, with the teetotallers immediately forming their own society: the Maine Temperance Union.[43] The members of a Massachusetts society, located in Hillsborough County, managed to stay in harness until 1839, at which point a majority voted in favour of teetotalism. In doing so they expressed the hope, one destined never to be realized, that the two factions might yet "harmoniously cooperate."[44] As late as 1844, it took almost no coaxing to get some "temperance men" in Lowell, Massachusetts, to accept a glass of wine. The newspaper reporting the story considered this a "violation of their temperance principles"; the men in question did not.[45]

Among the holdouts was the original temperance society in nearby Moreau. Its surviving members waited until 1843 to take the new pledge. Billy Clark, now an old man, took it, as did Lebbeus Armstrong.[46] They had travelled far from the days when hard liquor was the only enemy and backsliding was all but expected.

Most of the people who took the teetotal pledge were not problem drinkers. This was true first and foremost of the hundreds of thousands of women who drank little or no alcohol but who nonetheless embraced the cause of temperance.[47] Many committed themselves in hope of reforming improvident husbands and wayward sons, but few did so out of a need to reform themselves.[48] Like the long-suffering wife in "Why Don't He Come" (1849), they often seemed to have no vices at all:

> Until the waning moon was high,
> A silent watch I here did keep;
> But slow, the long, long hours went by,
> And I returned, alone to weep.[49]

Some, like Frances Willard, had grown up in households in which nobody drank. "I never in my life saw wine offered in my own country but once," she recalled.[50] Of her friends and intimates in later life, only one drank: her beloved brother Oliver.[51] When she swore off drink in 1855 (she was just sixteen at the time) her life went on much as it had before.

The boys who grew up in these households were obviously exposed to the same messages, and for every Oliver Willard there was a pure-heart like William Andrus Alcott. Alcott recalled growing up in a house where distilled spirits and coffee were almost never drunk. Temperance, he had to admit, "was to me an easy virtue."[52] Neal Dow (1804–1897), the man who brought prohibition to Maine, was the "blindest man" in that state because the "adder, 'drink,' [had] never stung his heart, nor made him hang his head for shame, nor struck his wife's sweet face with its foul lash, nor goaded him to borrow, lie or steal; he has seen men and women but as trees walking, and has inhaled the hot breath of the saloon for a generation, and yet not seen it, save as one catches glimpses of some slimy, crawling thing and turns his eyes away no wiser."[53] When the American Temperance Society sent out a questionnaire in 1835, asking its members to describe how they felt now that they had given up drinking, many could offer no insights at all. Gerrit Smith (1797–1874), the wealthy abolitionist, was one such innocent. "I thank you for addressing to me a copy of your circular," he replied, "but, as my use of intoxicating liquor, even before the temperance reformation began, was very limited, my experience furnishes little of the information you desire." Samuel Miller (1769–1850), a professor of religious history at Princeton and a big believer in the benefits of fasting, was yet another innocent: "I was never in the habit of using ardent spirits; and during the earlier period of my life, seldom drank wine."[54]

There were so many of them, respectable men and women, signing pledges that were absurdly easy to keep. The people who threatened them the most were not drunks. The real threat lay closer at hand, in the parlours of the moderate and outwardly respectable drinkers who lived next door, across the street, down the road. True inebriates were object lessons, living proof of alcohol's capacity to ruin lives. But moderate drinkers were not so easily categorized. Their ability to drink without coming to ruin threatened to put the lie to the entire teetotal paradigm. "You teach the doctrine that it is needful, or useful, or innocent," the American Temperance Society lamented in 1834.[55]

Moderate drinkers offended on another level: they were neutrals in the ongoing war against sin. And this, for rigorists like Charles Grandison Finney, was as bad as siding with sin:

> It is not needful that a person should rail at the cold-water society, in order to be on the best terms with drunkards and moderate drinkers. Only let him plead for the moderate use of wine, only let him continue to drink it as a luxury, and all the drunkards account him on their side. If he refuses to give his influence to the temperance cause, he is claimed of course by the other side as a friend.[56]

A BAD EXAMPLE.

A Bad Example, as set in 1909.

Moderate drinkers were a persistent thorn in the side of the American temperance movement, which was reduced to telling them that they should stop drinking not because they were doing themselves harm, but because others might be encouraged to think that drinking was harmless.

C.E. Sargent did not mince words: any man who did not "advocate the temperance cause today in its boldest and most radical form" was "a coward, and in a certain sense a dead weight upon society."[57] The *National Temperance Orator* for 1877 had a ready rejoinder for everyone who abstained and yet refused to take the pledge: "Are you not a MAN?"[58] Terrence Powderly (1849–1924), the labour leader who tried unsuccessfully to get his union to embrace temperance, called the "man who remains neutral" a "coward at heart," undeserving of the "name of man or friend."[59]

The first major challenge to the American temperance movement came in 1840. That was the year actual drunkards, the group that had been so ill-served by the old American Temperance Society, started forming their own teetotal societies. Anticipating that their motives might be assailed, they gave themselves an unassailable name: the Washingtonians. Similar societies had already been launched in Britain, the first and most famous being the Preston Temperance Society. (One of that society's original members, a stammering plasterer named Dicky Turner, is supposed to have coined the term *teetotal* when he called for "tee-tee-tee-total abstinence.") The British and American groups had three things in common: their organizers and members were working class, the groups were not ostensibly religious, and they relied on drunkards to keep each other sober.

The Washingtonians started with six men, all friends and each with a serious drinking problem. During one of their bouts, in Chase's Tavern in Baltimore, it occurred to them that they should give up drinking. The group's leader, a tailor by the name of William Mitchell, came up with an idea straight out of the

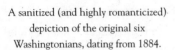

A sanitized (and highly romanticized) depiction of the original six Washingtonians, dating from 1884.

Preston Temperance Society: each man should tell his story by way of encouraging other drunkards to take heart and take the pledge. The idea, of drunkards reaching out to other drunkards, caught on. By the end of the year, there were upward of three hundred Washingtonians. By 1841, there were independent societies in every major town in the northeast United States. The group grew because it did the one thing that no one else did: it helped common drunkards, men who had, up to now, been "held up to public indignation and reprobation."[60] By one estimate, some 600,000 men ended up taking the Washingtonian pledge, of whom 150,000 managed to stay sober.[61]

It did not last. By 1847, just seven years after their first meeting in Chase's Tavern, the Washingtonians had all but faded from view. The organizers, for all their good intentions, had made several strategic mistakes, starting with the decision to allow non-drinkers to join their ranks. The desired effect, of allaying the suspicions of the mainstream temperance movement, was not achieved. Nor, given the depth of those suspicions, could it ever have been achieved. As far as one New Hampshire newspaper was concerned, all Washingtonians were scoundrels. Certainly this was the point of an article the newspaper ran in 1844. The villain of the piece was a reformed drunkard named William Rich. At the behest of Washingtonians of Lynn, Massachusetts, Rich had been released from the state prison with the understanding that he would deliver temperance lectures about his struggles with alcohol. The editors were unimpressed. Perhaps their readers remembered the "person who lectured through this section of the state last winter, and who became famous for relating disgusting stories"? Soon Rich was back to his old tricks, repaying a bene-factor's kindness by breaking into his store. This, the newspaper editorialized, "sets in a strong light the impolicy of the haste with which Washingtonian lecturers are made."[62]

Middle-class reformers wasted no time in remaking the Washingtonian societies in their own image. First men still in the throes of drink were locked out, then reformed drunkards were kept from telling their "disgusting stories." But the Washingtonians themselves must bear the blame for their own demise, if only because they were so anxious to keep the churches from co-opting them. This was an understandable goal. But it also left the organization without a sustaining ideal. At the end of the day, after all the meetings, parades, and cold-water picnics, nothing stood between the drunkard and his desire to drink. John Gough, who joined the Washingtonians in 1842, was one of many to try and fail to stop drinking on his own. It was only after he had put "forth all his energies," trusting in "God's mercy and grace," that he succeeded in sticking to his pledge.[63]

Gough would go on to make a career out of telling his life's story to the world, becoming the most beloved temperance lecturer of his day. He was tireless. From 1843 to 1886, when he collapsed from a stroke in the middle of a lecture, hardly a day passed in which he did not fill an auditorium, mesmerizing his middle-class audiences with an endless succession of homely stories.[64] He was legendary for his theatrics, honed in the days when he fancied he might become an actor. Frances Willard could watch him for hours. She remembered "That lithe form . . . always in motion up and down the immense platform; that sallow, bearded face, framed in a shock of iron-grey hair, was of protean aspect, now personating the drunkard, then the hypocrite, anon the saint. Those restless, eager hands, supple as India-rubber, were always busy, flinging the hair forward in one character, back in another, or standing it straight up in a third; crushing the drunk fiend, pointing to the angel in human nature."[65]

He had almost no formal schooling, a quality that recommended him to his American audiences. In a passage suspiciously reminiscent of John Wesley ("I design plain truth for plain people"), Gough claimed to know "nothing of grammar or rhetoric," that "Logic was a term to me that I could not define." Far from being embarrassed by his lack of learning, he was forever calling attention to it. In this he was more than a little disingenuous. He was far smarter and subtler than he let on, and those who condescended to him did so at their own peril. This was demonstrated early in his career, in 1854, when he persisted in delivering a temperance talk to students at Oxford. He had been warned not to go. But he relished the challenge of matching wits with people more privileged than himself, and so for twenty minutes he "spoke in pantomime amid the deafening catcalls of the boys."[66] They were a tough crowd. An earlier lecturer who had come to talk about the evils of tobacco had been forced to flee after the students, puffing on pipes and cigarettes, filled the hall with smoke. But Gough stood his ground. "What is the cause of the intemperance of Great Britain?" he asked. "Tempewanth thothietieth," somebody replied, and even Gough had to laugh.[67] He made no converts that day, but he made no enemies either.

Gough was the exception, the working-class man who could charm the middle-class leaders of the mainstream temperance movement. The *New York Observer* gushed: "A natural sense of propriety, refined and exalted by divine grace, preserves him from those ways and manners which have seriously crippled . . . the Washingtonian reformers with public assemblies."[68] Polite society did more than just accept him: it lionized him. Even Lyman Beecher, the old venerable of the movement, called Gough a *friend*.[69] What was not to love? Gough did not blame other people for his troubles. His personal philosophy was upbeat and inoffensive. "We cannot create circumstances, but we can make the best of them when they come," he said. "Their power is not despotic, and, by God's help and our own endeavor, we may make them our servants."[70]

If Gough was the genial face of the early temperance movement, the bootstrap apostle of suasion, Neal Dow was its face at mid-century, stilted, self-righteous, and mistrustful of human perfectibility. He was unlike Gough in every possible way. He had been born into wealth. He had never had a problem with alcohol. He had no faith in the ability of ordinary people to grasp the logic of abstinence. He had an unattractive personality and was a miserable orator. Even the official journal of the American Temperance Union found it hard to like his public persona: "He is not a noisy and loose disclaimer. But while he is a man of order, he is a man of correct statistics and useful facts. He speaks like a man of business rather than the studied orator."[71] It puzzled him that everyone else was not as successful as he – until he put two and two together. The reason was obvious: other people drank and he did not. From his carriage he could see scenes of poverty and misery. "Rum did that!" he would exclaim.[72] He "saw that, as a rule, neither industry, thrift, prudence, saving nor comfort was to be found where indulgence in intoxicants prevailed." In 1827, inspired by Justin Edwards and Lyman Beecher, he committed himself to temperance. By the early 1830s, he had taken the next step and aligned himself with the radicals who were calling for teetotalism.

He was even then coming to believe that the movement's earlier initiatives had not gone far enough. Moral suasion did not impress him. His pessimism was leading him to a different conclusion: "that any permanent change for the better in the habits of the people would be improbable, if not impossible, without the suppression by law of the traffic in intoxicating liquors."[73]

What was missing was a bully pulpit. This Dow got when he was elected mayor of Portland in 1851. He used the position for all it was worth, ceaselessly agitating for statewide prohibition. He found allies among the abolitionists – and inspiration, learning from them how to roil public opinion by churning out propaganda and how to pressure the legislature by swamping it with petitions. The Maine legislature had already voted for prohibition five years earlier, but it had deliberately neglected to give the law teeth.[74] In 1851, the legislature again voted for prohibition. This time there was someone committed to its enforcement. The new law, moreover, did have teeth – crippling fines for first-time offenders, jail time for recidivists, a mechanism for obtaining search warrants, and a provision for seizing black market liquor. Dow's Maine Law was not the first

Neal Dow as a colonel in the Union Army.

"*At the outbreak of the war,*" he would later confess, "*I had had no military experience, not even such as might have been obtained in the state militia.*" This did not keep him from raising his own regiment and placing himself at its head. Dow ran his regiment according to strict temperance principles, forbidding all drinking and swearing. Courtesy of the Maine State Archives.

state law to prohibit alcohol, but it was the first attempt to make prohibition work.

And for that Dow paid a high price. His businesses were boycotted. His house was vandalized. He was harassed in the courts. In 1852, his effigy and that of another temperance crusader, both saturated with turpentine, were found hanging from a tree on the Boston Common.[75] In 1855, rattled past endurance, he ordered the militia to open fire on a mob in Portland. One man died as a result and seven were wounded. The *Farmers' Cabinet* rushed to his defence. Was it not better "for one man to die by a *bullet*, rather than a thousand by the *bottle*"?[76]

The real threat to prohibition lay in the passive resistance of the middle classes who continued to drink in cheerful defiance of the law. No one could stop them from importing supplies from elsewhere. Nor did the Maine Law ban hard cider, as Dow himself had to concede in 1852.[77] The first of these loopholes was partially closed when other states and territories passed their own Maine Laws – Massachusetts, Minnesota, Rhode Island, and Vermont in 1852, Michigan in 1853, Connecticut in 1854, and New Hampshire, New York, Delaware, Indiana, Iowa, and Nebraska in 1855. But that same year Dow was booted out of office, and the legislature that had been the first to vote for statewide prohibition became the first to repeal it. Other states quickly followed suit.

That still left a majority of states and territories (twenty-nine out of forty-two as of 1860) that had not opted for prohibition, though many had come close. All six of the New England states had voted for it. But none of the Southern states had done so.[78] It was in vain that the American Temperance Union moved its headquarters closer to the South (from Boston to Philadelphia), in vain that it insisted that the friends of temperance were under no compulsion to take up any other causes.[79] Nor were many

The Maine Traveller's Satchel.

In this print a respectable matron is caught in the act of smuggling liquor into the dry state of Maine.

Southerners convinced by the organization's repeated assertions that it was only in the business of promoting temperance – and not abolitionism. The close links between the two causes were there for all to see, driving a wedge between Northern and Southern Methodists in 1844 and making many of the temperance movement's best speakers personae non gratae south of the Mason-Dixon Line.[80] Even if those speakers had been welcome in the South, it is by no means clear that they would have made much headway, for once there they faced a series of obstacles for which they were ill-prepared. What good were their tracts when so many people were illiterate? How were they to reach large numbers of people when so much of the population was dispersed? Who among them could convince Southerners to abandon their obsession with personal honour and instead embrace the Yankee virtues of thrift, industry, and self-restraint?[81]

But the biggest division of all was as much theological as it was ideological, which is to say that Southern evangelicals already had a radically different understanding of Christian perfection, one whose pietism and extreme conservatism were diametrically opposed to the all-encompassing activism of the Oberlin reformers. That this understanding also served to protect the status quo – slavery in the years before the war, segregation after it – need not be belaboured.[82] Northern temperance reformers would have to pay a high price for Southern support, and that was to abandon their dream of achieving a perfect society.

In 1885, Frances Willard, now into her sixth year as president of the Woman's Christian Temperance Union, made a pilgrimage to the grave of Benjamin Rush. There she planted a tree and placed a marble tablet commemorating the hundredth

anniversary of Rush's famous pamphlet. She had already planted
a tree outside Washington's tomb at Mount Vernon, after which
she and the women accompanying her sang "My Country, 'Tis
of Thee." Washington was the father of his country, but Rush,
in Willard's eyes, was something just as important: he was the
father of the American temperance movement.

The gesture ignored how little she actually had in common
with Rush. To Rush, very much a man of the Enlightenment,
temperance had meant moderation. To Willard it meant the
opposite. It meant abstinence. This was brought home most
spectacularly when an Episcopalian matron made the mistake
of offering Willard a glass of wine. Willard made a scene: "The
blood flushed in cheek and brow as I said to her, 'Madam,
200,000 women would lose somewhat of their faith in humanity if I should drink a drop of wine.'" In her autobiography,
written for the benefit of those 200,000 women, the incident
becomes a teachable moment, one that affirms their superiority
to the non-evangelical upper classes: "Evidently this lady lived
in a world so different from my own that it did not occur to her
that a temperance woman was a total abstainer!"[83]

The progression from Rush's position to Willard's was sub-
stantially complete by 1836, the year the American temperance
movement forever turned its back on all forms of drink. From this
point forward it had a new enemy: the moderate middle. In a
certain sense, the radicals were devouring their own, respectable
men and women who resembled them in every way except their
drinking habits. But as long as the moderates could lay claim to
the temperance mantle, they were a reproach to the movement in
its newly constituted form. By their example they suggested that
there was more than one way to deal with drinking, that cutting
back might be nearly as good as stopping altogether.

Behind these debates lurked an even deeper fault line: between the North and South. The North, with its broad interpretation of Christian perfection, was receptive to temperance; the South, with its narrow interpretation, was not. Even at this early juncture, however, the seeds of doubt were being sown in the North. Or so one might infer from the movement's abandonment of moral suasion in favour of coercion. Implicit in that abandonment was a loss of faith in a cornerstone of the Second Great Awakening: the idea that all Americans were equally capable of overcoming the dead hand of sin. Those who could not or would not embrace abstinence on their own would now have it imposed on them – in the form of prohibition.

THREE

SYLVESTER GRAHAM, VEGETARIANISM, AND THE PURSUIT OF PERFECT TEMPERANCE

First goes the tobacco, most filthy of all,
Then drugs, pork and whisky, together must fall,
Then coffee and spices, and sweetmeats and tea,
And fine flour and flesh-meats and pickles must flee.

Roswell Cottrell, "Oh, Yes, I See It Is So" (1867)

Health reform, which first became a fad in the 1830s, was the second of America's abstinence movements. The list of things it proscribed was long – tobacco, coffee and tea, meats and spices, pickles, oysters, and sweets, and, of course, alcohol. Unlike temperance, it has never really gone away, returning every few years in a new guise and fading just as quickly. The most demanding and thoroughgoing of America's abstinence movements, it was also, in its first incarnation, the movement that came closest to embodying the high ideals of the Oberlin perfectionists.[1] Why did Ellen G. White (1827–1915), the revered

The strict dietary restrictions of the original perfectionists were picked up by Ellen G. White and the Seventh-Day Adventists, who were expected to "bear positive testimony against tobacco, spirituous liquors, snuff, tea, coffee, flesh-meats, butter, spices, rich cakes, mince-pies, a large amount of salt, and all exciting substances used as articles of food." Courtesy of the Willard Library in Battle Creek.

prophetess of the Seventh-Day Adventists, make diet a centre-piece of her teachings? Because the "subject of temperance in all its bearings has an important place in the work of salvation."[2] Mary Tyler Peabody Mann (1806–1877), wife of the reformer and educator Horace Mann, wrote an entire cookbook (*Christianity in the Kitchen*) around the idea that "we are not to eat to gratify our ignoble appetites, but to build up purely and devoutly those temples of the Holy Spirit which our bodies are designed to be."[3] The "laws of health," Catharine Beecher (1800–1878) pronounced in 1855, are the "laws of God."[4]

Those laws – and the demands they placed on those who followed them – extended well beyond the kitchen. Eat only twice a day and never before bed. Let at least five hours elapse between meals. Shun "all dalliance with females, and all lewd books, and obscene conversation, and lascivious images, and thoughts." Sleep on a "hard bed, and rise early in the morning," "no matter if the hour be somewhat early."[5] Rub your body "briskly and freely with a good stiff flesh-brush, and then exercise vigorously in the open air, or in the gymnasium, for an hour before breakfast."

The goal, one that took its cue from the doctrine of Christian perfection, was to achieve purity on all fronts – physical, mental, and sexual. All of the reasons the health reformers gave for doing as they said, all of their appeals to the laws of nature, were secondary to this one goal. Sylvester Graham, the leading figure of the early health reform movement, could and did object to meat on humanitarian grounds. So did Ellen G. White.[6] But the suffering of animals was always overshadowed by the suffering of the people who ate them. Carnivores daydreamed. They thought lustful thoughts. They acted on those thoughts. In short, they sinned. That was what made meat morally objectionable – not the animals that went to the abattoir, but the souls that went to hell. Only occasionally does one find sensitive souls like Amos Bronson Alcott (1799–1888), unable to enter a butcher's shop without feeling sick to his stomach.* "The death-set eyes of beasts peer at me and accuse me of belonging to the race of murderers," he confided in his journal.[7]

The movement's goal was quintessentially evangelical, and so was its basic premise: that the individual could overcome every adversity, poverty as well as disease.[8] The essential contribution of the early health reform movement was to cast disease as a sin, as something the individual brought on himself or herself. It is the flip side of this equation Americans keep returning to:

---

* Alcott was father to Louisa May Alcott and cousin to the health reformer William Andrus Alcott.

if disease is a sin, if it is a choice, then it is also something individuals can overcome on their own.[9]

Health reform owed its inspiration to Christian perfection. But it owed its start to the misfortunes of one man: the Reverend Sylvester Graham. To his enemies (and these by far out-numbered his friends), he was the "apostle of saw-dust puddings and cob-meal bread," an "itinerant lecturer-general for the public good so far as his own pecuniary profit is regarded."[10] William Andrus Alcott, Graham's better-educated rival, described him as "far-famed, and very far-hated," elsewhere observing that the "bare mention of his name, in almost any part of the country, is to awaken the prejudices, if not the hostilities of every foe, and of some friends (supposed friends, I mean), of 'temperance in all things.'"[11] Theodore Weld, an early convert to Graham's regimen, was all too aware of his hero's failings, noting that he had "unpleasant peculiarities about him in some respects," that he was "vain and egotistic in some measure."[12] What did Isaac Lyons think of the man who had once kept a shop in Parsippany, New Jersey? That he was a poseur and a fop, "an eccentric and wayward genius from first to last."[13] Graham's surviving siblings went out of their way to avoid him – Isaac by refusing to respond to his letters, Jerusha by cutting off all contact, Harriet by withdrawing into her own family.[14]

Graham's call to the ministry came only after he had failed at a succession of jobs. At the age of twenty-nine, a man among boys, he was admitted to the Amherst Preparatory Academy. The person who had written on his behalf, the Reverend James Richards of Newark, New Jersey, could say only that the applicant's talents were "above mediocrity" and that "Should he set himself down to study for a few months, and his conduct be such as to commend itself to the pious and judicious – I should think it safe to patronize him."

Graham lasted only six or eight months at Amherst – the records differ on how long. The academy's director, the Reverend Daniel Clark, explained: "Mr. Graham sometimes thinks too loud for this dishonest world." Another instructor mentioned "some peculiarities," yet another his "quick sense of right and propriety." His classmates were less judicious. Piqued by the "apparent sense of superiority which it is generally thought Mr. Graham displays," they simply called him a "vile fellow, without specifying any traits of character in which that vileness consisted," and bided their time. Their opportunity came when Graham was charged with assaulting a young woman in broad daylight. There was a trial – it is unclear whether Graham was actually convicted – and after that he was booted out of the academy.

Graham still hoped to become a minister. But each time he applied for a position, questions were raised about his contretemps at Amherst. The Reverend Henry Ludlow was especially blunt in turning down Graham's application, telling him that he "must give up the idea of entering the ministry, 'because . . . the Association are unanimous in the opinion, that you are not a proper person for that office. Every member of that body . . . thinks you ought never to be licensed to preach the gospel. You had therefore better relinquish the idea, and go to New York and take a school.'"

Graham next surfaces back in Amherst, where he went about collecting letters testifying to his good character. These were tepid at best. Gamaliel Olds, a professor at the academy, could only "certify that Mr Sylvester Graham, whilst resident in this town, may have fallen into imprudences, yet, so far as my knowledge extends, he did nothing to impeach his moral character." The Reverend Ebenezer Gay struggled to find the right words: "As to his piety, though I must confess I did not see so much evidence of it as I could have wished, there was nothing, so far as I know, directly to the contrary." Perhaps the most astonishing thing in all of this was Graham's obliviousness to what was being said about him. Olds's letter, Gay's letter, the countless rebuffs – Graham copied them all into a letterbook under the heading "Testimonials Concerning the Character of Sylvester Graham, Relative to his Entering the Christian Ministry."

Graham had yet another problem: he had too little formal schooling to qualify as a Presbyterian minister. He tried studying on his own after being expelled from Amherst, but was nonetheless turned down when he applied for a position in Springfield, Massachusetts. For once his character was not an issue. This time it was "because my time of study did not come up to their requirements." A congregation in Mendon, Massachusetts, was more easily impressed, going so far as to say that "Although he has not a collegial education, we think he has a good knowledge of *most* if not *all* the branches of science attended to at college."

Just as things were at long last looking up, his past again caught up with him. The Mendon Association, which had been on the verge of ordaining him, balked, relenting only after Graham threw himself on their mercy, asking them to take pity on "My little family . . . afloat in the world without a home, and without any other means of support than my labour."[15] In 1829, he is to be found in the New Jersey town of Bound Brook, where his appointment was again blocked, this time by the New Jersey Presbytery after hearing "things unfavourable to Mr. Graham's character."[16]

Sometime after this Graham moved farther south, to Philadelphia. There, at a safe remove from Amherst, he hoped to make a fresh start. He started to dabble in physiology, studying, as best he could, the works of the French physiologists François Broussais (1772–1838) and Xavier Bichat (1771–1802).[17] This sudden interest in physiology is not readily explained. Graham's father, the Reverend John Graham, had been a physician (after a fashion), but he died when the boy was only two. Another possible influence was the Reverend Heman Humphrey (1779–1861), Graham's preceptor at Amherst.

Humphrey was an early convert to the cause of temperance, having delivered and printed a sermon on the subject in 1814, and he is known to have had strong opinions about diet as well.[18] He also happened to be a member of the American Temperance Society.[19] Graham himself was a confirmed teetotaller, and it was presumably on this basis that the Pennsylvania Society for Discouraging the Use of Ardent Spirits hired him as a lecturer in 1830. Six months later, he resigned to try his luck at lecturing on a wider range of issues: human physiology, diet, courtship and marriage, the treatment and prevention of cholera. By 1832, he had already worked out the rudiments of the regimen that would bear his name.[20] When he started lecturing on sexual habits, peppering his talks with frank words on masturbation, he created a sensation.[21] These talks he delivered in 1833, publishing them a year later under the title *Lecture to Young Men on Chastity*. Other publications followed in rapid succession: *Aesculapian Tablets of the Nineteenth Century* (1834), *A Defense of the Graham System of Living* (1835), the *Graham Journal of Health and Longevity* (1837–1839), and *Lectures on the Science of Human Life* (1839).

Graham had finally found his calling. His limited education, the thing that had held him back for so long, was now his biggest asset, the thread connecting him to a public that mistrusted learning for learning's sake.[22] "My desire is to carry my instruction into every family, and to be understood by every individual of ordinary capacities," he wrote in the preface to *Lectures on the Science of Human Life*. Making a virtue of necessity, he boasted that it had been "nearly twenty years" since he had "read any work on intellectual and moral philosophy." He was not ashamed to say that he often relied on friends who "furnished me with such extracts as they thought would be serviceable to me."[23]

Graham himself was no populist. He was too vain for that, too stiff and uncomfortable in his dealings with other people. But he was perfectly capable of using populism to his own advantage. If he had a role model, it was almost certainly Samuel Thomson, the self-styled "people's doctor." Thomson had started with even less education than Graham, peddling botanical cures and a self-help manual (*New Guide to Health; or Botanic Family Physician*) to people just like himself.[24] Now Thomson was rich, and, just as important, famous.

Doctors had no place in Samuel Thomson's system. Still less did they have a place in Graham's. But where Thomson had peddled cures, Graham peddled prevention. People could choose to be well, or they could choose to be ill – it was entirely up to them.[25] Nor were the things doctors knew all that complex; with a little elbow grease, anyone could master the basics of physiology. This part of Graham's message was evangelicalism by any other name, placing, as it did, boundless confidence in the common sense of ordinary Americans. It also made them solely responsible for their well-being.[26] And like evangelical Christianity, it held out

the promise of perfection in this life. If only "mankind always
lived precisely as they ought to live, they would – as a general
rule – most certainly pass through the several stages of life, from
infancy to extreme old age, without sickness and distress, enjoying through long protracted years, health, security, peace, and
individual and social happiness." When people died, and alas,
even Graham could not prevent *that*, they would do so in their
sleep, "without an agony, without a pain."[27]

And what was abstinence, if not the ultimate form of prevention? Hence its centrality in Graham's system – abstinence
from masturbation and sexual fantasies, from pickles and spices,
from sweets, milled flour, tea, coffee, tobacco, alcohol, and meat
in any form. Because each carried risks, all had to be shunned.

It is, at first glance, an incongruous list. Why masturbation
and sexual fantasies, and why their inclusion alongside pickles,
bacon, and apple pie? To Graham the link was obvious.
Stimulants, and these included rich foods as well as beverages
containing alcohol or caffeine, excited sexual desire, and sexual
desire, even when limited to the realm of fantasy, enervated the
body, making it vulnerable to every imaginable illness:

> Langour, lassitude, muscular relaxation, general
> debility and heaviness, depression of spirits, loss of
> appetite, indigestion, faintness and sinking at the pit
> of the stomach, increased susceptibilities of the skin
> and lungs to all the atmospheric changes, feebleness
> of circulation, chilliness, headache, melancholy,
> hypochondria, hysterics, feebleness of all the senses,
> impaired vision, loss of sight, weakness of the lungs,
> nervous cough, pulmonary consumption, disorders

of the liver and kidneys, urinary difficulties, disorders of the genital organs, spinal diseases, weakness
of the brain, loss of memory, epilepsy, insanity,
apoplexy, abortions, predispositions, and early death
of offspring. . . . [28]

In Graham's system, the body has only so much vital energy,
and a little is lost with each sexual act. The idea was old (it can
be traced all the way back to Hippocrates and Galen) but it took
on new life in the eighteenth century with the publication of two
books that demonized masturbation. The first, *Onania; or, the
Heinous Sin of Self Pollution*, was published anonymously in 1711
or 1712 (the author was probably John Marten, a London surgeon
who had been charged previously with publishing obscene mate-
rials). The second was *Onanisme*, published by Samuel-Auguste
Tissot in 1760. Unlike Marten, Tissot was a respected physician,
and his credibility was such that more than a century would pass
before his theories were seriously challenged.[29]

Graham's contribution lay in extending the same logic
to the marriage bed.[30] Where Marten had played up the role of
sexual pleasure in marriage, Graham played it down. The only
difference between it and masturbation was one of degree.
Graham, married since 1824, explained: "It is not the mere loss
of semen, but the peculiar excitement, and the violence of
the convulsive paroxysms, which produce the mischief; and
these are exceedingly increased by the actions of the mind."
Not so with husband and wife: "They become accustomed to
each other's body, and their parts no longer excite an impure
imagination, and their sexual intercourse is the result of the
mere natural and instinctive excitements of the organs
themselves – and when the dietetic and other habits are such

as they should be, this intercourse is very seldom."[31] This was a far cry from saying, as Calvin and the Puritan divines once had, that sexual pleasure was a vital – and indispensable – part of marriage.[32]

The theory left the couples who took it seriously wondering how often was too often. Graham gave them a bitter pill: no more than once a week. The gold standard, one even Graham did not expect many to live up to, was once a month. To those who chafed under these restrictions he had a ready answer: "Recollect that the *final cause* of your organs of reproduction – the propagation of your species – requires but seldom the exercise of their function!" Elsewhere in the *Lecture to Young Men on Chastity*, Graham shows his hand more clearly and reverts to the man who had once dreamt of becoming a minister. "How philosophically adapted to the nature, and condition, and welfare of man," he rhapsodizes, "is the requisition of the gospel, which demands *spiritual chastity*; and forbids even the look of lust, and the lascivious thought!"[33]

History has not been kind to Graham's theories. Of these, none has been more thoroughly lampooned than his insistence that masturbation was destroying the health of America's youth. And yet he was in good company. Countless Europeans had been gulled by *Onania* and Tissot's *Onanisme*. As late as 1922 the *Larousse médical illustré* was still describing the act in the bleakest possible terms, equating it with a "great physical weakening" and a "state of intense degradation."[34] The theory, moreover, was not without a certain logic. What made it so plausible for so long was that it linked an activity that was common to diseases and disorders that were just as common – consumption, insanity, blindness, incontinence, seizures, idiocy, in short, anything for which there was no cure. Graham was not so benighted as to offer a cure for these or any other maladies. By singling out masturbation, by denouncing it again and again, he was merely offering the one thing he could: a sure means of prevention to a society that was short on cures.

How many people actually subscribed to Graham's sexual theories is an open question. That there were so many books urging compliance would suggest a high degree of non-compliance.[35] Nor were all doctors on board. Far from it. Many, probably most, took a more benign view of sexual pleasure. Dio Lewis's (1823–1886) colleagues did. One is supposed to have told a patient that "Every healthy man has sexual desires, and he might as well refuse to satisfy his hunger as deny them." Another, with a "large and very profitable" practice, was in the habit of advising young men to "keep a mistress," if only to avoid the "danger of an accumulation of semen."[36] Orson Fowler (1809–1887), the popular phrenologist, was not willing to go that far. Mistresses and masturbation had no place in his scheme. But sexual passion most emphatically did, provided that it was confined to marriage (he himself married three times). He could not even begin to count the benefits of the sexual act; how could he, when it "electrifies every other function in man"? Going without was almost too terrible to contemplate: "As nothing breeds other diseases equally with inertia, so dormant love diseases both itself and the entire body and mind."[37] Then there was Dr. Andrew J. Ingersoll (b. 1818), who ran a clinic for women in Corning, New York. They came to him frigid; they left orgasmic, convinced that "sexual life is the sustaining force of body and mind, and that through this life, if it is reverenced as a holy gift, the spirit of the Creator will work the regeneration of body and soul, which is the second birth." Ingersoll still disapproved of masturbation, laying rheumatism, paralysis, and insanity at its doorstep, but in every other respect his approach was the exact opposite of Graham's.[38]

Graham's star faded as quickly as it had risen. In the late 1830s, he ceased lecturing altogether. Graham's most controversial work, *Lectures on Chastity*, would remain in print for fifteen years, but it, too, eventually faded into obscurity, leaving Graham to be remembered by something more tangible: his eponymous cracker.

The fad he had unleashed was also fading. The biggest stumbling block was meat, which even Graham did not seriously expect everyone to forgo.[39] Many of the people who adopted his diet allowed it back into their lives, albeit in smaller quantities than before. Dr. N.J. Knight of Truro, Massachusetts, confessed that "Since last November I have, at times, taken animal food, in order that I might be absolutely satisfied that my mode of living acted decidedly in favor of my perfect health; and that a different course would produce organic derangement." Joseph Rickeston, who lived with his wife and aging mother in New Bedford, Massachusetts, "adopted what is called the Graham or vegetable diet, though not in its fullest extent. We exclude animal food from our diet, but sometimes we indulge in shell and other fish." Sometimes, too, the Rickestons used a spice. And sometimes they enjoyed desserts in the form of puddings, custards, and pies, the latter with just enough shortening "to make it a little tender."[40]

The regimen was especially popular among valetudinarians. When Ellen G. White had her first health reform vision, in 1863, she was "weak and feeble, subject to frequent fainting spells."[41] "Most of these individuals were more or less feeble,"

William Andrus Alcott said of the original members of the American Physiological Society, "and a very large proportion of them were actually suffering from chronic disease when they became members of the society. Not a few joined it, indeed, as a last resort, after having tried everything else, as drowning men are said to catch at straws."[42] He could just as well have been describing himself, for his own health, while improving after he removed all stimulants from his diet, was never good.[43] Graham's *Aesculapian Tablets* (1834), published as a defence of his system, consists entirely of valetudinarian testimonials – "From infancy, my health was delicate, and violent fits of sickness were my lot," "My own health has been quite delicate, from my childhood; and I have always been very subject to colds and coughs," "I was subject to frequent turns of debility, and a good deal of languor, and an indefinite kind of indisposition," and so on.[44]

They all said they had never felt better. But the cure, giving up the habits and indulgences everyone else took for granted, turned their lives upside down. To adopt the Graham system of living was to choose the life of an ascetic, to break with everyone who was less enlightened and less virtuous. It meant carrying Graham's own cross, which is to say that followers were exposed to ridicule and scorn. Even Graham, otherwise the most oblivious of men, had to admit as much. He expressed himself in verse:

> What have I done – what crime have I committed?
> Why should I be so roughly, rudely treated?
> I respect all, male and female, black and white,
> But oh, the *horrid* thing! "*She is a Grahamite!*"
> . . . Those old friends who seemed most true,
>   now from me run,

> And even *parents*, too, their own dear daughter shun.
> But do not blame them – they think they're doing right,
> For oh! The *cruel* thing! *"She is a Grahamite!"*[45]

Small wonder that Graham's regimen found its most loyal following among the radical abolitionists. Had they not already placed themselves beyond the pale of polite society, risking, like Graham, life and limb to promote a cause that was as unpopular as it was right?[46] Charles Grandison Finney, Theodore Weld, William Lloyd Garrison, the Grimké sisters Sarah and Angelina, the Tappan brothers Arthur and Lewis, and William Goodell – all were Grahamites at some point in their lives.[47] So was the freethinker Amos Bronson Alcott. When the Concord sheriff came to haul him off to jail for refusing to pay taxes to a government that supported slavery, Amos's wife (Abby May) proceeded to pack food for him. The prison fare was too rich, they explained – and it contained meat.[48]

Abby May Alcott's patience would be tested to the breaking point when Amos set up a commune at Fruitlands, a farm in eastern Massachusetts.[49] For seven months, from June 1843 to January 1844, the family attempted to live off what they could grow. Louisa May Alcott described her ordeal in a thinly fictionalized story ("Transcendental Wild Oats") that appeared in the *Independent* in 1873. "Every meal should be a sacrament," intones Timon Lion, who is none other than Amos Bronson Alcott. "Neither sugar, molasses, milk, butter, cheese, nor flesh are to be used among us, for nothing is to be admitted which has caused wrong or death to man or beast." The daily routine, one that faithfully followed Graham's precepts, made monks of them all:

We shall rise at dawn, begin the day by bathing, followed by music, and then a chaste repast of fruit and
bread. Each one finds congenial occupation till the
meridian meal; when some deep-searching conversation gives rest to the body and development to the
mind. Healthful labor again engages us till the last
meal, when we assemble in social communion, pro-
longed till sunset, when we retire to sweet repose,
ready for the next day's activity.[50]

The Graham regimen also was hugely popular at Brook
Farm, the transcendentalist commune that lasted from 1841 to
1847. There were special tables for the community's Grahamites,
and one of the members, George C. Leach, left in 1843 to start
a hotel based on Graham's regimen.[51] Rebecca Codman, who
stayed on the farm from 1843 until the bitter end, recalled "few
delicacies." Gingerbread was the "only cake; meat was only occasionally furnished, never but once a day, and the food, though
healthful and well cooked, was not equal to that ordinarily found
upon a mechanic's table."[52] From 1855 there is the even more
ambitious Vegetarian Kansas Emigration Company, founded in
hope of starting whole communities of vegetarians, teetotallers,
and abolitionists in that territory. It, too, failed.[53]

Graham, whose health had never been good, died in 1851. He
was just fifty-seven years old. His enemies pointed out the obvious:
that his regimen had failed him. In the months before his death
he was often seen in a wheelbarrow, being carted along the streets
he used to walk. His plight, far from rousing pity, was eagerly
reported on in the local newspaper, the *Northampton Courier*:

The people of Northampton were amused one day last week by seeing this philosopher of sawdust pudding trundled on a wheelbarrow from his house to the barber's house, he being infirm and unable to walk the distance. To be sure, he occupied a low place but has done so much to enlighten the present and especially the future generations in science and philosophy that the wheelbarrow was dignified as such a vehicle never was before.[54]

Few mourned his demise, physicians least of all.[55] The *Boston Medical Surgery Journal* took the occasion of his death to say that he "wore everybody out who listened to him," that his vanity exceeded belief, that even his friends found him "obtusive."[56] *Harper's* summed up his life's work in one equivocal paragraph:

Rev. Sylvester Graham, the founder and untiring advocate of the Vegetarian System of dietetics, died at Northampton, Mass. on Thursday, 11 inst. Dr. Graham was chiefly known for his strict adherence to the system which, for some time, bore his name. His writings on the subject were numerous and popular, and his labors as a lecturer were incessant. . . . Of his theories, each will form his own judgment; the projector, at least, was undoubtedly honest and sincere in sustaining them.[57]

Graham's old enemies, the physicians, appropriated his theories, thus ensuring their survival into the early years of the twentieth century. For all their hostility to Graham, many were already convinced of the benefits of a vegetarian diet. William

Andrus Alcott, who had received his medical training at Yale, became a vegetarian in the 1820s.[58] In 1838, he set out to show that he was not alone, collecting the testimonials of more than a hundred people who had adopted a vegetarian diet or a variant of it. Of these, more than fifty were physicians (the sample was skewed to the extent that Alcott had posted his request in Graham's old nemesis, the *Boston Medical and Surgical Journal*).[59] After Alcott came Larkin Baker Coles, Russell Thatcher Trall, Augustus Gardner, Dio Lewis, Mary Wood-Allen, Emma

John Harvey Kellogg, the brother of the cereal magnate W.K. Kellogg, repackaged Graham's theories for the Progressive era, turning the Seventh-Day Adventists' sanitarium in Battle Creek into a popular destination for middle-class valetudinarians. In 1879, convinced that the nation's health was being undermined by "sexual excesses of all kinds," he wrote Plain Facts about Sexual Life, *later issued under the more anodyne title of* Plain Facts for Old and Young. *For Kellogg, masturbation was so serious an offence that he suggested small boys who persisted in the habit should be circumcised without the benefit of anesthesia, "as the brief pain attending the operation will have a salutary effect upon the mind, especially if it be connected with the idea of punishment." Courtesy of the Willard Library in Battle Creek.*

Frances Drake, and John Harvey Kellogg, all doctors, and all, whether they acknowledged it or not, Grahamites. Gardner, writing in 1874, was sure that "much of the worthlessness, lassitude and physical and mental feebleness attributable to the modern woman" could be blamed on masturbation. Wood-Allen, writing in the early years of the twentieth century, was still warning women that if the "procreative act" "does not kill, it exhausts, and no doubt takes from the vital force of those exercising it. One can feel justified to lose a part of her own life if she is conferring life upon others, but to indulge in such a waste of vital force, merely for pleasure is certainly never excusable, and least excusable of all is the arousing of pleasurable emotions by a direct violation of natural law."[60]

Their differences with Graham were ones only of degree. William Andrus Alcott went one step further than Graham and dropped yeast from his recipe for coarse bread. It was too stimulating, he said.[61] John Cowan, whose theories were warmly commended by the abolitionist William Lloyd Garrison and the feminist Elizabeth Cady Stanton, held married couples to an even higher standard than had Graham. Where Graham had been willing to permit sexual intercourse as often as once a week, Cowan told couples to limit themselves to once a month and then desist for at least two years after the birth of each child. Some physicians, like Dio Lewis, recommended that couples place a curtain between their beds "to protect you from each other's observation when bathing and dressing." Not that this was a barrier to earnest conversation, far from it – "Two narrow beds, separated by the curtain, will make conversation as easy as though you occupied the same couch."

On one point they were all agreed: no vice existed in isolation. Each was linked to all others in a Gordian knot of snares, gateways, and loops. Dio Lewis had some blunt advice for any woman contemplating matrimony: "As you would shun ship-wreck, shun the victims of tobacco, alcohol and lust. These evils constitute the BAD TRIO. They are rarely separated."[62] The variables were so numerous, their connections so multifarious, that John Cowan sometimes wondered if he would ever get to the bottom of it all:

> So closely is the nature of licentiousness interwoven with that of alcoholic liquors, opium and tobacco, that it is difficult to tell which depends upon the other for its stimulus; but be that as it may, it is required as an absolute necessity that the individual give up the use of tobacco in all its forms, and ale, wine, whisky, cider, and all other alcoholic liquors; for a man or woman cannot possibly live a chaste life, sexually or otherwise, who uses these soul-debasing articles; and if the individual cannot or will not give up these habits, it is almost useless for him to read further.[63]

The stress remained on prevention. William Andrus Alcott believed that consumption, scrofula, rheumatism, and a host of other common afflictions could all be kept at bay if only people would take proper care of themselves. What they needed was "plain food and water," combined with "faith, and hope, and cheerfulness."[64] If this formula could not always "prevent such diseases as cancer, gout, epilepsy, scrofula, and consumption," it could at the very least "prolong life under them."[65] Alcott's message, like that of American evangelicalism, managed to be both optimistic and pessimistic at the same time – optimistic because it held out the hope of near-perfect health, but pessimistic because there was only one way to achieve this goal, and that was through unstinting personal effort. If good health was a personal achievement, its loss was a personal failing.

This message moves from the periphery to the centre in the writings of Larkin Baker Coles and John Harvey Kellogg. Both were intimately associated with the Seventh-Day Adventists, the first as an inspiration for the Church's prophetess, Ellen G. White, the second as a one-time follower. "More than nineteen twentieths, probably, of all the diseases of which complaint is made, are created, directly or indirectly, by the people who suffer from them," Coles proclaimed in his hugely popular *Philosophy of Health* (1851). He offered another startling statistic, one in keeping with a book that promised *Health and Cure without Drugs*: "Probably in nine cases out of ten of all the diseases in the world. . . . Nature requires no help from medicinal agents."[66] Kellogg went even further. There was simply no excuse for ever getting ill. He could, after twenty years in practice, "truthfully say that I have never met with a single instance in which disease of any kind was present as the result of a pure or continent life."[67] From this it was but a short leap to Ellen G. White's pronouncement that "The human family have brought upon themselves diseases of various forms by their own wrong habits."[68] With doctors casting doubt on medicine, it was inevitable that some people would take the next logical step and make themselves solely responsible for their health. Ellen G. White chose this route at first (she later relented, consulting a physician in 1854).[69] But Mary Baker Eddy (1821–1910), founder of the Church of Christ, Scientist, remained true to her principles to the very end. Frances Willard, who was raised in a strict Methodist household, remembered that "A physician was an unknown visitant to our home in early days." Isolated on a remote farm in Wisconsin, the

Willards trusted their health to a modified version of the Graham system of living, confident that "God had but about half a dozen laws of health," and that if they lived by these laws they "would have a happy, well-to-do life."[70]

As intertwined as health reform was with the temperance movement, it never had the same staying power or appeal. The American Physiological Society, founded with such high hopes in 1837, was gone by 1841. The American Vegetarian Society, founded in 1850, had to drop its journal just four years later for lack of subscribers.[71] As a fad, health reform was fated to come and go, largely because its regimen, in sexual practice no less than in diet, was both demanding and complex. Where temperance had been honed down to one simple rule by the mid-1830s (teetotalism), the health reform movement was from the start burdened by elaborate rules and endless variations. Few stuck with it for long. Horace Greeley (1811–1872), who met his future wife in a Graham boarding house, could only laugh at the effect the diet had on their houseguests: "Usually, a day, or at most two, of beans and potatoes, boiled rice, puddings, bread and butter, with no condiment but salt, and never a pickle, was all they could abide; so, bidding a kind adieu, each in turn departed to seek elsewhere a more congenial hospitality."[72] A Georgia physician, writing in 1837, knew of a "gentleman in an adjoining county, who with his lady [had] been living for some time past on a purely vegetable diet." He could not, however, say whether the regimen was a success – the couple simply had "not continued it long enough . . . to make the experiment a fair one."[73] Even Charles Grandison Finney eventually broke down, announcing, in 1845, that he would henceforth "prefer those things which are most consistent with and conducive to the best physical state of our bodies, not hesitating, however for conscience sake to eat such things as are set before us in our journeys and wanderings, provided they are not positively injurious."[74] But the biggest backslider of all was Sylvester Graham. Toward the end of his life, he began drinking. There were also rumours that he had succumbed to his wife's rich cooking.[75]

The movement's small successes were a function of its high goals. The endless rules were daunting in and of themselves. But the goal, the spiritual regeneration of the individual, was even more daunting. Healthy habits did not by themselves impress Ellen G. White: what was also needed was a "reformation in the heart."[76] She was writing in 1896, when health reform was already more than a little passé. But this had been no less true in the movement's earliest days, in the 1830s. It was then that William Andrus Alcott came to the awful realization that he was surrounded by Pharisees, by polite men and women who were outwardly upright but inwardly corrupt. They could give up liquor and tobacco, they could give up everything else, and still never be saved:

> Purity of character goes much deeper than has sometimes been supported. It is not sufficient that we abstain from open and gross misconduct at every age and in all circumstances. Nor is it sufficient that we avoid the use of words which have an acknowledged signification of this kind. I have seen those whose conduct was, thus far, for a time, unexceptionable. And all this, too, while there was ample evidence – short of words or overt acts, it is true, but still obvious – of impurity within.[77]

That the extreme asceticism of the early health reform movement bore a striking resemblance to that of the old Church was no accident. In both cases asceticism was the child of perfectionism, of the need to prove one's worthiness to God. Graham, of course, would have bristled at the suggestion that he harboured crypto-Catholic tendencies. But in taking asceticism to a dizzying extreme, in pushing it far beyond anything the Puritans ever could have imagined or even wanted, Sylvester Graham and the early health reform movement are yet another reminder that American evangelicalism has as much – or more – in common with Catholicism as it does with the Protestantism of Calvin and Luther.

FOUR

ABSTINENCE WITHOUT IDEALISM

Yes, deliverance will come, but it will be from the sober
and august Anglo-Saxon south, unspoiled and
unpoisoned by the wine-tinted, beer-sodden,
whiskey-crazed, sabbath-desecrating, God-defying
and anarchy-breeding and practicing minions from
over the sea and from the vast and virile countrysides
where the bible is not yet effete, nor Christ a myth.

From an Anti-Saloon League publication, 1903[1]

So far, this has been a story about just one region of the
United States: the Northeast. It is here, in New England
and the Burned-Over District of upstate New York, that one
finds the first local temperance society (founded in Moreau in
1808 or Andover in 1810), the first national temperance organization (founded in Boston in 1826), the first temperance hotel
(opened in Boston in 1837),* the first groups to embrace
Sylvester Graham and his peculiar blend of vegetarianism, teetotalism, and sexual continence.[2] The Northeastern states were

---

* The Marlborough Hotel.

also the first to ban all sales of alcohol, starting with Maine in 1851. From the Northeast the cause of temperance spread westward, with Indiana, Iowa, Minnesota, and Nebraska all voting themselves dry shortly after Maine had done so.

The one region that held out was the South. This is not to say that antebellum Southerners took no interest in temperance.[3] They did. But their temperance societies had not the zeal, numbers, nor influence of their Northern counterparts. Nor, in those early years, did Southerners equate temperance with total abstinence. When Henry Scomp, writing in 1888, set out to prove that his fellow Southerners had always supported temperance, he was able to adduce only the most equivocal of examples. One dates from 1843, when Georgia Baptists congratulated themselves on how few of their ministers drank distilled spirits. There was, however, still work to be done, for "among the uninformed and less intelligent classes this odious vice (drunkenness) still prevails." Five years later, the oldest of Georgia's Baptist churches, the Kiokee Baptist Church, thought that it would be just as well if members stopped making and selling spirits, "Yet, in view of the independence of the churches, and the great delicacy involved in this subject, we would, in all cases, recommend to our brethren the exercise of that Christian charity and forbearance which the gospel enjoins."[4] The Methodist Episcopal Church, South also had a poor track record in its early years, dragging its feet while its Northern counterpart flirted with making teetotalism binding on all members. As far as Henry Wheeler (1835–1925) was concerned, the secession of the Southern Methodists was a positive boon to the Northern Church, allowing it to advance temperance without the constant "obstructions" that had doomed earlier initiatives.[5]

By the early twentieth century, a dramatic change had

occurred. The South, once the laggard in the temperance movement, had become its biggest supporter, the Northeast its biggest
scoffer. This pattern, moreover, has continued up to the present
day. The South now has the highest proportion of teetotallers in
America – 42.6 per cent in the Southern states that border the
Atlantic, 52 per cent in the four states (Alabama, Kentucky,
Mississippi, and Tennessee) that comprise the East South-Central
region of the U.S. census. New England and the mid-Atlantic
states, by contrast, now have the lowest proportion of teetotallers
(less than one-third of the adult population).[6] Southerners also
have the lowest rate of illicit drug use in the country.[7] And no
region has done more to promote sexual abstinence until marriage. The New Virginity originated in the South, in the late
1980s, while slightly over half of that region's school districts
teach abstinence-only sex education, compared to just one-fifth
in the Northeast.[8]

America, in short, is still living with the effects of a cultural
shift that occurred in the late nineteenth and early twentieth
centuries. Because of this shift, abstinence has gone from being
a force for change to a force against it, a path back to the world
as it existed before Darwin, before modernism, before the New
Deal, and, most of all, before the sexual revolution. Just as important, this shift has given abstinence a new lease on life, for had
the idea fallen out of favour in the Northeast without being
picked up by the South, it would have been one of history's dead
ends, fading into obscurity as the nineteenth century gave way to
the twentieth. Abstinence was not only saved, it was reinvented.
And to understand how this happened is to understand the
meaning today's conservative evangelicals attach to that virtue.

Frances Willard, the revered president of the Woman's Christian Temperance Union.

Miss Willard, the New York Times eulogized, "was a woman of attractive presence. She possessed that unknown quantity often called magnetism, which was felt in her private conversation as well as in her public addresses." From the Library of Congress Prints and Photographs Division.

One of the first people to see that a new era had dawned was the always prescient Frances Willard. The insight occurs almost as an afterthought to "Home Protection" (1879), one of her most influential essays on behalf of temperance. Here, just as she is winding down, she suddenly makes a special appeal to the "women of New England," but the harder she pushes, the more she goads them to "lead us in this fight for God and home and native land," the more she is in fact acknowledging that the opposite is true, that the region that once led the fight has been reduced to the role of an increasingly reluctant follower.[9]

The Civil War, with its savagery and unprecedented carnage, was the most obvious turning point for the Northeast.[10] But the decay had set in long before then. It was writ large in the Maine Laws, in their tacit acknowledgment that large numbers of Americans were essentially intractable. The abolitionists must also bear part of the blame, if only because the war of words over slavery forced them to interpret the Bible in increasingly creative ways. The Bible contained numerous mentions of slavery: did this mean that the institution was fixed for all time? There was only one way out of this conundrum and that was to say that slavery was an historical artifact and not part of the divine plan. But if this was true of slavery, it could be true of anything and everything in the Bible. God, in other words, was capable of promulgating a potentially infinite succession of laws, each tailored to a specific moment in time.[11] From this it was but a short step to reject the inerrancy of the Bible, and with it, the very premise of evangelical Protestantism.

This distressing tendency to judge a thing by its context took on a life of its own after the war. Among the many New Englanders it infected were the members of the Free Congregational Society in Florence, Massachusetts. In 1874, they were unable to decide which hymn to sing at the opening ceremonies for their new lyceum. "O God, Our Help in Ages Past" was an old favourite (such a beautiful melody), but the lyrics, which had been composed in the early eighteenth century, had a dated feel. The solution was obvious: the congregation would supply lyrics more in keeping with the times. The result was so startling as to be a travesty of the original:

> Among the faiths of bygone years
> Our minds no longer stray,
> But they may guide some wand'ring soul
> To find the broader way.[12]

Context becomes the touchstone in the writings of the future Supreme Court justice Oliver Wendell Holmes, Jr. (1841–1935). A passionate abolitionist, he enlisted in the Massachusetts Militia when war broke out. The war changed him, forever shaking his faith in moral certitudes.[13] Was there even such a thing as the truth? At most the truth "is what I can't help believe" – far be it from him to make "my can't helps . . . compulsory for the universe."[14] The relativism that Holmes applied to the law, William James (1842–1910) would apply to psychology. If "no two 'ideas' are ever exactly the same," if "*no state once gone can recur and be identical with what it was before*," then evangelical Protestantism, with the faith it placed in unerring truths, was the grandest delusion of them all.[15]

James and Holmes were the vanguard, arguably more representative of Harvard and the Pragmatists than of the Northeast as a whole. That region's evolution, from a bastion of idealism to an island of skepticism, is better represented in the apostasy

Henry Ward Beecher, the Beecher who wandered furthest from the strict evangelical morality of his father Lyman. In 1875, he was charged with adultery, only to be acquitted after the jury deadlocked. His sister, the feminist Isabella Beecher Hooker, never forgave him. His parishioners, however, did, raising money for his defence and excommunicating his alleged mistress when she persisted in accusing their beloved pastor. When asked how to live well, he is supposed to have replied, "Eat well, sleep well, and laugh well." From the Library of Congress Prints and Photographs Division.

of Henry Ward Beecher (1813–1887), the most notorious of Lyman's children. Young Henry began his career following in his father's footsteps. He became a Congregationalist minister. He supported the Maine Law.[16] He found it baffling that there were still people who had yet to make up their minds about the temperance movement.[17] He pressed Lincoln to emancipate the slaves. But a very different man starts to unfold after the war. He began delivering sermons that were pleasing and genial, so much so that British guidebooks directed tourists to his thriving church in Brooklyn. In 1870, he was accused of having an affair with a married woman. In 1882, he attempted to reconcile Darwinism with Christianity, exulting that "Religion has much to hope, and the old theology much to fear from scientific disclosures."[18] And in 1886 he scandalized Frances Willard, now seven years into her presidency of the Woman's Christian Temperance Union. When she had first sought him out, in 1876, he was a confirmed teetotaller. He disapproved of tobacco and shunned the theatre. Yet already he showed signs of wavering. He had come to accept a scenario in which the liquor trade could continue, albeit in a highly restricted form. A decade later, he was still a teetotaller. But he had ceased to expect everyone else to follow suit. This was too much for Willard. She confronted him in the most public of places, right after one of his famous services and "as the throng pressed upon him." His answer ("I have no harsh word for my brethren in the ministry who do not see as I do"), his equivocal theology – everything about him now seemed to disappoint her. He had, in short, a "most inconvenient capacity for seeing both sides."[19]

Nowhere was the disaffection of the Northeast more in evidence than in Boston, the city where Lyman Beecher once had presided over a prosperous congregation and where the American Temperance Society had first set up shop. The Boston

Brahmins that Anthony Trollope (1815–1882) visited in 1861 drank in open defiance of Massachusetts's own Maine Law.[20] When Josephine Butler (1828–1906), the great figure of the Victorian sexual purity movement, sent two organizers to that city, they encountered nothing but skepticism. "Even the women, usually the quickest to come to the aid of our cause, were cautious and doubtful."[21] William Lloyd Garrison, now close to death, did his best to help the two men, but the idealism that had roiled the city in his youth was gone.[22] That city was also becoming more Catholic with each passing year, so much so that by the time of the Civil War, with three hundred thousand Irish immigrants, it had already become the nation's second largest diocese.[23]

As Boston went, so went Massachusetts. The great women's crusade of 1873 to 1874, the precursor to the Woman's Christian Temperance Union, spawned almost no demonstrations in that state (11 in all, compared to 307 in Ohio).[24] In 1874, Massachusetts overturned its own Maine Law, returning to a system of strict licensing.[25] Twenty years later, in 1894, the state legislature flirted with the idea of following the example of Gothenburg, one of several Scandinavian cities to remove the profit motive from the drink trade by placing it in the hands of regulated monopolies.

Purists hated the Gothenburg system because it eliminated the villains from the equation. Gone were the greedy saloon-keepers who kept plying their customers with drink, and gone, too, were the seedy dives that gave drinking a bad name. In place of the first were bland civil servants, in place of the second, halls that were brightly lit, antiseptic, and devoid of all attractions. John Granville Woolley (1850–1922), member of the Prohibition Party since 1888, was having none of it. He knew what every other temperance man knew: that the cause depended on having

A scene from the women's temperance crusade of 1873 to 1874.

This crusade, which originated in Ohio, relied on matrons shaming the men who ran and patronized local saloons. In this scene, the matrons of Logan, Ohio, have gathered outside one such saloon to sing hymns. Frances Willard participated in two of these demonstrations when she was working in Pittsburgh, braving "abundant fumes, sickening to healthful nostrils," to kneel and pray among a "crowd of unwashed, unkempt, hard-looking drinking men." From the Library of Congress Prints and Photographs Division.

clear-cut villains. Let the saloon-keeper stay just as he was: "As we have it now, no saloon-keeper even aspires to recognition by good men and women except in their own congenial circles and in politics; labour societies, Knights of Pythias, Free Masons, Catholic societies, churches, nearly all condemn and despise them. They ought to be kept so."[26]

The scheme's European pedigree also rendered it suspect. Woolley never let his audiences forget this. "Who vouches, upon knowledge, for the character of this alien thing?" he asked. People

Gerrit Smith, one of several wealthy abolitionists to underwrite both the American Temperance Society and Oberlin College.

Smith also lent his support to John Brown, going so far as to give him a farmstead in the Adirondacks. In 1869, Smith helped launch the Prohibition Party, supplying it with a slogan that for several decades would doom its chances in the South: "Slavery is gone, but drunkenness stays." From the Library of Congress Prints and Photographs Division.

like the Bishop of Chester, whose opinions "even in his own diocese, would lay an anti-liquor project under suspicion." People like William Gladstone, a known wine-drinker and a politician beholden to voters in the "South of Ireland." Groups like the House of Lords, the "most worthless, not to say disreputable, legislative body on the face of the earth, excepting the last congress." Worse even than the scheme's popularity in Europe was its popularity among academics. Their considered approval, far from recommending the scheme, rendered it even more suspect. Who could trust anyone who asked "How does it work?" when the real question was "How does it square with righteousness?"[27]

If the Northeastern establishment was starting to lose its idealism, so, too, were the groups who still believed in the attainability of Christian perfection. The first step down this slippery slope was taken when Northerners, who had up to this point construed perfection in the broadest possible terms, started to downplay its activist dimension. The person who contributed the most to this process was Phoebe Worrall Palmer, a New Yorker who had grown up in a strict Methodist household. For sheer strictness, however, little Phoebe outdid them all, so much so that she was "sometimes smiled at for my well-intentioned scrupulousness, and at other times almost censured for carrying it to a troublesome excess."[28] In 1827, she married another devout Methodist: a homeopathic doctor by the name of Walter Palmer. Walter's practice thrived, but when their first three children died in rapid succession, Phoebe fell into a severe depression. Desperate for solace, the couple embarked on a study of Wesley's collected writings, convinced that the way forward was to be found in his numerous (and often contradictory) pronouncements on Christian perfection. In 1837, Phoebe was finally satisfied that she had attained that state. She started talking about her experiences in the weekly prayer meetings she hosted along with her sister Sarah Lankford, and six years later she put them down in writing.

The book, *The Way of Holiness*, was a hit. By 1854 it had gone through thirty-four editions and still it was flying off the shelves.[29] What made the book so popular was that it offered a streamlined and seemingly foolproof way of achieving Christian perfection. Wesley's remarks on the subject never had been entirely satisfactory. But on one point his writings were un-ambiguous: the road between conversion and sanctification was almost always long and hard.[30] Phoebe Palmer was sure there was a "shorter way," that a heartfelt commitment to Christian perfection was tantamount to attaining it.[31] As one scoffer put it, "Believe that ye have it and ye have it."[32] This did not protect against backsliding. Nor did it exempt the believer from continuous striving. On the contrary. The "way of holiness" lay in "making *daily* advances in the knowledge and love of God." She herself could find "no Scriptural reason why each successive day might not witness the heavenly traveler at a higher point of elevation in his homeward course than the day previous."[33]

Phoebe Palmer's approach to achieving Christian perfection may have been novel, but her understanding of it was not. It broke no new ground, said nothing that had not already been said by earlier American perfectionists. Her relationships with them were entirely cordial. Timothy Merritt raised no objections when the Palmers purchased his *Guide to Christian Perfection* and installed Phoebe as the magazine's editor.[34] Asa Mahan, the renowned Oberlin perfectionist, was a frequent visitor at the Palmers' Tuesday Meetings for the Promotion of Holiness, and his endorsement of *The Way of Holiness* was prominently displayed in its many editions.[35] In 1867, both Palmers were to be found in Oberlin, paying their respects to the now elderly Charles Grandison Finney.[36]

One thing, however, was missing from Palmer's formulation: the social activism of the Oberlin perfectionists. Her passion for temperance, her hatred of slavery – these were things she downplayed. The great religious revival she helped launch, the so-called "Businessman's Revival" of 1857 to 1858, steered clear of slavery.[37] So did the periodical she published, now rechristened the *Guide to Holiness*. Who should the sanctified Christian vote for in the 1856 presidential election – the Democrat who favoured doing nothing about slavery or the Republican who wanted to keep it from expanding into new states and territories? The editor, Henry V. Degen, could offer no advice, even though he himself was a known abolitionist.[38] Vote for God's man, he said, without, however, saying who that man might be. The whole question irritated him. "We have naturally but little relish for politics," he explained, "and if we had, we are not disposed to leave our appropriate mission, and enter the political arena."

The result was a doctrine that was as personally demanding as it was politically passive.[39] On the surface, nothing had changed. The people who were attracted to Phoebe Palmer's holiness movement were the same sorts of people who had always been drawn to Christian perfection. There were college presidents (Stephen Olin of Wesleyan, Mahan of Oberlin), professors (Thomas Upham of Bowdoin), even the occasional Episcopalian (the Boston physician Charles Cullis). But in transforming Christian perfection into a doctrine that was inward-looking and socially neutral, Phoebe Palmer, the housewife from New York City, was helping to push that doctine in a new – and more conservative – direction.[40]

One of the people who heard Phoebe Palmer preach was Frances Willard, now settled in Evanston, Illinois. Willard was twenty-seven at the time, and she was so moved by the experience that she stood up and professed herself sanctified.[41] But where Palmer had inherited the thoroughgoing piety of the Oberlin formula, Willard had inherited its restless activism. Her commitment to "Do Everything," her insistence that the Woman's Christian Temperance Union take on such causes as woman's suffrage and higher wages and better conditions for industrial workers – all marked a return to a youth lived in the shadow of Oberlin. Her father, Josiah, had moved the family there in 1841, studying for the ministry under Finney and Mahan, without, however, completing his studies. Willard's mother, Mary, also attended classes at Oberlin. Young Frances was kept busy, mastering the rudiments

of reading from the *Slave's Friend*.[42] When the family moved to
Wisconsin, in 1846, Mary subjected the children to a "whole
system of calisthenics that she learned at Oberlin, which she
used to put us through unmercifully, as I thought," while Josiah
kept them to the Oberlin regimen of "Simple food, most of veg-
etables, fish and fowls."[43]

Willard's moral compass was the Social Gospel, a liberal theology that embodied many of the high ideals of the Oberlin
perfectionists.[44] But where the original perfectionists had practised a faith that placed as much weight on individual redemption
as it did on social activism, the proponents of the Social Gospel
practised a faith that was overwhelmingly activist. For Walter
Rauschenbusch (1861–1918), the leading theologian of the
Social Gospel, God was to be approached not in isolation, not
through the solitary conversion experience, but by bringing "men
under repentance for their collective sins." Rauschenbusch's God
"made us for one another, and our highest perfection comes not
by isolation but by love. The way of holiness through human fellowship and service is slower and lowlier, but its results are more
essentially Christian."[45] Armed with this conviction, Willard
committed herself and her followers to much more than just temperance. Lynching, tobacco, yellow journalism, prostitution, the
Armenian genocide – these were but some of the injustices
the Woman's Christian Temperance Union took on under
Willard's leadership. Few, one admirer would write upon her
death, "even now have gained the clear vision of the social
mission of Christianity to which Miss Willard had ten years ago."[46]

How few would be shown in the years that followed. Absent
its charismatic leader, the Woman's Christian Temperance
Union quickly retreated from her ambitious agenda.[47] The first
convention held after her death dropped several of her pet

causes, including workers' rights and equal pay for women. The organization remained committed to woman's suffrage, but its other planks – prohibition, strict blue laws, sexual purity – were all evangelical hobbyhorses.[48] By 1909, the organization that had once stood shoulder to shoulder with the Knights of Labor was urging "working men and women who work for wages to cultivate a sense of responsibility in the thoroughness of their work and to consider their employer's welfare as their own."[49] By the 1920s, it was even applauding the Ku Klux Klan's efforts on behalf of Prohibition.[50] The Woman's Christian Temperance Union had travelled far from the days when it could boast of having African Americans among its members, and further still from the time, in 1897, when its members had passed a resolution condemning lynching. That its African-American members were few, that the sainted Miss Willard had been slow to condemn lynching, is beside the point.[51] Civil rights had never been a front-burner issue for the Progressives, and by these limited standards, Frances Willard had behaved better than most.[52]

One is left to wonder what role disillusionment played in Willard's decision to spend much of the 1890s in England. There were many reasons for her long absences – her infatuation with Lady Isabella Somerset, her poor health, squabbles with the rank and file of the Woman's Christian Temperance Union over the wisdom of building new headquarters in Chicago.[53] But I think that Willard's reasons went deeper than that, that behind the myriad of excuses she gave for going abroad was the realization that her brand of Christian activism was outside the American mainstream. Certainly the Social Gospel was destined to remain on the fringes of America's religious life, appealing to an educated and increasingly isolated elite.[54]

Lady Isabella Somerset, circa 1902.

Lady Isabella and Frances Willard first met in 1891, and instantly became fast friends. "Why must Isabel & I be separated?" reads the last entry in Willard's journal. "Because we put our Work before our Love." From the Library of Congress Prints and Photographs Division.

The so-called Temperance Temple, which served as the headquarters for the Woman's Christian Temperance Union.

Located in Chicago's business district and completed in 1893, it strained both the organization's finances and Willard's relations with the rank and file. The building was demolished in 1926. From Anna Gordon, *The Beautiful Life of Frances Willard* (1898).

Frances Willard, for all her Progressive ideas, looked backward in time, to the enthusiasms and restlessness of the Oberlin perfectionists. If she was the old face of American evangelicalism, Billy Sunday (1862–1935), the baseball player turned revivalist, was its new face – barely educated, socially conservative, and as committed to Prohibition as he was suspicious of all other government initiatives. Where Willard talked of "mother love," Sunday was the prophet of muscular Christianity, extolling well-ordered families and striking pugilistic poses as he preached. "His words come in a torrent," the *Des Moines Register and Leader* reported in 1914, "and it is largely by means of the 'antics' by which he is well known, that his meaning is made clear. He hops from one side of the platform to the other, he pounds everything in the pulpit that has a flat surface with his fists, and almost every sentence is reinforced by a vigorous gesture."[55] The words flattered him. "I'm still pretty handy with my dukes," he was fond of saying, "and I can still deliver the goods with all express charges prepaid."[56]

Billy Sunday's physicality was on display even on this visit to the White House in 1922.

Here he is striking a pose for the benefit of reporters eager to get a taste of the theatrics for which he was so justly famous. The expensive coat and impeccably tailored suit mark him as a successful businessman, an identity he actively cultivated. From the Library of Congress Prints and Photographs Division.

Sunday's was an essentially negative Christianity, long on proscriptions, long on enemies, and more focused on heaven and hell than on the here and now. The vision he paints of heaven is strikingly vivid, as much a tribute to his priorities as to the sincerity of his belief. "Oh, what a place Heaven is":

> Fruits without one speck upon them.
> Pastures without one thistle or weed . . .
> Harps all in tune.
> The river without a torn or overflowed bank.[57]

Sunday's pessimism cannot be separated from his social conservatism. Naturally he was the enemy of the Social Gospel. When the Federal Council of Churches, meeting in 1912, urged its ministers to tackle social problems, he scoffed. "We've had enough of this godless social service nonsense," he told a reporter.[58] There was a simpler way to end poverty and crime: work hard and believe in God.[59] In 1935, already on death's doorstep, he still had the energy to criticize the New Deal. The "brainstorms" and "alphabetical set-ups" that were coming out of Washington were causing "more trouble than the dust storms in the West."[60] He hated feminism. It was impossible to raise the "standard of women's morals by raising their pay envelope." The problem went "deeper than that."[61] He had no patience for women who shirked maternity. He was "sure there is not an angel in heaven that would not be glad to come to earth and be honored with motherhood if God would grant her that privilege." He was a "Roman Catholic on divorce."[62] The man who had once reached out to African Americans turned his back on them once his popularity started to wane. In the 1920s, he allowed hooded members of the Ku Klux Klan to march into his signature tabernacles. By the 1930s, he was telling his audiences that "there can be no social equality between the black and white races."[63] He was the sworn enemy of higher criticism. "There are men in hell because they wasted too much time in trying to find out where Cain got his wife." Darwin's theory of evolution was an abomination. "If by evolution you mean advance, I go with you, but if you mean by evolution that I came from a monkey, goodnight!"[64]

He was the friend of free enterprise. His own business acumen, his ability not only to stage slick revivals but to turn a profit on them, was legendary. "The Bible, my friends, hasn't one word to say against success," he would say. Abraham, David, and Solomon would have been billionaires had they walked the earth today.[65] One of the selling points of Christianity was that it "reduces jails and penitentiaries and aids the police force, and in a thousand ways serves the state and nation."

The same bootstrap Protestantism made him a friend of Prohibition, its loudest booster in the years leading up to it, its biggest defender once it started to come undone. Nine-tenths of the "misery, poverty, wrecked homes and blighted lives were caused by booze." In 1933, on the eve of repeal, he was still boasting that he had personally "put twelve states dry before we voted on the Eighteenth Amendment."[66]

There were, of course, other vices that bothered Sunday, starting with smoking and gambling. When petting started to become acceptable, he railed against that, too. "You must be a moral idiot if you haven't brains enough to know that a 'petting party' is a secondary sexual love feast."[67] But already the list of sins had been reduced, which is to say that Sunday's brand of Christian perfection set the bar so low that the averagely obser-vant evangelical could reach it without overmuch effort. Sunday himself let slip that he enjoyed the occasional glass of wine.[68] He drank weak tea and watered-down coffee. But food was his real weakness. He claimed that he ate only nutritious foods, but the list was long and suspect: "mashed potatoes, boiled beef, codfish, dried beef, smoked herring, stewed tomatoes, hard, dry toast," plus his favourite dish: apple pie sprinkled with cinnamon.[69] The night he died he ate his "special ice cream."[70] Where Charles Grandison Finney had once railed against red meat, Billy Sunday held it up as bait:

> Come on; I'm going to line up the drunkards. Everybody fall in. Come on, ready, forward march, right left, here I come with all the drunkards. We will line up in front of a butcher shop. The butcher says: "What do you want, a piece of neck?"
>
> "No; how much do I owe you?"
>
> "$3.00."
>
> "Here's your dough. Now give me a porterhouse steak and a sirloin roast."
>
> "Where did you get all that money?"
>
> "Went to hear Bill and climbed on the water wagon."[71]

With Billy Sunday the idealism of the Oberlin perfectionists is reduced to a system of proscriptions that are careful not to ask for too much, to an ever-shrinking list of taboos. How few is hinted at in "Abstinence from Evil," a sermon composed by John Granville Woolley. The title no doubt would have appealed to Finney, but that is where the similarities end. Surely it was no coincidence that Woolley had got his start as a lawyer, for who else could split hairs quite so finely?

Ohio. It was only fair, he wrote. The defendant had been acquitted on a technicality. Besides, *"Every man in town knew he was guilty."*[74] By 1908, a compilation edited by another party member, Ohio's George M. Hammell, could seriously say that prohibition was needed in the South because the "black man, made drunken by unscrupulous white men engaged in the liquor trade, had become a peril to the womanhood of the dominant race."[75] The Anti-Saloon League was no better. Why, it asked in 1908, were there so many lynchings in the South? Because the "primitive negro field hand" "sits in the road or in the alley at the height of his debauch, looking at the obscene picture of a white woman on the label, drinking in the invitation it carries."[76] By 1924, the superintendent of one of the state leagues, Edward Shumaker of Indiana, was endorsing Klansmen for state office.[77]

The more the temperance movement backpedalled on civil rights, the more traction it gained in the South. But this was not the only reason why old enemies were flocking to the cause. In the years after the war, Phoebe Palmer's holiness movement made enormous strides in the South, and as it spread, so did the desire to achieve sanctification. Palmer herself visited the region in 1867 and was pleasantly surprised to find large numbers of "Southern ministers acquainted with us, by reputation, and disposed to be affectionately appreciative." One is even supposed to have broke down and wept upon meeting her, "saying that for years he had been interested with our writings on the precious theme of holiness, and had longed to see us."[78] Three years later, the Methodist Episcopal Church, South was actively promoting Palmer's brand of holiness.[79] A year later, in 1871, William Baker, a minister from the Northern Methodist Episcopal Church, started a holiness periodical in Tennessee. Called the *Home Altar*, it had the distinction of being the first such publication in the

South.[80] The following year, the North-based National Camp Meeting Association for the Promotion of Holiness made its first foray into the South, hosting a meeting in Nashville.[81]

The holiness movement began within the older churches, and had it stayed there, it almost certainly would have remained the decorous affair that it had been under Phoebe Palmer. But by the 1870s these churches were faced by a revolt from within. The rebels' objections fell under two broad headings – laxity on the one hand, formality and ritualism on the other – and when they were kept from voicing their concerns, they broke off to form their own holiness churches. Dozens of churches still answer to this label, the largest group being the various Pentecostal denominations.

The holiness revolt was by no means limited to the South. The Free Will Baptists originated in New England, and even Massachusetts had several of its own holiness churches by the 1880s.[82] Nor were all of the breakaway churches rural. On the contrary. Many of the early holiness churches sprang up in cities, catering primarily to recent immigrants, whether from Europe or Mexico or the American countryside (the so-called "Azusa Street Revival," which took place in Los Angeles between 1906 and 1909, is the most obvious example).[83] But it was in the South, among the poor in the countryside and small cities, that the holiness movement made the greatest inroads. The first Pentecostal churches – the Church of God in Christ, the Pentecostal Holiness Church, the Church of God, the Assemblies of God – all originated in the South. The first two generations of Pentecostals were also overwhelmingly Southern, and not until 1936 did as many Pentecostals live outside that region as in it.[84]

Other Southern churches, including, most notably, the Methodist Episcopal Church, South, preached temperance.

That Church welcomed speakers from the Woman's Christian Temperance Union, supported the Anti-Saloon League, and said, at its General Conference in 1890, that it would settle for nothing less than prohibition."[85] But for sheer strictness none of the established churches could match the early holiness churches. Their rules fairly bristle with proscriptions. All were opposed to alcohol and tobacco. Many forbade meat, sweets, "medicinal foods," cosmetics, neck ties, jewellery, and other "worldly ornamentations."[86] The lists varied, but "The Lot in Canaan's Land," a holiness hymn dating from 1906, covered the basics:

> *The lot has no tobacco,*
> *No clubs, no cards, no ball;*
> *All dwell in peace together,*
> *With love for one and all;*
> *They set no fads or fashions,*
> *They pay all debts they owe;*
> *The men vote prohibition;*
> *Saloons, they say, must go.*[87]

The discussions were both heated and endless. Scarcely a year passed in which the Church of God was not called on to consider a new ban. It was simply assumed that its members did not drink alcohol. Tobacco was not so easily eradicated. For eight long years, from their first general assembly in a private home in Cherokee County, North Carolina, the congregation wrestled with the issue. They disapproved, but was it fair to hold everybody to the same high standard? They proceeded cautiously. At first they asked only that pastors and deacons "deal tenderly and lovingly with those in the church who use it, but insist with an effectionate [sic] spirit that its use be discontinued as much as possible." Two years later, they ratcheted up the rules. Now deacons were forbidden from using tobacco in any form. By 1911, total abstinence from tobacco had become a pre-condition for membership. A year after that, all members were enjoined from growing or selling tobacco. The final blow came in 1913. Those members who still used tobacco were to be "given ample time, only a few weeks, and if they fail to abstain they are to be disfellowshiped."

No sooner had tobacco been laid to rest than other sub-stances competed for the members' attention. Was it a "sin to drink coffee, eat meat etc. and wear collars and ties?" the dele-gates wanted to know. The questions were so sweeping that they caught the general overseer off guard. "I believe our folks would be better off without it," he ventured, "but we cannot bring it in the Church as a doctrine." The same principle applied to pork: it "may not be good for some people and we might all be better off if we did not use it, but if one wants to eat it and another does not there should be no fault-finding with each other about it." As for collars and ties, they were unobjectionable. In 1917, even as America was entering the war, the members agonized over Coca-Cola and "other cold drinks" ("I hope none of our people are guilty of drinking such things, but if they are I hope they won't do it any more"), chewing gum ("This is not a test of member-ship, but our people should not use it"), and coffee (the general overseer disapproved but stopped short of banning it outright).[88]

Sexual behaviour was the occasion of still more earnest discussions in the holiness churches. All urged married couples to limit sexual intercourse to the bare minimum necessary for procreation ("If licentiousness on the part of those that are unmarried deserves punishment . . . does not the same law hold just as binding in the sight of God on those that have been granted a legalized marriage certificate by man?").[89] Some held that divorcees should be made to return to their original spouses. Others said that they should be barred from ever marrying again. Still others, recalling the extreme asceticism of the Oberlin perfectionists, recoiled at the idea of non-procreative sex and wondered aloud if the sanctified should refrain altogether.[90]

The intensity of these debates was a tribute to just how seriously the early holiness churches took Christian perfection. One looks in vain for comparable outpourings in the mainstream Methodist churches. The Northern Methodists, for all the support they gave the Anti-Saloon League, had been known to be less than zealous.[91] Their General Convention stood by and said nothing when President McKinley refused to discontinue sales of liquor in army canteens. The Pennsylvania Conference expelled the editor of its newsletter for being a prohibitionist.[92] The Methodist Episcopal Church, South was slower still to warm to teetotalism (as late as 1882 it was still temporizing over hard liquor, forbidding its preachers from manufacturing and selling it, but saying nothing against their actually drinking it). When that Church finally came around to temperance as it was understood and preached in the North, it nonetheless remained conspicuously silent on tobacco, that most Southern of commodities. When a "treatise upon this wonderful weed" was published in 1868, the New Orleans *Advocate* used the occasion to take a potshot at the Northern Church. Had the author belonged to the North Ohio Conference, he doubtless would have been forced to "make many confessions, promises of amendment, besides eating an enormous quantity of codfish."[93]

One of the reasons why the holiness churches could commit themselves so wholeheartedly to Christian perfection was that they did not bear the taint of slavery. They were too new for that and too poor. Many of their churches, moreover, catered to African Americans. Of the old Southern churches, the Southern Baptists were arguably the most tainted. Strong supporters of slavery before the war, they would remain committed to strict segregation in the decades that followed.[94] When, for example, Theodore Roosevelt invited Booker T. Washington to the White House in 1901, the editor of the *Biblical Recorder*, a North Carolina Baptist paper, canvassed several prominent Southerners. What, he asked, was the "right and reasonable attitude of Christian white people toward the members of the colored race"? The responses were unanimous: it was one thing to be civil, but under no circumstances should the two races socialize.[95]

This is not to say that the early holiness churches were socially liberal. Far from it. Their inward focus, their commitment to transforming themselves rather than their society, made them conservatives by default, upholders of the status quo rather than a threat to it.[96] The strictures that kept poor white members from joining the Ku Klux Klan also kept them from joining labour unions. To the extent that they could even see a role for government, it was of the populist sort associated with William Jennings Bryan and the agrarian populism of the 1890s (no fewer than twenty-three holiness churches were founded during that calamitous decade, while the most radical of these, the Fire-Baptized Holiness Church, did best in those states where farmers felt themselves most threatened, in Florida, Georgia, North Carolina, South Carolina, Virginia, Texas, Oklahoma, and Kansas).[97]

Small, isolated, and militantly apolitical, the early holiness churches were neither able nor willing to take the lead in bringing the South into the temperance fold. That task fell to the largest and most powerful of the Southern churches, the

Southern Baptist Convention. It was a latecomer to the cause.[98] Individual Baptists had been speaking out against liquor since the early nineteenth century, but only in 1890, after years of going back and forth on the issue, did the Convention formally ask its members to practise teetotalism and lobby for prohibition.[99]

After that, however, there was no turning back. An alliance with the Woman's Christian Temperance Union was out of the question.[100] That group's links to the Social Gospel movement, its unabashed feminism, its sympathy for labour unions – all rendered it suspect to the Convention's conservative members. As one aggrieved Baptist put it, "The whole spirit of the 'W.C.T.U.' is to turn Christianity into a set of 'reforms' – anti-liquor, anti-tobacco, 'social purity,' 'female suffrage,' and what not."[101] The temperance organization that *was* acceptable to the Convention was the Anti-Saloon League. Unlike its rival, the League had only two planks – prohibition and woman's suffrage – and the second was clearly subordinated to the first. Just as important, the League had already demonstrated that it was more than willing to turn a blind eye to racial injustice.

When the fight against liquor was won, in 1920, the Convention would set its sights on the sins of the cities, on crime, the "divorce evil," Sabbath-breaking, salacious movies, and, most of all, dancing.[102] Much later in the century, it would be a major player in the New Virginity movement, launching the Christian Sex Education Project in 1987, and True Love Waits in 1992. And after all these years, the Convention has not dropped its opposition to alcohol. The issue came up as recently as 2006, at which time a reaffirmation of the Church's commitment to teetotalism was carried by a four-fifths vote.

By the end of the nineteenth century the South had embraced temperance. But it was still far from being in a position to lead, and by the time it was, in 1912, the fight was already close to being won.* With the South still weak and the North increasingly wobbly, the leadership of the temperance movement defaulted to a region that was by no means fully committed to the cause: the Midwest. Three-quarters of the actions the women's temperance crusade staged took place in the Midwest, more than a third in Ohio alone.[103] The organization that grew out of the women's crusade, the Woman's Christian Temperance Union, had its headquarters in Chicago.[104] The Anti-Saloon League was started in Oberlin (in 1893) and was based in Westerville, a suburb of Columbus. Wayne B. Wheeler (1869–1927), the league's general counsel, was one of many Oberlin alumni to work for that organization.[105]

Yet already there were cracks in the facade. By the 1870s, the Independent Order of Good Templars, a teetotal organization committed to advancing prohibition, was not only losing members in the Northeast: it was also losing them in the Great Lakes region.[106] Nor did it help that the Northeasterners who had poured into the Midwest before the war, evangelicals like Asa Mahan and Charles Grandison Finney and Josiah Willard, were dying out – or that most of the immigrants who came after them happened to be Catholic. Chicago, which by 1916 was more than two-thirds Catholic, was the worst offender.[107] The surrounding

♦

* The South's political exile effectively ended in 1912, the year the Democrats, taking advantage of a split in the Republican vote, swept the White House and both houses of Congress. The president (Woodrow Wilson) was a Southerner, as were five of his ten Cabinet appointees, while the key congressional committees were also picked up by Southern Democrats.

suburbs – Evanston, Oak Park, and Blue Island – all voted them-selves dry, but not Chicago.[108] Even in 1919, with national Prohibition a foregone conclusion, Chicago voters, male as well as female, overwhelmingly rejected an initiative that would have shut down the city's saloons.[109] When Prohibition was forced on them a year later, they started making their own wine (one esti-mate, dating from 1925, put the amount at 15 million U.S. gallons a year). Purchases of sacramental wine rose by eight hundred thousand U.S. gallons a year.[110]

Chicago's intransigence is a reminder that the divide over Prohibition was as much regional as it was cultural, with the countryside, small towns, and suburbs on one side, and the large and ethnically diverse cities on the other.[111] The fact that most of the leaders of the Anti-Saloon League lived in cities did not keep them from pandering to the people who did not.[112] Certainly they never missed an opportunity to say that the cities, with their saloons, corrupt politicians, and hordes of immigrants, were their real enemy, the only thing standing between them and their goal.[113] It is also instructive that Billy Sunday, the revivalist most associated with Prohibition, could never quite breach America's largest cities. This was not for want of trying. He staged revivals in Philadelphia, Boston, and Buffalo in 1915 and 1916, and in 1917 he led a ten-week crusade in New York City. But the revival he held in Chicago, in 1918, was his last foray into Sodom until 1934, and for the last sixteen years of his life he would limit his circuit almost entirely to the South and his native Midwest.

Prohibition merely widened the divide between the cities and the rest of America.[114] It was a godsend to writers like H.L. Mencken, providing him with endless fodder: "There are single acres in Europe that house more first-rate men than all the states south of the Potomac," "We are not only to abandon the social customs of civilization at the behest of a rabble of peasants who sleep in their underclothes; we are now to give up all the basic ideas of civilization and adopt the gross superstitions of the same mob," and so on. Mencken was perhaps closer to the mark when he warned that Prohibition would serve only to convince sophisticates of their own superiority. Certainly it had that effect on him.[115] Clarence Darrow, the scourge of William Jennings Bryan, also had the satisfaction of having his prejudices confirmed. "There would be no literature, no art, no music, no statesmanship if we relied on the prohibitionist for works of genius." His hero was Brand Whitlock (1869–1934), one-time ambassador to Belgium. Whitlock had gone into exile rather than live under "prohibition fanaticism." Lucky Whitlock – fated to spend his days flitting between Belgium "in the summer and the Riviera in the winter, writing, traveling, leisurely enjoying the day and the morrow as they pass by."[116]

Support for Prohibition had been weakest in the Northeast, and it was here that it was first allowed to lapse. By 1924, New York City had ceased to enforce the law.[117] The New York Times was forever running articles showing up the law's failure to keep people from drinking.[118] In 1932, Mayor Jimmy Walker led two "beer parades" on a single day. "We want beer!" the marchers chanted. One, a young mother, had attached a banner to her infant. "My daddy had beer," it read. "Why can't I?"[119] In 1926, New York State voters, by a margin of three to one, voted in favour of softening the Volstead Act. Massachusetts voters did so twice, in 1920 and 1928.[120] The state later repealed its own enforcement law. Rhode Island, which had never ratified the Eighteenth Amendment, followed suit in 1932.[121] It was a Connecticut senator, Hiram Bingham, who introduced a bill allowing sales of beer with an alcohol content of 3.2 per cent or lower. The Bingham Beer Act became law in March of 1933, eight months before Prohibition was formally repealed.[122]

The South and rural Midwest stood firm. The Ku Klux Klan, which had been resurrected in Georgia in 1915, was a conspicuous supporter. When Prohibition went into effect, Atlanta's Klan joined with the local Anti-Saloon League to celebrate the death of "King Barleycorn."[123] But the Klan's activities on behalf of Prohibition (it collected information on violators and bullied authorities into prosecuting them) were by no means restricted to the South. It was especially active in Indiana, the state that happened to have the largest Klan membership in the nation (one-fourth to one-third of all native-born white Hoosiers are supposed to have joined in the 1920s).[124] Even after repeal, temperance still enjoyed considerable support in the South and the rural Midwest. Of the six states that voted against repeal, four (South Carolina, Georgia, Louisiana, and Mississippi) were Southern and two (Kansas and North Dakota) were Midwestern. Of the three states that opted to remain dry after repeal, two (Georgia and Alabama) were Southern. The other state, Kansas, was Midwestern.[125]

The most curious example of all dates from 1936, when the Virginia General Assembly commissioned two professors, James Alexander Waddell and Harvey Bernhardt Haag, to prepare a scientific report on alcohol's effects on the human body. The state's public schools were required to teach a course on the subject (the goal was to discourage children from drinking), and Waddell and Haag had the job of bringing the curriculum up to date. This is not the unusual part of the story: many other states offered similar courses, a legacy of the pedagogical work carried out by the Woman's Christian Temperance Union, and if anything,

Virginia's Board of Education was being more conscientious than most by initiating a review of the latest literature. The unusual part was the report's fate: when it was at long last released, in 1938, the Assembly, deeming it insufficiently critical of drinking, ordered all one thousand copies burned in the State Capitol's furnace.[126]

If evangelicalism has a motto, it is certainly not "Live and let live." A thing is right or wrong, and that is all there is to it. This was true of evangelicalism in its earliest and most idealistic form, and it is just as true of evangelicalism today. There is, however, one crucial difference. The vision of the antebellum evangelicals was for the most part post-millennial, which is to say that it was suffused with optimism. The basic idea was that society was constantly getting better, paving the way for a millennium of peace and prosperity. It was only after that millennium, at some vague and distant point in the future, that Christ would return and be reunited with his saints. This optimism is what made the Oberlin perfectionists such passionate activists.[127]

Post-millennialism was the impulse behind the early temperance movement.[128] But it was already losing steam in the run-up to Prohibition. There were still believers – the Progressives and the proponents of the Social Gospel come first to mind – but what is most striking is the growing pessimism and conservatism of late nineteenth- and early twentieth-century evangelicals. Their vision, in other words, was increasingly pre-millennial. This view holds that Christ will return to earth before the millennium of peace and prosperity can begin. The worse society becomes, the sooner Christ will return to set it aright. The most a Christian can do is to lead a sinless life to ensure that he or she will be counted among the saints. The underlying assumption can be summed up in one sentence, in this case the motto that adorned Aimee Semple McPherson's "Gospel Car": "Jesus is coming soon – get ready."[129] To reform society is not only futile: it thwarts God's plan and merely delays Christ's return.[130] As one evangelical preacher put it during the presidential election of 1988, "The next event on the eschatological clock is the return of Christ. Things in society should get *worse* rather than better. If Christians worked to turn our nation around, that would be a humanistic effort and delay Christ's return."[131] This gloomy thought runs through the teachings of Dwight Moody (1837–1899), Billy Sunday, Tim LaHaye* – and conservative evangelicals in general.

Just as post-millennialism lends itself to activism, pre-millennialism lends itself to retrenchment, to an almost obsessive focus on individual moral failings. It is also the natural ally of laissez-faire capitalism, a fact that goes far toward explaining why religious conservatives and libertarians, who otherwise have very little in common, have nonetheless been able to rally behind the Republican Party.[132]

To an outsider, this difference – whether Christ will return before or after the millennium – seems trivial. Both camps, after all, believe in sanctification, and both make a virtue of abstinence. But they abstain for entirely different reasons – the post-millennialist out of hope, the pre-millennialist out of fear, out of the conviction that it is only a matter of time before Christ

---

* LaHaye is best known for his writings on the last dispensation, otherwise known as the "Rapture." This is the moment at which the millennium is supposed to begin and all faithful Christians are to be reunited with God, leaving the rest of humanity to suffer under the Antichrist.

returns to sit in judgment of humanity. To appreciate this sense of urgency is to appreciate the huge appeal of Phoebe Palmer and her "shorter way" to achieving Christian perfection.[133]

It takes no particular imagination to see why Southerners were drawn to pre-millennialism in the bitter years following the Civil War.[134] Here, in the most lurid form imaginable, was an assurance that their miseries would soon end – and that they would be both avenged and vindicated. Nor can the South's embrace of bootstrap Protestantism be separated from the shape of its social institutions. If Southerners of the post-Reconstruction era gravitated to a moral code that made a virtue of self-sufficiency, this was at least in part because their state and local governments did so little for them, stinting on education, hospitals, public health, and prisons.[135]

Much was lost in the new and distinctly Southern formula, starting with any real engagement with society. The criticism of Walter Rauschenbusch is especially apropos: "To be afraid of hell or purgatory and desirous of a life without pain or trouble in heaven was not itself Christian. It was self-interest on a higher level."[136] Lost, too, was the enormous faith the original evangelicals had placed in the individual, the assumption that there was no end to the good ordinary men and women could do. In its place was a system of crabbed and increasingly disconnected rules and proscriptions. What had been a religion of the New Testament had become a religion of the Old Testament.

FIVE

JOHN STUART MILL AND THE BRITISH ALTERNATIVE

That these proposals would solve, absolutely and defini-
tively, the entire problem of intemperance, is neither
claimed nor believed. This no single scheme can effect.

Joseph Rowntree and Arthur Sherwell,
The Temperance Problem and Social Reform (1899)[1]

We must never think we cannot hold two inconsistent
views.

Lady Isabella Somerset[2]

American temperance reformers were forever being dis-
appointed by their European counterparts. It baffled
them that perfectly intelligent people could read the same
science and the same statistics and yet fail to see that the only
possible solution was abstinence for everyone. The French, who
waited until 1916 to ban distilled liquors in kindergartens
and primary schools, were a lost cause.[3] But even the British,
the people Americans most admired, were never fully on board.
How could the Church of England Temperance Society, formerly

the Church of England Total Abstinence Society, throw open its door to non-abstainers (something it did in 1872) and still say it stood for temperance?[4] How could the United Kingdom Alliance, an organization committed to prohibition, take money from people who had no intention of becoming teetotallers?[5] How could Frederic William Farrar, author of the best-selling *Life of Christ* (1874), sign a teetotal pledge and then say he had no quarrel with "those who think that a little wine is conducive to their happiness or necessary to their health"?[6]

That British temperance reformers had started from the same premise, Christian perfection as it had been handed down by Wesley, merely added insult to injury. Their words were the same, and yet their goals were always subtly different. Even Josephine Butler was not all she appeared to be. Her life's work, realized in 1886, was the repeal of the Contagious Diseases Acts (these subjected prostitutes in port and garrison towns to routine medical inspections). Her hero was William Lloyd Garrison and she liked to call herself an abolitionist.[7] But that is where the similarities ended. Butler's focus was in fact exceedingly narrow, the exact opposite of the "Do Everything" philosophy of Frances Willard and the Woman's Christian Temperance Union.[8] Unlike her American counterparts, Butler had no interest in criminalizing non-marital sex.[9] She was also chary of the temperance movement: she herself was not a teetotaller, and in 1897, after a highly publicized falling-out with Frances Willard and Lady Isabella Somerset, she resigned her position in the World's Woman's Christian Temperance Union.[10] Somerset, in turn, ran into difficulties when she proposed to broaden her association's mandate to include such issues as workers' rights, opium addiction, and social purity.[11]

British reformers were not only more narrowly focused than their American counterparts: they were also likelier to accept imperfect outcomes. Butler, who consistently refused to compromise with her opponents, was the great exception. Everywhere else one finds Britons taking a more roundabout path to their goals. Slavery was abolished in 1833, but the slaves themselves were not fully emancipated until 1838. England's Vice Society was more lackadaisical than the New York Society for the Suppression of Vice, Anthony Comstock's (1844–1915) pet project – or so one might infer from the volume of smut each organization impounded.[12] And the British medical establishment was less horrified by masturbation.[13]

But nowhere were the differences more apparent than in the two countries' approaches to the age-old problem of drunkenness. The British had their own temperance movement, which for the first three decades of its existence gave every appearance of marching in lockstep with its American counterpart, going through the same phases at roughly the same time – abandoning moderation for teetotalism in the 1830s, abandoning suasion for coercion in the early 1850s. In both countries, moreover, there was the same clustering of temperance with other radical causes: abolitionism, feminism, vegetarianism, and the like.[14]

The appearance of unity was reinforced by the constant exchange of speakers and news, each fanning the hope that whatever worked on one side of the Atlantic could be transplanted whole to the other. The *Christian Observer*, a newspaper representing the evangelical wing of the Church of England, had high hopes after the American Temperance Society was founded in 1826. And the good news from America did not stop there.

The students of Yale College had unanimously agreed that intemperance was a bad thing. Citizens in the New Hampshire town of Lyme had "abstained entirely from the use of ardent spirits during the whole of the year 1827, and many others [had] used but little." In one Connecticut township 612 men had promised to "abstain entirely from distilled liquors."[15] The American Temperance Society repaid the compliment by excitedly reporting on developments in Britain, including, most notably, the founding of the first teetotal society (the famous Preston Temperance Society) in 1832.[16]

The turning point came in 1851, when Maine became the first U.S. state to ban all sales of liquor. This was followed, in 1853, by the appearance of a new temperance organization in Britain: the United Kingdom Alliance. Headquartered in Manchester, it was far better organized than its predecessors. It was also far more militant, for its stated goal, the "suppression of the traffic in all intoxicating liquors," amounted to prohibition.[17] By 1857, however, the Alliance already had lowered its sights, for from this point it is to be found putting all of its efforts into drying up Britain one town at a time. This was the idea behind the local veto, which required the vote of two-thirds of a town's ratepayers. Whether this incremental approach eventually would have resulted in nationwide prohibition is debatable. There was no guarantee that all towns would go along, and each ban, moreover, was binding for three years only.

Even this went too far. When the bill was first introduced, in 1864, it was resoundingly defeated, by 282 votes to 35, and while subsequent votes were closer, the Alliance, after more than six decades of lobbying and petitioning, would have exactly two things to show for its efforts: Sunday closings in Wales and parts of Ireland, and the passage, in 1913, of legislation giving Scottish towns the local veto.

What went wrong? Otherwise put, why did the temperance movement encounter so little resistance in America and so much in Britain? This is an old question, and there is no shortage of good answers.[18] The most obvious, one to which historians keep returning, is political: America's governmental structure was far more decentralized, allowing temperance reformers to postpone a showdown at the federal level while steadily advancing their agenda at the local and state levels. Just as important, religious dissenters, the group most associated with temperance in Victorian Britain, remained outside the political mainstream, and their inexperience cost them dearly each time they tried to advance their agenda through Parliament. The structural variables in Britain were also all wrong: the drink trade was more entrenched and better organized, while the rural population (the biggest supporter of prohibition in America) was its biggest enemy.

These explanations, compelling though they are, skirt the larger question of why the ideal of the temperance movement, universal abstinence, sparked so little enthusiasm in Britain. For without that vital spark the movement could never quite get off the ground. What was missing, in short, was a commitment to Christian perfection in its most rigorous – and most American – form. British temperance reformers laboured under a double handicap. Though the Protestant version of that doctrine had originated in that country, with Wesley and the Methodists, it never attracted as many adherents as it did in America. Nor did the doctrine undergo the same startling transformation that it did on the other side of the Atlantic, which is to say that it was less radical, less all-encompassing, and, by inference, less capable of inspiring people to fight for it.

Nothing illustrates the point quite so well as tea. For the longest time, American temperance reformers were dead set against this mild beverage, and only much later in the century does one start to find people like Frances Willard drinking it without guilt.[19] The objection, one that took its cue from the Oberlin perfectionists, was that tea was a stimulant and therefore "inconsistent with perfect temperance."[20] Ellen G. White was emphatic: "Tea, coffee, and tobacco, as well as alcoholic drinks, are different degrees in the scale of artificial stimulants."[21] Amherst's Edward Hitchcock could accept that coffee and tea were less pernicious than alcohol and tobacco, but the "exciting principle is essentially the same; that is, it is a narcotic."[22] William Andrus Alcott was unable even to make this small concession. Caffeinated beverages stimulated the "brain and nervous system, just as other intoxicating liquors do. And what difference does it make whether the excitement be produced by one drink or another?"[23]

To George Gabriel Sigmond, an English doctor and author of *Tea; Its Effects Medicinal and Moral* (1839), it made all the difference in the world. Tea made people "sober, careful and provident." They worked harder. Their heads were clearer, their minds sharper. In short, they were "healthier, happier, and better," all because they had "given up a debasing habit for an innocent one."[24] What Sigmond said, British temperance reformers repeated. More than that, they acted on his advice, drinking tea in vast quantities and throwing tea parties to raise money for the cause.

It may be countered that the British had a perfectly corrupt motive for promoting tea (the East India Company), and that the habit was, in any event, past extirpating (Friedrich Engels, writing in 1844, found that only the poorest of England's house-holds went without tea, and this with the greatest reluctance).[25] All of which is true. But it does not change the fact that the British started from a completely different premise: that there were many areas of life into which the writ of Christian perfec-tion did not extend (an argument Wesley himself had once made) and that tea was one of them.

There were, of course, pockets of Christian perfection in Victorian Britain. The Primitive Methodists, who had broken with the Methodist Conference early in the century, come first to mind (they would later take credit for the Preston Temperance Society, claiming that it had been their idea all along).[26] William and Catherine Booth, the founders of the Salvation Army and easily the most famous teetotallers in late Victorian Britain, were as strict in their personal lives as anyone in America. This was especially true of Catherine. Like William, she had been raised in a strict Methodist home. She fussed when William ate meat, and scolded him when he had the occasional glass of wine or port, a habit he gave up entirely when they married.[27]

But even the Primitive Methodists were at first wary of teetotalism.[28] A Brother Marriott was censured in 1840 for "preaching politics and teetotalism at Hyde [Park]." In 1845, a Brother Compton was told that he "must not deliver Teetotal lectures when he should preach the gospel."[29] William Antliff (1813–1884), writing in 1873, recalled how one local preacher used to rail against teetotalism, calling it "just *a trick of the devil*, to cause people to be satisfied with something else than the Gospel."[30] The official Methodist Church, the Connexion, was warier still, consistent with its growing conservatism.[31] When

James Caughey (1811–1891), the Irish-born American revivalist, called on British Methodists to embrace teetotalism, the
Connexion ordered its chapels closed to teetotal meetings.[32]

Also revealing is that American revivalists, for all the
crowds they attracted in Britain, had little success in getting
those same crowds to commit to a life of Christian perfection.[33]
Caughey had only 9,000 sanctified souls to show for his
six years in Britain. Phoebe Palmer could garner only 2,287
sanctified souls after preaching non-stop for four years (how
she arrived at these numbers she does not say). The number of
conversions was much higher – perhaps 20,000 for Caughey
and exactly 17,643 for Palmer – again suggesting that many
were called but few were chosen.[34] Both revivalists, moreover,
ran into difficulties whenever they went off message and
started to espouse temperance as Americans understood
it.[35] Even Harriet Beecher Stowe, as popular as she was in
Britain, alienated many well-wishers whenever she changed
the subject from *Uncle Tom's Cabin* and abolitionism to the
evils of intemperance.[36]

The results are even more dispiriting when one considers
that the Americans were shopping for souls among the Britons
who most resembled them, that is, among the Methodists
and other nonconformists. Anglican strongholds (the south,
London) were a lost cause. But even without these the potential
pool of fellow travellers was vast. This was brought home by the
religious census for 1851, which showed that there were nearly
as many Christians (48 per cent) outside the Church of England
as there were inside it. The established Church, moreover, harboured a sizable evangelical wing at this time.[37] The Methodists,
now split into several factions, were the second largest denomination, accounting for just over 20 per cent of all professed

Christians, followed by the Congregationalists at 11 per cent, and the Baptists at 8 per cent.[38]

Of all the problems facing the British temperance movement, the biggest was its core assumption: that everyone should be held to the same high standard. This message had played well in nineteenth-century America, complementing, as it did, that country's religious and political ideals. Just as important, America's class structure was still relatively flat, and to that extent, evangelical morality, with its insistence that God's rules were simple, changeless, and equally binding on all Christians, had considerable charm. America, of course, was *not* a classless society. Far from it. The hero of Justin Edwards's *Well-Conducted Farm* was not just anyone: he was a landowner, and the objects of his foray into temperance were the men who worked for him.[39] But these divisions were far more pronounced – and far more ideological – in Britain than they were in America. The Alliance's own allegiance, to middle-class nonconformists, was clear. But by the same token it had not one enemy but two: the working classes who resented any attempt to reform them from above, and the Anglican elites who resented any attempt to reform them from below.

The growing cohesion and radicalism of the working classes also mitigated against passing unpopular laws.[40] If they could not vote, they could riot. This they did most spectacularly in 1855, after Parliament had made one concession to the nation's evangelicals and was about to make another. The first, the Wilson-Patten Act of 1854, curtailed the pubs' opening hours on Sundays. The second, the Sunday Trading Bill, proposed to make Londoners observe the Sabbath by closing all but a handful of their stores on Sundays. This prospect was enough to spark large-scale riots in the capital. A rattled Parliament responded by repealing the Wilson-Patten Act and shelving the Sunday Trading Bill. The lessons of that year may have been wasted on the Alliance, but they were not wasted on Parliament.[41]

And the Alliance's difficulties did not end there. It was bad enough that so many Britons failed to see the light, that so many professed Christians, factory workers, and aristocrats refused to stop drinking. Worse even than their wilfulness was the mindset that could never quite accept the implications of evangelicalism in its most radical – and most American – form. It is telling that Wilberforce and his vice society were not out to reform the morals of the working poor: they were out to reform their *manners*.[42] The goal was entirely Pharisaic, for unlike American evangelicalism, it asked only for obeisance – and not for a thoroughgoing trans-formation and uplifting of the individual. Hence Sydney Smith's (1771–1845) criticism that Wilberforce was doing everything to compel "outward compliance" and nothing to "raise up the inward feeling which secures the outward compliance."[43]

This still does not answer the question of *why* Britons like Wilberforce set the bar so low. Much of the answer lies in the levelling tendencies of American evangelicalism, in its mistrust of everything that stood between the individual and God – tradition, hierarchy, and learning.[44] Small wonder that so many nonconformists were attracted to evangelicalism in its American form. Were they not the victims of privilege, of Parliament, of the Church of England (a "thing apart, as distinct from the life of the race as the House of Lords or the monarchy"), and of an aristocracy that was as corrupt as it was immoral?[45] The result, however, was disastrous for British evangelicals, for in copying the form more than the substance of American evangelicalism they ended up with the worst of both worlds: their energy never quite equalled the Americans' and yet the association was sufficiently strong to stiffen the resistance of the nation's political and cultural elites.[46]

The foes of temperance had motive and opportunity, but most important, they had the means: the working classes in the form of menace and violence, the chattering classes in the form of wit and irony. The last two arguably mattered more, for they supplied what was so painfully lacking in antebellum America: a counterpoise to an argument whose emotional appeal exceeded its intellectual merit. Both rhetorical devices carried the corrosion of doubt, complexity, and absurdity; both had been used already to undermine the authority of the Church of England, and both would be used again to blunt the twined forces of evangelicalism and temperance.[47] Where in antebellum America was there a George Eliot, herself a lapsed evangelical, to deconstruct the most popular evangelical writer of her day, a Dickens to parody the sanctimonious Pecksniff, a Matthew Arnold to remind the public that there was more to life than just God?[48] Emerson was too ponderous, Thoreau too serious, Melville too sodden.

The hill was twice as steep in Britain. Not only did the Alliance have to overcome the contempt and apathy of the nation's elites, it also had to endure their barbs, puns, and *bons mots*. The Maine Law was a favourite target. In November 1851, just after that law had taken effect, *Punch* printed the minutes from a fictional teetotallers' society, noting that the members had met "to enjoy a little excitement derived from hearing everybody abused, instead of from the abuse of fermented liquors." Mr. Belloway spoke, then Messrs. Screamer,

Earsplit, and Stunner.[49] In 1853, *Punch* took on the venerable
John Gough. "If he bears out the reputation he brings with him,
his lectures will be no laughing matter; for he is, as it were,
pledged to set all the men and women off into so many watering-
pots, by drawing from them such a series of wailings and sobs, as
will not only drown the voice of the orator, but threaten even to
drown those who are assembled to hear him."[50] When a group of
ministers attended a temperance meeting in Birmingham, *Punch*
took the occasion to compose a sermon of its own, reminding its
readers that "there are many kinds of intemperance, and not the
least disgusting sort is that which blurts forth upon others a stream
of fierce and fiery trash."[51] In 1856, with the Maine Law already a
dead letter, *Punch* gloated: "Since the mockery of the Law, it is no
longer said in America of a drunken man, that 'He is in a shock-
ing state of liquor,' but 'He is in a frightful State of Maine.'"[52]

Punch was but one of many. *Blackwood's Edinburgh Magazine*
also weighed in, describing the law as "unreasonable, tyranni-
cal, and unconstitutional."[53] The *Manchester Guardian* dismissed
it as ineffective and counterproductive.[54] The *News of the World*
reprinted *Punch's* many witticisms, and on a scarcely more
serious note reported how easy it was to get a drink in Maine, law
or no law.[55]

But it was the London *Times*, in volume no less than venom,
that outdid everyone else: "The drunkard has his drawl, the
puritan his whine, and the teetotaler, and others of his class,
have their long stream of watery prose, trickling so tediously that
you never know when you got to the last drop," "to moralize is
one thing; to fill the frothed tankard is another," and so on.[56] In
October 1856 the *Times* alarmed its readers with news that
certain people in Gloucester had met to lobby for the "adoption
of the Maine Law in this country."[57] When a member of the

Alliance wrote an impassioned letter to the editor, defending the Maine Law and urging the notoriously Tory paper to lend its support to "this great social reform," the response was both immediate and withering. It appeared in the same issue, and was twice as long as the letter that had provoked it. The letter's writer was accused of being unsubtle to the point of stupidity, of "always pushing admissions to their consequences," of not letting "you rest till he has fixed you either in the clouds or in the pit. He sees only one line, up and down, and you are a fool if you don't make an absolute decision to go one way or the other."[58] The following year, in 1857, the *Times* gleefully reported the defection of Joseph Barker (1806–1875), "who for so many years advocated temperance and the Maine Law." A chastened Barker was quoted as saying that the Maine Law was a "failure in America," and that "nothing but moral suasion [would] make a people sober, good, and happy, either here or in any other country."[59]

The ridicule that was heaped on the British temperance movement had no counterpart in antebellum America. Nor could it, what with the quintessentially Jacksonian mistrust of anyone who was idle, facile, or conspicuously educated – in short, of anyone who aspired to belong to the chattering classes. William Andrus Alcott's ideal wife was none of these things, cultivating instead "great plainness of language, dress and manners – an entire artlessness and freedom from everything which savors in the smallest degree of cunning or duplicity." The ideal husband was no less dour. He shunned people who told dirty jokes, told no jokes of his own, and avoided "at all times, and in all places and circumstances, every appearance of evil."[60] These proscriptions made it all but impossible for the Americans who observed them to take in a play while in London. Alexander

Slidell Mackenzie (1803–1848), a sea captain and presumably a man of the world, could not decide which was worse, the "amorous feats" or the "low, coarse, traditional stage-jokes, execrable, atrocious puns and playing upon words, and vulgar and indecent equivoques."[61] Joseph Ballard (1789–1877), a Boston merchant, clearly enjoyed himself at the Covent Garden Theatre (there were "some fine dancers at this house"), but felt guilty nonetheless ("these ladies are so thinly clad and throw themselves into such indecent postures that I think a New England audience would not have tolerated them").[62]

Nothing the Americans said seemed to move the Anglican establishment. Their words were too earnest, their stories too mawkish, their prayers too sincere. *Blackwood's Edinburgh Magazine* went so far as to deconstruct one of "their tearful tales." It was all about a boy who had bought rum not once but "as many as ten or a dozen times." In the original, the boy's story reduces the grown men who hear it to tears. *Blackwood's* editors were made of sterner stuff:

> This, we believe, is what in literary criticism is called spasmodic, and in theatrical criticism, melodramatic. It is the expression of a strong sentiment without a cause: it is feeling without a base of reality. If people go off into the melting mood, and waste away in tears when they learn that a little boy bought rum for his father on a Sunday, what is to become of them before the greater calamities of life?[63]

John Gough was also taken to task for appealing to hearts rather than minds. As one Scottish journal observed, "His arguments are practically no arguments."[64] Gough had to agree. "The English

No. 22

LOOK OUT FOR THE TRAP!

BY MRS. J. P. BALLARD.

SIDE by side on the mossy forest log, what a happy brace of squirrels were Brownie and Grayback! To be sure, they had no names but Squirrel in their woods home but they did not always live there, as I shall tell you. One day they espied on their favorite log something nicer than acorns, more juicy than beechnuts or walnuts.

Oh! what a feast the fresh, cool turnips proved. They never stopped to wonder about the new food, but, carefully smelling it, and then tasting—rather doubtfully at first

---

Look Out for the Trap!

The sentimentality that brought so many nineteenth-century American women into the temperance camp provided the British chattering classes with an endless source of fodder. In this temperance allegory by Mrs. J.P. Ballard, the squirrels Brownie and Grayback are about to be confronted with a temptation unlike any they have ever encountered. Courtesy of the Brown University Library.

and Scotch people require argument," he wrote in his auto-biography. "I cannot argue, for I want logic; I am no logician, I have no education. I can only tell them just what I believe to be the truth in my own way, and I fear I shall not succeed."[65]

Had the war of words been waged by wits and wags alone, the cause of temperance might conceivably have made more progress in Britain. But there were also perfectly thoughtful people who objected to holding an entire society to a single – and exceedingly narrow – code of conduct. Most of all they objected to the evangelicals' conviction that they and they alone were in possession of the truth. They did more than object: they offered a viable alternative. If the evangelicals offered a religion that made a virtue of certitudes, they would offer a philosophy that made a virtue of pluralism and doubt. The more ideas, the merrier, the more points of view, the richer society was for it. This was one of the key points in Matthew Arnold's *Culture and Anarchy* (1867–68). In it he took aim at the nonconformists, accusing them of pursuing religion to the exclusion of all else. Religion was important to Arnold (he is short on specifics), but not all-encompassing. There were whole areas of life into which its writ did not extend, most notably to the thing that he valued the most: the arts. And that, in Arnold's estimation, was where the nonconformists had failed. They had "developed one side of their humanity at the expense of all others," so much so that they had become "incomplete and mutilated men." The Americans were even worse. He himself had never visited America, but he could say, "without much fear of contradiction," that its inhabitants were excessively religious, and religious "in a narrow way."[66]

Arnold did not take on the temperance movement per se. That task fell to an even more formidable thinker: John Stuart Mill. In 1855, when the Alliance still had hopes of crafting a

John Stuart Mill, from a pen-and-ink
by Harry Furniss.

In his essay On Liberty, *Mill took direct
aim at the evangelicals of his day, calling
their understanding of Christianity
"negative rather than positive; passive
rather than active; Innocence rather than
Nobleness; Abstinence from Evil, rather
than energetic Pursuit of Good."* Courtesy
of the National Portrait Gallery in London.

Maine Law for Britain, Mill started work on an essay that posed
a fundamental question: how far can society go in regulating the
behaviours and morals of its members? By the time his essay *On
Liberty* appeared, in 1859, prohibition was no longer a threat in
Britain. But what Mill did, perhaps better than anyone before or
since, was to question the very notion of moral certitude.[67]
Where the proponents of prohibition had offered their followers one way toward one goal, Mill made the case for a healthy
competition among ideas, arguing that "only through diversity
of opinion is there, in the existing state of human intellect, a

chance of fair play to all sides of the truth." In doing so, he rejected the very basis of Judeo-Christian morality: truth, no less than human behaviour, could not be defined in absolute terms, and was instead "a question of the reconciling and combining of opposites . . ." The freedom to *think* as one pleased went hand in hand with the freedom to *do* as one pleased, providing only that one's actions did not harm others.[68]

Mill reserved his harshest criticism for the Alliance, holding it up as an example of what can happen when one group attempts to impose its morality on everyone else.[69] Warning that it was "by no means impossible that persons of these sentiments may at some time or other command a majority in Parliament," he asked,

> How will the remaining portion of the community like to have the amusement that shall be permitted to them regulated by the religious and moral sentiments of the stricter Calvinists and Methodists? Would they not, with considerable peremptoriness, desire these intrusively pious members of society to mind their own business? This is precisely what should be said to every government and every public, who have the pretension that no person shall enjoy any pleasure which they think wrong.

On Liberty is not a work of systematic philosophy. It is an essay, passionate, polemical, and not entirely logical. At what point do an individual's actions cross the line and cause harm to others? Where does the state draw the line between taxing liquor and deliberately limiting its consumption? Mill provides no satisfactory answers. Nor could he, after saying that all ideas – and by implication all solutions – were relative. Mill admitted as much in a letter published in the London *Times* in 1868. His approach, he wrote, "did not pretend to be adequate." He was merely making the point that the "use or non-use of alcoholic liquors is a subject on which every sane and grown-up person ought to judge for himself under his own responsibility."[70]

What Mill did provide was a secular counter-argument to the perfectionism that is at the heart of American evangelicalism and its particular understanding of abstinence. Just as important, Mill offered a definition of freedom that was fundamentally opposed to that of the American evangelicals. Where Mill banished virtue from his system, identifying any attempt to impose it as a threat to freedom, American reformers gave it pride of place. The individual was free *only* to be good, a definition that effectively placed roadblocks in the way of his or her being bad.[71] This was the only solution that the residents of Cedarville, the fictional setting for *Ten Nights in a Bar-Room*, could come up with after several of their neighbours had succumbed to drink. In the novel's last chapter, Joe Morgan, now a model of sobriety, convinces everybody that there is "but one remedy": "The accursed traffic must cease among us. You must cut off the fountain, if you would dry up the stream. If you would save the young, the weak, and the innocent – on you God has laid the solemn duty of their protection – you must cover them from the tempter." Anticipating that some people might not like having restrictions placed on their freedom, Morgan tells the townspeople that virtue must take precedence over freedom. Who, he asks, "has any right to sow disease and death in our community? The liberty, under sufferance, to do so, wrongs the individual who uses it, as well as those who become his victims."[72]

know. She did not. Did she "wish to make everybody a tee-totaler"? She did not. Did she favour "Prohibition by act of Parliament"? She did not.[74] To change one's mind (which she did on numerous occasions), to change one's religion (which she also did, switching from Anglicanism to Methodism and back again), to limit one's weapons to suasion – all marked her as a true disci-ple of John Stuart Mill. Even the London *Times*, the scourge of the temperance movement, could see that, seizing the occasion of her death to take a potshot at American-style Prohibition. Lady Isabella, the obituary read, "saw that (whatever may be the case in America) you cannot in England make people sober by Act of Parliament, and she therefore worked mainly by persuasion."[75]

In 1893, Lady Isabella, having long since concluded that the drink problem could not be solved without first doing something about poverty, joined the British Fabian Society. Frances Willard, now her constant companion, also joined at this time. "We are New Testament Socialists," Willard exclaimed in her diary.[76] The gesture's significance was twofold. It repudiated the old temper-ance equation (that it was drunkenness that caused poverty and not the other way around), and it signalled a willingness to enter-tain solutions that fell short of prohibition. This was true espe-cially of Lady Isabella, but an element of doubt had by now also crept into Willard's thinking, for in these, the final years of her life, she found herself increasingly at odds with the hard-liners in the Woman's Christian Temperance Union.[77] There was much unhap-piness when she cautiously endorsed the idea of regulating sales of alcohol, if only as an intermediate step toward their eventual elim-ination.[78] This small step backward also placed her at odds with Christian socialism in its American form (the Social Gospel). Its leading lights, Walter Rauschenbusch, Washington Gladden, and Josiah Strong, remained committed to prohibition, and while all three were critical of the idea of individual sanctification, a lingering perfectionism can be detected in everything they themselves refused to do – to compromise, to fix just a few things at a time, to accept that change was something that might be achieved through small steps rather than all at once.[79] What was the "end of Christianity" for Gladden? A "perfect man in a perfect society."[80] One must look long and hard to find common ground with their contemporaries among the Fabians. How many American reformers believed in the "inevitability of gradualism" (Sidney Webb's famous phrase) or that "moderate

SIDNEY WEBB.
Photographed by Elliott & Fry.

MRS. SIDNEY WEBB.
Photographed by Elliott & Fry.

A GROUP OF ENGLISH SOCIALISTS.

Sidney and Beatrice Webb, as photographed by Elliott and Fry in 1894.

The couple's characteristic response to the drink problem was to study it – hence The History of Liquor Licensing in England Principally from 1700 to 1830, *which they co-authored in 1903. Their research notes, now housed in the London School of Economics and Political Science, show them to have been meticulous scholars.* From the Library of Congress Prints and Photographs Division.

reforms" were preferable to "heroic remedies" when it came to reducing drunkenness?[81]

That the Fabians could even talk about reducing drunkenness (as opposed to eliminating it altogether) spoke to an unbridgeable divide. The Fabians' studiousness, their penchant for going back to the archives and undertaking fact-finding trips, was yet another rebuke to the American approach, for it made facts – and not abstract principles – the touchstone for reform.[82] The Webbs wrote a whole *History of Liquor Licensing in England* (1903). Edward Pease (1857–1955) felt unable to comment on the subject without first summarizing what had been tried in other countries; hence the lengthy preamble that appears in Fabian Tract 85, otherwise known as *Liquor Licensing at Home and Abroad.* The same impulse lay behind the exhaustive studies undertaken by Joseph Rowntree (1836–1925) and Arthur Sherwell: *The Temperance Problem and Social Reform* in 1899, *Public Control of the Liquor Traffic* in 1903, *The Taxation of the Liquor Trade* in 1906. Arthur Shadwell (1854–1936) was yet another practitioner of this weighty genre, producing such classics as *Drink, Temperance and Legislation* (1915), and *Drink in 1914–1922: A Lesson in Control* (1924). Only the New York-based Committee of Fifty, with its study groups and criticisms of prohibition, could match this level of critical enquiry, and even in that group there was considerable dissent from within the ranks, most notably from Gladden, and Harvard's Charles W. Eliot.[83]

The Fabians' contribution lay not in their accomplishments but in their underlying assumptions. They wanted to do so many more things than they did, to municipalize the drink trade, along with just about everything else – milk, bread, fire insurance, bathhouses, and burials.[84] They dreamt of building "people's palaces" that would compete with the pubs by offering wholesome entertainments and uplifting lectures, on science, mechanical inventions, history, biography, and travel. Precious little came of these schemes, but as thinkers they were both formidable and practical. Where the temperance crusaders talked about solving problems, the Fabians talked about managing them. Most important, they were open to trying several different approaches at the same time, and that, more than any single thing they taught or believed, was the highest tribute they could have paid to John Stuart Mill.

In 1899, the Royal Commission on the Licensing Laws, the same commission Lady Isabella had testified before two years earlier, released two reports. Both called for a reduction in the number of licensed establishments, a proposal that effectively shelved the local veto, but only one, the majority report, called for full compensation to the publicans who would find themselves without a livelihood. Lord Salisbury, whose heart never had been in the enquiry, took the occasion of this seeming impasse to do nothing.[85] That the debate had been reduced to this – to how many pubs were too many and to how much compensation was too much – spoke volumes. Lady Isabella came out in favour of the minority report, and in 1900, after much arm-twisting, the British Women's Temperance Association did so as well. This remained the association's official stance even after Lady Isabella was forced out. The United Kingdom Alliance, in turn, split on the issue: should they agree to a plan that would make some inroads into the trade, or should they hold out for the local veto?

The disarray of the British temperance movement at this time is the subject of several excellent monographs, and its retelling here would merely repeat the two points that have emerged so far: that the British movement operated in an infinitely more hostile environment than its American counterpart, and that its history was therefore one of half-measures. Defeat was as good as admitted when the Alliance set its sights on the local veto, a solution no one seriously expected all towns to adopt, while the recommendations of the Royal Commission on the Licensing Laws backtracked still further.

The Alliance's last hurrah came during the First World War. Ads in the newspapers urged Britons to "follow America's method and achieve America's success." They could start by shutting down the distilleries. It was too much to ask that the breweries also be put out of business, but surely they could be prevailed upon to produce "non-intoxicating beer or other useful products." As for the public houses, let them be converted to "people's cafes, social clubs, national kitchens, or other similar places of real recreation and refreshment." None of these goals were realized in their entirety. But the pubs' hours were curtailed, a restriction that only recently was relaxed under the Licensing Act of 2003, and an important (and quintessentially Fabian) principle was established: the government's right to control the drink trade for the public's benefit.[86]

The war years were auspicious in yet another way: for the first time in its history, the Alliance had one of its own in office. That man was David Lloyd George, and one of his first acts upon becoming minister of munitions in 1915 was to push through a series of emergency measures limiting both the manufacture and consumption of distilled spirits.[87] As prime minister, from 1916 to 1922, he used his office as a bully pulpit for temperance. On one occasion he told the faithful that "we are fighting Germany, Austria, and drink and the greatest of these deadly foes is drink." On another he spoke approvingly of the closure (in 1918) of all breweries in America.[88] After the war, he invited the remnants of the temperance movement to Number 10 Downing Street to discuss how best to keep the old wartime restrictions in place.[89] Before leaving that address, in 1922, he twice doubled the duties on spirits.[90]

But nowhere was there talk of prohibition. The delegation that met with Lloyd George after the war bristled at the suggestion. Its members were, in one reporter's words, anxious to "rid themselves of the imputation that they were prohibitionists."[91] The most they could hope for was a continuation of the wartime restrictions, the rationale for which was receding with each passing year.

Britain handily avoided American-style prohibition, but several other Western countries did not. The Canadian federal government banned sales of alcohol during the First World War (several provinces had already voted themselves dry), but allowed breweries and distilleries to continue to produce for the export market. A de facto prohibition remained in effect throughout most of Canada after the war; Quebec and British Columbia, as one might expect, were the outliers, the first voting against prohibition in 1919, the second in 1920. Finland and Iceland both opted for prohibition at the end of the war. Swedish voters rejected it by the narrowest of margins in 1922. Norwegians imposed yet more restrictions on the trade, stopping just short of actual prohibition. The Nordic experiments, however, were to prove short-lived, with Iceland and Finland both repealing prohibition one year before America did. By then, too, most Canadian provinces had long since resumed sales of liquor.[92]

The idea that there can be more than one response to a problem lives on in the British National Health Service's approach to alcohol abuse. Abstinence remains the ideal, but controlled drinking, an imperfect and riskier outcome, is offered as an alternative in most British treatment facilities.[93] Flexibility – sobriety for those who are up to the challenge, harm reduction for those who are not – is also the hallmark of the services available to drug addicts.[94] The same principle can be detected in the Rolleston Report (1926), which upheld the right of physicians to prescribe opiates to addicts who cannot or will not abstain. A more careful reading shows that what its authors were really recommending was a two-tiered approach: complete withdrawal whenever possible, and maintenance only after every effort "has been made, and made unsuccessfully, to bring the patient to a condition in which he is independent of the drug."[95]

If only it worked. The British, for all their much-vaunted reasonableness, have been no more successful than the Americans in stemming drug and alcohol abuse. Heroin dependence, once a rarity in Britain, is now as widespread there as it is in America.[96] And the British have had no better luck with alcohol. Their rates of alcohol dependence, though measured by different criteria, are roughly comparable to the Americans' (6.9 per cent compared to 4.6 per cent) while their rates of abstention are far lower (12 per cent compared to just under 39 per cent).[97] Nor, with the recent relaxation in opening hours, are there any immediate prospects for improvement.[98]

The reality is that the range of options for controlling alcohol and drug problems is small, and that over time, all – abstinence, prohibition, and different combinations of regulations – have been tried. Only one, abstinence, can be said to work in its entirety, and even then only for motivated individuals. Nor do attempts to match alcoholics with individually tailored treatments seem to have a significant effect on the outcome, making this a case where motivation trumps theory.[99] Mill's model, in other words, is a poor one for alcohol and drug problems. It assumes that there is a crowded marketplace of good ideas (which in this case there is not) and that after a fair fight, the best one eventually will emerge.

A century and a half later, it is perhaps time to say that a better idea has not come along because it does not exist. What the British example shows is that an intellectual elite can, with enough determination and self-confidence, play a decisive role in checking the advance of prohibitionism and the perfectionist impulse that fuels it. What it cannot offer is a demonstrably better alternative.

FROM ABSTINENCE'S PAST TO ITS PRESENT

If you are as seriously alcoholic as we were, we believe there is no middle-of-the-road solution.

From the "Big Book" of Alcoholics Anonymous

"Truth's motto," John Granville Woolley once said, "is 'all or nothing.'"[1] Woolley, the Prohibition Party's presidential candidate in 1900, was explaining why he was opposed to any scheme that stopped short of eliminating liquor altogether. But he could just as easily have been explaining why he himself, after a lifetime of heavy drinking, had suddenly opted for teetotalism in 1888.[2] For Woolley, as for millions of Americans before and after him, it was impossible to meet a problem halfway.

This assumption has persisted even as the link between abstinence and evangelicalism has progressively weakened. Few of the Americans who now go without meat or poultry or milk or all of these things would answer to the label *evangelical*. And yet they are in many ways the descendants of the abolitionists and feminists who once tried to save themselves and the world by giving up their favourite foods.[3] The direct link to Christian

"Take That Meat Away

We will have no more meat or heavy,
hard-to-digest foods on our breakfast
table this Summer. We never felt so
well in our lives as we did last Summer, when
we made EGG-O-SEE the foundation of every meal."

If you do not use EGG-O-SEE for EVERY meal, you should at
least make it the LAW OF YOUR BREAKFAST TABLE, and
insure Summer Health and vigorous happiness for your entire household.

EGG-O-SEE is Nature's own food—the whole
wheat in its most tempting, delicious and sustaining form.

More EGG-O-SEE is eaten each day
than all other similar foods combined.
This is the strongest endorsement ever
accorded any food by the American people.

Costs no more than the ordinary kinds—
large package 10c.

FREE—our "-back to nature" book—tells how to
get well and keep well by natural means. Sent free
on application—write today.

EGG-O-SEE CEREAL COMPANY, Chicago

"Take that meat away," reads this advertisement for Egg-O-See cereal. "We will have
no more meat or heavy, hard-to-digest foods on our breakfast table this summer." Cold
cereals came into vogue in the late nineteenth century, fuelled by a revival of interest in
Sylvester Graham's theories and by a growing concern over tainted meat. John Harvey
Kellogg liked to prescribe large doses of his own cereals, along with bran, zwieback,
Graham crackers, and caramel cereal coffee. Courtesy of the Warshaw Collection of
Business Americana.

perfection is gone, so much so that vegetarianism has been touted as a way to "enhance your love life," but the formula is otherwise the same one Sylvester Graham used to hawk to the antebellum ascetics.[4] Today there is the same conviction that health is a matter of choice (the word that repeats is *lifestyle*), the same sense that if only one were to get enough exercise and avoid the wrong foods and eat the right ones, life would go on – if not forever, then well past its appointed span.[5] One need look no further than *Prevention* magazine: "bib up, beat cancer," "carrots crush diabetes," "smile away sickness," "diligence fixes depression," "be your own best coach."* The same formula accounts for the phenomenal success of Kevin Trudeau's *Natural Cures "They" Don't Want You to Know About* (2004). To read this book is to "know categorically, absolutely, with a hundred per cent certainty that there is a natural cure for your disease and you will know exactly what to do to cure yourself of your disease and remain healthy for life – all without drugs or surgery."

The modern health reform movement, moreover, is not without its idealists, and if it has aged out of its roots in the counterculture of the 1960s and 1970s, it still has its share of people whose abstinence, whether from meat or eggs or milk or non-organic foods, is a matter of conscience.[6] A gesture against globalization, a show of solidarity with farm workers and peas-ants, a protest against the mistreatment of animals and the

---

* That magazine's founder, Jerome Rodale, liked to collect testimonials from satisfied readers. A particularly miraculous tale concerns a Mrs. H.J. Schauer of Roseville, California, who claimed that ever since she had taken up organic gardening her teeth were no longer "inclined to decay, and believe it or not, within the last six months a nice hard shining cap of new enamel has com-pletely covered the exposed dentine."

degradation of the environment – all, one suspects, would have resonated with the pure-hearts who formed the core of the original health reform movement. There is a certain irony in this, for what linkage there still is between abstinence and idealism is not on the right but on the left.

Alcoholics Anonymous, easily the most successful abstinence movement to come out of twentieth-century America, is another hybrid, retaining parts of the evangelical formula while explicitly rejecting the idea of human perfectibility.[7] Members might become better, happier, and more spiritual, but they will not become saints. Nor are they expected to act like saints. Bill Wilson, the group's co-founder, overcame his compulsion to drink, but this still left him with a multitude of other bad habits. He was a womanizer. He dabbled in LSD. He was a chain-smoker. He was famous for his sweet tooth.[8]

Just as important, the alcoholic who undertakes a "searching and fearless moral inventory" does so without the benefit of hard-and-fast rules. This is the case even when taking stock of one's sexual history. Was a relationship "selfish or not"? – that is what really matters, not whether it occurred before marriage, outside it, or with someone of the same sex. Even this guideline, cautious and equivocal though it is, is hedged with caveats: "We tried to be sensible on this question," "We do not want to be the arbiter of anyone's sex conduct," "We avoid hysterical thinking or advice."[9]

Where Alcoholics Anonymous has remained true to the evangelical model is in its understanding of abstinence. Abstinence was always a means to an end for the evangelicals, a means of getting closer to God by vanquishing the sins that separated one from the other. Sobriety occupies a similar theoretical position in the thinking of Alcoholics Anonymous. The word *sin* is gone, though the language that has replaced it – the "misuse of willpower," "our vengeful resentments, self-pity, and unwarranted pride," "derelictions," and the like – is a watered-down version of the original. Yet the goal itself has lost none of its old spirituality, none of the old wish to surrender to God and in so doing achieve peace of mind.[10] Sobriety is a foundation and nothing more. It is rarely mentioned in the group's literature, and to be a "dry drunk" (an alcoholic who has merely stopped drinking) is to invite the scorn of alcoholics who define recovery as a spiritual process.[11]

But on one point Alcoholics Anonymous is both emphatic and unambiguous: the alcoholic can never drink again. A "long period of sobriety and self-discipline" is not enough, and even one drink is one too many.[12] This refusal to compromise comes from only one place, and that is from the moral absolutes of American evangelicalism.

Where evangelicals *have* compromised is in their understanding of what constitutes Christian perfection. The trend, which was already well underway in the nineteenth century, has been to set the bar progressively lower, to subtract one thing after another – first the social activism of the Oberlin perfectionists, next their dietary restrictions, then their objection to coffee and tea. By the First World War, evangelical groups like the Young Men's Christian Association were cheerfully distributing cigarettes to the troops. The rationale they gave, that they were substituting a lesser vice (tobacco) for a greater one (alcohol), was many things – ingenious, pragmatic, Jesuitical even – but it was not evangelical.[13] Temperance lay at the bottom of this slippery slope, for each step away from Christian perfection made it that much easier to give up the fight against alcohol. That fight continues, to varying degrees, within the

Cousin Sallie Served Coffee from a Silver Urn Owned by Thomas Jefferson.

In this print, dating from 1916, the rehabilitation of coffee is complete, down to the patriotic association with Jefferson himself. From the Library of Congress Prints and Photographs Division.

The Methodist circuit preacher as he appeared to a later and
more genteel generation of Americans.

*By the time this print appeared, in 1867, the Methodists were well on their way to
becoming a mainstream and solidly middle-class Church, prompting cries that "some of
you Methodists who were once poor and unknown, but have grown rich and prominent
in the world, have left the narrow way in which you walked twenty or thirty years
ago, have ceased to attend class-meetings, seldom pray in your families or in
prayer-meetings, as you once did, and are now indulging in many of the fashionable
amusements of the day, such as playing chess, dominoes, billiards, and cards, dancing
and attending theatres, or allowing your children to indulge in them." From the Library
of Congress Prints and Photographs Division.*

The most important change has occurred in how conservative evangelicals think about pleasure. They have not simply
shortened the list of taboos: they have also repudiated the idea
that the pursuit of pleasure is inherently sinful. Nowhere is this
shift more apparent than in their relationship to food. Mike
Huckabee, Southern Baptist preacher, Republican presidential
candidate, and self-described "recovering foodaholic," objects
to obesity not on moral grounds but on health grounds.[18] Gwen
Shamblin, the founder of the hugely popular Weigh Down
program, tells Christian dieters that there are no "bad" foods and
that a good rule of thumb is to eat half of whatever might be on
their plate. Those who follow the program are not just "laying
down sin": they are also rediscovering the pleasure of eating.[19]
And while there is no shortage of evangelical diet books, one
would be hard-pressed to find a church that does not have a
kitchen – or one that does not sponsor picnics and bake sales.[20]

Sexual pleasure too has been rehabilitated, so much so that
teenagers are no longer told to stop thinking about sex: they are
told to think how much better it will be once they are married.
"Sex is great fun!" writes Dannah Gresh, author of *And the Bride
Wore White* (1999). "*If* you will wait, *then* it will be exciting!"[21]
Wade Horn, one-time president of the National Fatherhood
Initiative and assistant secretary for Children and Families,
under George W. Bush, likes to tell teenagers that "really good,
satisfying sex" "happens when you're married and you're fully
committed – and it's even better if you were a virgin when you
were married."[22] Where previous generations of evangelicals were
barely reconciled to the sexual dimension of marriage, today's
evangelicals positively celebrate it, and in so doing betray just
how much they have been corrupted by the very thing they hate:
the sexual revolution.[23] There are evangelical sex manuals –

*Intended for Pleasure: Sex Technique and Sex Fulfillment, Sexual
Intimacy in Marriage, Romancing Your Marriage: Keeping Your
Marriage Alive and Passionate after the Honeymoon Years Are Over,
Lonely Husbands, Lonely Wives: Rekindling Intimacy in Every
Marriage, Dealing With a Spouse's Diminishing Sex Drive,* and more.
There are evangelical workshops for couples.[24] There are evan-
gelical sex surveys. (In one, appearing in *Marriage Partnership*,
readers were asked to share their "Secrets of the O." Did they
ever have anal sex? the editors wanted to know. Or watch
pornography or engage in oral sex?)[25]

What is left, in short, is a code whose scope is almost
entirely limited to the sexual habits of the unmarried. It asks for
little beyond that, matching rather than challenging the habits
of the averagely observant evangelical. This tendency finds its
supreme expression in the advice Tim and Beverly LaHaye dis-
pense to married couples:

> Everything a Christ-controlled Christian does is
> spiritual. That includes eating, elimination, spank-
> ing children, or emptying the trash. Why isolate sex
> in marriage as if it were in a category all by itself?
> Many spiritual Christians pray before going to bed,
> then in a matter of minutes engage each other in
> foreplay, stimulation, coitus, and finally orgasm.
> Why isn't that just as spiritual as anything else
> couples do?[26]

Whether this lowered standard is enough to hold the current
generation of evangelicals and attract the next remains to be
seen. But it does suggest that the very thing that has sustained
evangelical Protestantism in America – the high standards it

sets both for itself and for the society at large – has been irre-deemably compromised.

Nor do today's conservative evangelicals assume that every-one might still be saved. This happy post-millennial thought, the cornerstone of the Second Great Awakening, has vanished along with the old belief in human perfectibility. Or so one might infer from the huge efforts that have gone into saving the *next* generation, into catching the young before they fall. The New Virginity does not target the old reprobates of the sexual revolution: it targets high-school and college students whose sexual histories are short or non-existent.

Yet if the attack on the sexual revolution has been led from the right, it is not without its allies on the left. One need only recall Andrea Dworkin's diatribes against Kinsey, her celebration of virginity, her uncompromising stance against pornography ("We will know that we are free when the pornography no longer exists").[27] Or the feminist Catharine MacKinnon's willingness to enter into alliances with anti-feminists, defying her critics to tell her "exactly what is sinister about women uniting women across conventional political lines against a form of abuse whose poli-tics are sexual."[28] This convergence at the fringes is a reminder that abstinence, contrary to present appearances, is not the exclusive property of the American religious right: the most radical of solutions, abstinence is the eternal property of radicals, of Malcolm X no less than Billy Sunday, of Andrea Dworkin no less than George W. Bush.

ACKNOWLEDGMENTS

To Jack Blocker, John Cunningham, Griffith Edwards, David Fahey, William Plum, Ron Roizen, Robin Room, William Rorabaugh, and Mariana Valverde for their gracious and learned critiques of the manuscript.

To Joanne Cordingley, Michelle Murphy, and Helen Suurvali, who proofread the manuscript, and in so doing saved me from still further embarrassment.

To the Social Sciences and Humanities Research Council of Canada for funding the project. To the Department of Psychiatry at the University of Toronto for supplementing those funds.

To Jenny Carson and Janine Riviere, who did so much of the research.

To all the librarians and archivists who gave their time and shared their knowledge, but most of all to the library staff at the Centre for Addiction and Mental Health.

To a patient agent, Peter Straus, and a smart editor, Trena White.

And to Reese, who read, listened, and went with me to Battle Creek.

NOTES

PREFACE

1   Lois Romano, "Son on the Horizon; Gov. George Walker Bush Is
    Running Hard. But Is He Heading in His Father's Direction?"
    Washington Post, 24 September 1998, B01; Nicholas D. Kristoff, "How
    Bush Came to Tame His Inner Scamp," *New York Times*, 29 July 2000;
    "Bush Says Faith Helped Him to Stop Drinking," *Associated Press*,
    30 January 2008.
2   "Bush Recounts Personal Recovery," *Join Together*, 12 December 2007
    (http://www.jointogether.org/news/headlines/inthenews/2007/
    bush-recounts-personal.html). Reference courtesy of Professor Laura
    Schmidt of the University of California at San Francisco.
3   David S. Broder, "Bush Defends Gun Record, Pushes Teen Sex
    Abstinence in S.C. Foray," *Washington Post*, 21 June 1999, A04.
4   As criticized in Douglas Clark Kinder and William O. Walker, "Stable
    Force in a Storm: Harry J. Anslinger and the United States Narcotic
    Foreign Policy, 1930–1962," *Journal of American History* 72, no. 4
    (1986), 908–27; Ethan A. Nadelmann, "U.S. Drug Policy: a Bad
    Export," *Foreign Policy* 70 (1988), 83–108; and the essays in Jurg
    Gerber and Eric L. Jensen, eds., *Drug War, American Style: the
    Internationalization of Failed Policy and Its Alternatives* (New York:
    Garland Publishing, 2001).
5   http://www.cdc.gov/nchs/data/nhis/earlyrelease/earlyrelease200612.pdf.
6   Everett M. Rogers, "Diffusion and the Re-Invention of Project
    D.A.R.E.," in *Organizational Aspects of Health Communication
    Campaigns: What Works?*, eds. Thomas E. Backer and Everett M. Rogers
    (Newbury Park: Sage, 1993), 142; Mary Brophy Marcus, "More Young
    People Go the Vegetarian Route," *USA Today*, 15 October 2007.
7   Jacqueline E. Darroch, David J. Landry, and Susheela Singh, "Changing
    Emphasis in Sexuality Education in U.S. Public Secondary Schools,
    1988–99," *Family Planning Perspectives* 32, no. 5 (2000), 204–11, 65;
    Jodi Wilgoren, "Abstinence Is the Focus of U.S. Sex Education,"
    New York Times, 15 December 1999, A18.

8   Laurence Michalak, Karen Trocki, and Jason Bond, "Religion and Alcohol in the U.S. National Alcohol Survey: How Important Is Religion for Abstention and Drinking?" *Drug and Alcohol Dependence* 87 (2007), 268–80; Louisa Degenhardt, et al., "Epidemiological Patterns of Extra-Medical Drug Use in the United States: Evidence from the National Comorbidity Survey Replication, 2001–2003," *Drug and Alcohol Dependence* 90, no. 2–3 (2007). Reference courtesy of Dr. Edward Adlaf.

9   A simplification of Everett M. Rogers, *Diffusion of Innovations*, 5th ed. (New York: Free Press, 2003).

INTRODUCTION

1   John S. Haller, *The People's Doctors: Samuel Thomson and the American Botanical Movement, 1790–1860* (Carbondale: Southern Illinois University Press, 2000), 37.

2   Max Weber, *Economy and Society: an Outline of Interpretative Sociology*, eds. Guenther Roth and Claus Wittich, vol. 2 (New York: Bedminister Press, 1968), 544 (1st ed. 1914); Michael Walzer, *The Revolution of the Saints: a Study in the Origins of Radical Politics* (London: Weidenfeld and Nicolson, 1966), 317; Nathan Leites and Charles Wolf, *Rebellion and Authority: an Analytic Essay on Insurgent Conflicts* (Chicago: Markham Publishing Company, 1970), 56; Edward P. Thompson, *The Making of the English Working Class* (London: Victor Gollancz, 1964), 58–9; James S. Roberts, "Alcohol, Public Policy, and the Left: the Socialist Debate in Early Twentieth-Century Europe," *Contemporary Drug Problems* 12 (1985), 309–30.

3   Clara Zetkin, *Reminiscences of Lenin* (New York: International Publishers, 1934), 50–1.

4   David M. Fahey and Padma Manian, "Poverty and Purification: the Politics of Gandhi's Campaign for Prohibition," *Historian* 67, no. 3 (2005), 489–506.

5   Andrea Dworkin, *Intercourse* (New York: Free Press, 1987), 96.

6   Frederick Douglass, *My Bondage and My Freedom* (New York: Miller, Orton & Co., 1857), 256.

7   Malcolm Little, *The Autobiography of Malcolm X*, ed. Alex Haley (New York: Grove Press, 1966), 223 224, 228. For the dietary politics of Elijah Muhammed, see R. Marie Griffith, *Born Again Bodies: Flesh and Spirit in American Christianity* (Berkeley: University of California Press, 2004), 157.

8   "The teetotal movement tended to attack Owenism and its belief that man is the creature of circumstance – and it has been pointed out

that Owenism itself, keen on temperance too, did not invoke environmental factors to explain working-class drinking. In an important sense, teetotalism and the 'pledge' (an act of individual resolve which is accounted adequate to surmount all circumstantial pressures) are plainly anti-environmental in spirit," Michael Mason, *The Making of Victorian Sexuality* (Oxford: Oxford University Press, 1994), 254. Also observed in Lilian Lewis Shiman, *Crusade against Drink in Victorian England* (New York: St. Martin's Press, 1988), 208–10, and John R. Greenaway, *Drink and British Politics Since 1830: a Study in Policy-Making* (Basingstoke: Palgrave Macmillan, 2003), 54–7.

9   *Twelve Steps and Twelve Traditions* (New York: Alcoholics Anonymous World Services, Inc., 1972), 48–9 (1st ed. 1953).

10   William Andrus Alcott, *The Young Man's Guide*, 20th ed. (Boston: T.R. Marvin, 1849), 318 (1st ed. 1833).

11   John Cowan, *Science of a New Life* (New York: J.S. Ogilvie & Company, 1869), 112; *Ministry of Healing* (1905), in Ellen Gould White, *Counsels on Diet and Foods* (Hagerstown, Maryland: Review and Herald Publishing Association, 1976), 430; George W. Bush, quoted in "Remarks to the Chamber of Commerce in Charlotte," *Weekly Compilation of Presidential Documents*, 4 March 2002, 307.

12   L. Penny, ed., *The National Temperance Orator* (New York: National Temperance Society and Publication House, 1874), 128–9.

13   John Granville Woolley, "Neal Dow at Ninety-Three," in *Civic Sermons* (Westerville, Ohio: American Issue Publishing Company, 1911), 29.

14   Harriet Beecher Stowe, *Sunny Memories of Foreign Lands*, vol. 1 (Boston: Phillips, Sampson, and Company, 1854), 172.

15   L. Penny, ed., *The National Temperance Orator* (New York: National Temperance Society and Publication House, 1874), 91.

16   Fulton J. Sheen, *Peace of Soul* (Garden City: Garden City Books, 1951), 194.

17   Wonderfully observed in Peter Brown, *The Body and Society: Men, Women, and Sexual Renunciation in Early Christianity* (New York: Columbia University Press, 1988), 442: "In Christian circles, concern with sexual renunciation had never been limited solely to an anxious striving to maximize control over the body. It had been connected with a heroic and sustained attempt, on the part of thinkers of widely different background and temper of mind, to map out the horizons of human freedom. The light of a great hope of future transformation glowed behind even the most austere statements of the ascetic position. To many, continence had declared the end of the tyranny of the 'present age.'"

18   John Harvey Kellogg, *Plain Facts for Old and Young: Embracing the Natural History of Hygiene of Organic Life* (New York: Arno Press, 1974), 502 (1st ed. 1877).

19   Judith E. Beckett, "Recollections of a Sexual Life: Revelations of a Celibate Time," *Lesbian Ethics* 3, no. 1 (1988), 33.

20   Robin Room, "The Liquor Question and the Formation of Consciousness: Nation, Ethnicity, and Class at the Turn of the Century," *Contemporary Drug Problems* 12, no. 2 (1985), 168–9; Ann Fairfax Withington, *Toward a More Perfect Union: Virtue and the Formation of American Republics* (Oxford: Oxford University Press, 1991), 15–16.

21   Elizabeth Malcolm, *"Ireland Sober, Ireland Free": Drink and Temperance in Nineteenth-Century Ireland* (Syracuse: Syracuse University Press, 1986), 318–19; George Bretherton, "Against the Flowing Tide: Whiskey and Temperance in the Making of Modern Ireland," in *Drinking: Behavior and Belief in Modern History*, eds. Susanna Barrows and Robin Room (Berkeley: University of California Press, 1991), 147–64; and more generally in John F. Quinn, *Father Mathew's Crusade: Temperance in Nineteenth-Century Ireland and Irish America* (Amherst: University of Massachusetts Press, 2002).

22   *Northern Star and Freeman's Advocate*, 17 February 1842, 17, quoted in Denise Herd, "The Paradox of Temperance: Blacks and the Alcohol Question in Nineteenth-Century America," in *Drinking: Behavior and Belief in Modern History*, eds. Susanna Barrows and Robin Room (Berkeley: University of California Press, 1991), 363. Also treated in Hanes Walton and James E. Taylor, "Blacks and the Southern Prohibition Movement," *Phylon* 32, no. 3 (1971), 247. Much the same argument was made by Joseph C. Price of the now defunct Afro-American League: "It is remarkable . . . to observe the steadfastness and persistency with which colored teachers, as a rule, hold to the idea that the race is to be uplifted morally, as well as materially and religiously improved, through total abstinence as a chief instrument," "The Negro and Prohibition," in *The Passing of the Saloon: an Authentic and Official Presentation of the Anti-Liquor Crusade in America*, ed. George M. Hammell (Cincinnati: Tower Press, 1908), 346.

23   David M. Fahey, *Temperance and Racism: John Bull, Johnny Reb, and the Good Templars* (Lexington: University Press of Kentucky, 1996), 8.

24   *Staying Clean: Living without Drugs* (Center City, Minnesota: Hazelden, 1987), 2.

25   Analyzed in Milton A. Maxwell, *The Alcoholics Anonymous Experience: a Close-up View for Professionals* (New York: McGraw-Hill, 1984), 38–9.

26 *Alcoholics Anonymous: the Story of How Many Thousands of Men and Women Have Recovered from Alcoholism*, 4th ed. (New York: Alcoholics Anonymous World Services, Inc., 2001), 152–3, 336, 276 (1st ed. 1939).

27 Catharine A. MacKinnon, "The Roar on the Other Side," in *In Harm's Way: the Pornography Civil Rights Hearings*, eds. Catharine A. MacKinnon and Andrea Dworkin (Cambridge, Massachusetts: Harvard University Press, 1997), 23; John Bartholomew Gough, *Sunlight and Shadow or, Gleanings from my Life Work. Comprising Personal Experiences and Opinions, Anecdotes, Incidents, and Reminiscences, Gathered from Thirty-Seven Years' Experience on the Platform and Among the People, at Home and Abroad* (Hartford: A.D. Worthington and Company, 1881), 472; Dio Lewis, *Chastity or, our Secret Sins* (New York: Arno Press, 1974), 229 (1st ed. 1874); Harry J. Anslinger and Will Oursler, *The Murderers: the Story of the Narcotic Gangs* (New York: Farrar, Straus and Cudahy, 1961), 32. Or this from Randy C. Alcorn, *Christians in the Wake of the Sexual Revolution* (Portland: Multnomah Press, 1985), 224: "Instead of talking about intentions in petting, we should talk about probable *results*. A man on a diet can go into a doughnut shop with the intention of only having coffee. The probable result, of course, is that he will also have several doughnuts."

ONE

1 Ednah D. Cheney, ed., *Louisa May Alcott: Her Life, Letters, and Journals* (Boston: Roberts Brothers, 1891), 32.

2 David W. Conroy, "Puritans in Taverns: Law and Popular Culture in Colonial Massachusetts," in *Drinking: Behavior and Belief in Modern History*, eds. Susanna Barrows and Robin Room (Berkeley: University of California Press, 1991), 29–60; Keith Wrightson, "Alehouses, Order and Reformation in Rural England," in *Popular Culture and Class Conflict 1590–1914: Explorations in the History of Labour and Leisure*, eds. Eileen Yeo and Stephen Yeo (Atlantic Highlands: Humanities Press, 1981), 1–27; Thomas Brennan, *Public Drinking and Popular Culture in Eighteenth-Century Paris* (Princeton: Princeton University Press, 1988).

3 The first is the theme of Gordon S. Wood, *The Radicalism of the American Revolution* (New York: Vintage Books, 1993), the second of Nathan O. Hatch, *The Democratization of American Christianity* (New Haven: Yale University Press, 1989), and, less successfully, of chapters 3 and 4 in Richard Hofstadter, *Anti-Intellectualism in American Life* (New York: Alfred A. Knopf, 1966).

4   Steven E. Ozment, *When Fathers Ruled: Family Life in Reformation Europe* (Cambridge, Massachusetts: Harvard University Press, 1983), 7.

5   Their remarks on sexual pleasure are especially revealing. If Luther was unable to divest himself of the old Pauline formula (at one point he compared marriage to a "hospital for incurables which prevents inmates from falling into graver sin"), he could nonetheless speak approvingly of couples indulging in sex more often than was strictly "necessary for the begetting of children." Calvin went further, describing the "intercourse of husband and wife" as "a pure thing, good and holy." Marriage, he wrote elsewhere, "allows husbands and wives to give each other delight." Drawn from Merry E. Wiesner-Hanks, *Christianity and Sexuality in the Early Modern World: Regulating Desire, Reforming Practice* (London: Routledge, 2000), 63–5; Martin Luther, "A Sermon on the Estate of Marriage," in *Luther's Works*, ed. James Atkinson (Philadelphia: Fortress Press, 1959), 9, 11; and William James Bouwsma, *John Calvin: a Sixteenth-Century Portrait* (Oxford: Oxford University Press, 1988), 136–7.

6   James Timberlake, *Prohibition and the Progressive Movement 1900–1920* (Cambridge, Massachusetts: Harvard University Press, 1963), 6; Wendy Mitchinson, "The WCTU: 'For God, Home, and Native Land': a Study in Nineteenth-Century Feminism," in *A Not Unreasonable Claim: Women and Reform in Canada, 1880s–1920s*, ed. Linda Kealey (Toronto: Women's Press, 1979), 151–67; Sidsel Eriksen, "Drunken Danes and Sober Swedes? Religious Revivalism and the Temperance Movements as Keys to Danish and Swedish Folk Cultures," in *Language and the Construction of Class Identities: the Struggle for Discursive Power in Social Organization, Scandinavia and Germany after 1800*, ed. Bo Strath (Gothenburg: Con Dis-Project, 1990), 55–94; Laura Schmidt, "'A Battle Not Man's but God's': Origins of the American Temperance Crusade in the Struggle for Religious Authority," *Journal of Studies on Alcohol* 56, no. 1 (1995), 110–21.

7   Jon R. Stone, *On the Boundaries of American Evangelicalism: the Postwar Evangelical Coalition* (New York: St. Martin's Press, 1997), 2–3.

8   Charles L. Wallis, ed., *Autobiography of Peter Cartwright* (New York: Abingdon Press, 1956), 38 (1st ed. 1856); Asa Mahan, *Scripture Doctrine of Christian Perfection: with Other Kindred Subjects, Illustrated and Confirmed in a Series of Discourses Designed to Throw Light on the Way of Holiness*, 11th ed. (Oberlin: James M. Fitch, 1850), 187 (1st ed. 1839); Lorenzo Dow, *The Life, Travels, Labors, and Writings of Lorenzo Dow; Including His Singular and Erratic Wanderings in Europe and America* (New York: R. Worthington, 1881), 19 (1st ed. 1857).

Analyzed in William James, *The Varieties of Religious Experience:
a Study in Human Nature* (New York: Modern Library, 1929) (1st ed.
1901–1902); and, more recently, in Chana Ullman, *The Transformed
Self: the Psychology of Religious Conversion* (New York: Plenum Press,
1989); and Julius H. Rubin, *Religious Melancholy and Protestant
Experience in America* (New York: Oxford University Press, 1994).

9 David William Bebbington, *Evangelicalism in Modern Britain: a History
from the 1730s to the 1980s* (London: Unwin Hyman, 1989), 3; and
Alister McGrath, *Evangelicalism and the Future of Christianity* (Downers
Grove, Illinois: InterVarsity, 1995), 55–6.

10 Charles Edwin Jones, *Perfectionist Persuasion: the Holiness Movement and
American Methodism, 1867–1936* (Metuchen, New Jersey: Scarecrow
Press, 1974), 1.

11 R. Newton Flew, *The Idea of Perfection in Christian Theology* (Oxford:
Oxford University Press, 1934); G.C. Cell, *The Rediscovery of John
Wesley* (New York: Henry Holt & Co., 1935); Umphrey Lee, *John
Wesley and Modern Religion* (Nashville: Cokesbury Press, 1936);
H. Richard Niebuhr, *The Kingdom of God in America* (New York:
Harper Torchbooks, 1959), 43 (1st ed. 1937); John Leland Peters,
Christian Perfection and American Methodism (New York: Abingdon
Press, 1956), 7–8, 19.

12 Henry Abelove, "The Sexual Politics of Early Wesleyan Methodism,"
in *Disciplines of Faith: Studies in Religion, Politics and Patriarchy*, eds. Jim
Obelkevish, Lyndal Roper, and Raphael Samuel (London: Routledge &
Kegan Paul, 1987), 86–99.

13 Bernard Semmel, *The Methodist Revolution* (New York: Basic Books,
1973), 18.

14 From *The Character of a Methodist* (1742), in Rupert E. Davies, ed., *The
Works of John Wesley*, vol. 9 (Nashville: Abingdon Press, 1989), 33–4.

15 Albert C. Outler, ed., *The Works of John Wesley*, vol. 2 (Nashville:
Abingdon Press, 1985), 271; Rupert E. Davies, ed., *The Works of John
Wesley*, vol. 9 (Nashville: Abingdon Press, 1989), 71. Preachers had
been denouncing tobacco for more than a century before Wesley joined
their ranks – John Downame in 1609, Richard Harris in 1619, and
Richard Young in 1638 – and in 1633 the Crown had actually banned
its sale in taverns and alehouses. Nor was Wesley alone in his opposi-
tion to distilled spirits. What he hoped to accomplish through suasion,
Parliament was already attempting to accomplish through coercion,
passing eight separate "gin acts" between 1729 and 1751. Examples in
John Downame, "A Disswasion from the Sin of Drvnkennes," in *Fovre
Treatises Tending to Diswade All Christians from Foure no Lesse Hainous*

then Common Sinnes; Namely, the Abuses of Swearing, Drunkennesse,
Whoredome, and Briberie (London: Imprinted for Felix Kyngston, for
William Welby, 1609), 80; Richard Harris, *The Drunkards Cup*
(London: Felix Kyngston for Thomas Man, 1619), 18; Richard Young,
The Drunkard's Character (London: R. Badger for George Latham,
1638), 269; James Holley Hanford, "Wine, Beere, Ale, and Tobacco: a
Seventeenth-Century Interlude," *Studies in Philology* 12, no. 1 (1915),
11; James F. Larkin, ed., *Stuart Royal Proclamations*, vol. 2 (Oxford:
Oxford University Press, 1983), 388–9; Jessica Warner, *Craze: Gin and
Debauchery in an Age of Reason* (New York: Random House Trade
Paperbacks, 2003).

16   Nehemiah Curnock, ed., *The Journal of the Rev. John Wesley, A.M.*,
vol. 6 (London: Epworth Press, 1938), 85; Edward P. Thompson, *The
Making of the English Working Class* (London: Victor Gollancz, 1964),
41; William G. McLoughlin, *Revivals, Awakenings, and Reform: an Essay
on Religion and Social Change in America, 1607–1977* (Chicago:
University of Chicago Press, 1978), 94–5; Richard Carwardine,
*Transatlantic Revivalism: Popular Evangelicalism in Britain and America,
1790–1865* (Westport: Greenwood Press, 1978), 10; Dee E. Andrews,
*The Methodists and Revolutionary America, 1760–1800: the Shaping of an
Evangelical Culture* (Princeton: Princeton University Press, 2000), 50–1.
Additional estimates in Roger Finke and Rodney Stark, "How the
Upstart Sects Won America: 1776–1850," *Journal for the Scientific Study
of Religion* 28 (1989), 27–44; and John H. Wigger, *Taking Heaven by
Storm: Methodism and the Rise of Popular Christianity in America* (New
York: Oxford University Press, 1998), 3–5.

17   The middle colonies, hardly the most backward region in America,
were without a seminary until 1726. That was the year William
Tennent (1673–1746) started his own school in the Pennsylvania
town of Neshaminy. For twenty years, until the founding of the future
Princeton University in 1746, Tennent's "Log College" was the region's
only seminary. Details in Marilyn J. Westerkamp, *Triumph of the
Laity: Scots-Irish Piety and the Great Awakening, 1625–1760*
(Oxford: Oxford University Press, 1988), 167–72; William R. Ward,
The Protestant Evangelical Awakening (Cambridge: Cambridge
University Press, 1992), 269–70. Connecticut's shortages persisted
well into the nineteenth century, as noted by Charles Roy Keller,
The Second Great Awakening in Connecticut (New Haven: Yale
University Press, 1942), 122.

18   Gordon S. Wood, "Evangelical America and Early Mormonism,"
New York History 61, no. 4 (1980), 369.

19   Nathan O. Hatch, *The Democratization of American Christianity*
     (New Haven: Yale University Press, 1989), 20.

20   Walter Bronlow Posey, *The Baptist Church in the Lower Mississippi Valley
     1776–1845* (Lexington: University of Kentucky Press, 1957), 23–4.

21   Ian C. Bradley, *The Call to Seriousness: the Evangelical Impact on the
     Victorians* (London: Jonathan Cape, 1976), 22.

22   Charles L. Wallis, ed., *Autobiography of Peter Cartwright* (New York:
     Abingdon Press, 1956), 11, 36–7, 65 (1st ed. 1856).

23   Phoebe Worrall Palmer, "The Doctrine of Entire Sanctification
     Simplified," *Guide to Holiness* 23 (1853), 53.

24   Hiram Mattison, *Popular Amusements: an Appeal to Methodists, in
     Regard to the Evils of Card-Playing, Billiards, Dancing, Theatre-Going, etc.*
     (New York: Carlton & Porter, 1867), 86.

25   David Sherman, *History of the Revisions of the Discipline of the Methodist
     Episcopal Church* (New York: Nelson & Phillips, 1874), 159.

26   Julius H. Rubin, *Religious Melancholy and Protestant Experience in
     America* (New York: Oxford University Press, 1994), chapter 5.

27   Horace Bushnell, *Christian Nurture*, ed. Luther A. Weigle (New Haven:
     Yale University Press, 1967), 233, 240 (1st ed. 1861).

28   Lyman Beecher, *Six Sermons on the Nature, Occasions, Signs, Evils, and
     Remedy of Intemperance*, 10th ed. (New York: American Tract Society,
     1833), 35 (1st ed. 1826).

29   Anna A. Gordon, *The Beautiful Life of Frances Willard* (Chicago:
     Woman's Temperance Publishing Association, 1898), 226.

30   "As castes disappear, as classes get closer to each other, as men are
     mixed tumultuously, and their usages, customs, and laws vary, as new
     facts come up, as new truths are brought to light, as old opinions
     disappear and others take their place, the image of an ideal and always
     fugitive perfection is presented to the human mind," Alexis de
     Tocqueville, *Democracy in America*, trans. Harvey C. Mansfield and
     Delba Winthrop (Chicago: University of Chicago Press, 2000), 427,
     from vol. 2 (1st ed. 1840).

31   Harriet Beecher Stowe, *Sunny Memories of Foreign Lands*, vol. 2
     (Boston: Phillips, Sampson, and Company, 1854), 123.

32   Merton M. Sealts, ed., *The Journals and Miscellaneous Notebooks of
     Ralph Waldo Emerson*, vol. 10 (Cambridge, Massachusetts: Belknap
     Press, 1973), 333 (entry for 23 July 1838).

33   Timothy Merritt, *The Christian's Manual, a Treatise on Christian
     Perfection; with Directions for Obtaining that State. Compiled Principally
     from the Works of Rev. John Wesley* (New York: Carlton & Porter, no
     date), 139–40 (1st ed. 1824).

34   John Leland Peters, *Christian Perfection and American Methodism*
     (New York: Abingdon Press, 1956), 98–100; Timothy L. Smith,
     *Revivalism and Social Reform: American Protestantism on the Eve of the
     Civil War* (New York: Harper Torchbooks, 1965), 115; Donald W.
     Dayton, *The Theological Roots of Pentecostalism* (Metuchen, New Jersey:
     Scarecrow Press, 1987), 65; John H. Wigger, *Taking Heaven by Storm:
     Methodism and the Rise of Popular Christianity in America* (New York:
     Oxford University Press, 1998), 20, 184.

35   The Methodists were also put off by the movement's Federalist
     leanings, as noted by Ian Tyrrell in *Sobering Up: from Temperance to
     Prohibition in Antebellum America, 1800–1860* (Westport: Greenwood
     Press, 1979).

36   Robert Emory, *History of the Discipline of the Methodist Episcopal Church*,
     ed. William P. Strickland, revised ed. (New York: Carlton & Porter,
     1857), 211, 223.

37   Henry Wheeler, *Methodism and the Temperance Reformation* (Cincinnati:
     Walden and Stowe, 1882), 112–22.

38   Background in Whitney Cross's *The Burned-Over District: the Social
     and Intellectual History of Enthusiastic Religion in Western New York,
     1800–1859* (New York: Harper Torchbooks, 1965).

39   Edward H. Madden and James E. Hamilton, *Freedom and Grace: the Life
     of Asa Mahan* (Metuchen, New Jersey: Scarecrow Press, 1982), 12–15.

40   A policy that fails to impress Ronald W. Hogeland, "Coeducation of
     the Sexes at Oberlin: a Study of Social Ideas in Mid-Nineteenth-
     Century America," *Journal of Social History* 6, no. 2 (1972–73),
     160–76.

41   Weld's particular hobbyhorse, as noted in Michael Newbury, "Healthful
     Employment: Hawthorne, Thoreau, and Middle-Class Fitness,"
     American Quarterly 47, no. 4 (1995), 688–9.

42   Garth M. Rosell and Richard A.G. Dupius, eds., *The Memoirs of Charles
     G. Finney* (Grand Rapids: Academie Books, 1989), 380, 411–12
     (1st ed. 1876); James Harris Fairchild, *Oberlin: its Origin, Progress and
     Results. An Address, Prepared for the Alumni of Oberlin College, Assembled
     August 22, 1860* (Oberlin: R. Butler, 1871), 18; *Oberlin: the Colony and
     the College* (Oberlin: E.J. Goodrich, 1883), 82–4; Robert Samuel
     Fletcher, *A History of Oberlin College from its Foundation through the Civil
     War*, vol. 1 (Oberlin: Oberlin College, 1943), 316–30; "Bread and
     Doctrine at Oberlin," *Ohio State Archaeological and Historical Quarterly*
     49 (1940), 58–67; James C. Whorton, *Crusaders for Fitness: the History
     of American Health Reformers* (Princeton: Princeton University Press,
     1982), 126. Examples of extreme fasting in Julius H. Rubin, *Religious*

Melancholy and Protestant Experience in America (New York: Oxford University Press, 1994), 191–2.

43 Benjamin Breckinridge Warfield, *Perfectionism*, ed. Samuel G. Craig, abridged ed. (Philadelphia: Presbyterian and Reformed Publishing Company, 1967), 24, 50.

44 Edward H. Madden and James E. Hamilton, *Freedom and Grace: the Life of Asa Mahan* (Metuchen, New Jersey: Scarecrow Press, 1982), 31–5.

45 Asa Mahan, *Autobiography: Intellectual, Moral, and Spiritual* (London: T. Woolmer, 1882), online at http://truthinheart.com/EarlyOberlinCD/CD/Mahan/Auto.HTM; Donald W. Dayton, *The Theological Roots of Pentecostalism* (Metuchen, New Jersey: Scarecrow Press, 1987), 66.

46 Asa Mahan, *Scripture Doctrine of Christian Perfection: with Other Kindred Subjects, Illustrated and Confirmed in a Series of Discourses Designed to Throw Light on the Way of Holiness*, 11th ed. (Oberlin: James M. Fitch, 1850), 12–13 (1st ed. 1839).

47 Asa Mahan, "Intimate Relation between Moral, Mental and Physical Law," *Graham Journal of Health and Longevity*, 11 May 1839, 153–8; Barbara Brown Zikmund, "Asa Mahan and Oberlin Perfectionism" (PhD Thesis, Duke University, 1969), 84–90; and Edward H. Madden and James E. Hamilton, *Freedom and Grace: the Life of Asa Mahan* (Metuchen, New Jersey: Scarecrow Press, 1982), 95–6.

48 Timothy L. Smith, "The Blessing of Abraham: Finney's Christian Perfection," *Christian History* 7, no. 4 (1988), 24–6.

49 Charles Grandison Finney, *Views of Sanctification* (Toronto: Toronto Willard Tract Depository, 1877), 108–9, 198–200 (1st ed. 1840). Recapitulated in his *Lectures on Systematic Theology* (Oberlin: James M. Fitch, 1847) (1st ed. 1846).

50 One is reminded of Howard Becker's moral crusaders: "Because of the importance of the humanitarian motive, moral crusaders (despite their relatively single-minded devotion to their particular cause) often lend their support to other humanitarian crusades," *Outsiders: Studies in the Sociology of Deviance* (New York: Free Press, 1966), 148.

51 Edward Beecher, "The Nature, Importance, and Means of Eminent Holiness throughout the Church," *American National Preacher*, June–July 1835, 194.

52 Garrison's commitment to perfectionism is touched on in Aileen S. Kraditor, *Means and Ends in American Abolitionism: Garrison and the Critics on Strategy and Tactics, 1834–1850* (New York: Pantheon Books, 1969), 29, 90–1.

53 Louis Ruchames, ed., *The Letters of William Lloyd Garrison*, vol. 2 (Cambridge, Massachusetts: Belknap Press, 1971), 260, 272, 367

(dated 6 May 1837, 16 June 1837, and 25 May 1838); Thomas H.
Le Duc, "Grahamites and Garrisonians," *New York History* 20 (1939),
189–91; Walter M. Merrill and Louis Ruchames, eds., *The Letters of
William Lloyd Garrison*, vol. 6 (Cambridge, Massachusetts: Belknap
Press, 1981), 407–8, 477, 522 (dated 29 May 1876, 3 June 1877, and
16 July 1878).

54   John Slater, ed., *The Correspondence of Emerson and Carlyle* (New York:
Columbia University Press, 1964), 283–84 (dated 30 October 1840).

55   Frances E. Willard, *Do-Everything: a Handbook for the World's White
Ribboners* (Chicago: Woman's Temperance Publishing Association,
1895).

56   Wilbur F. Crafts, "The 'Do Everything Policy,'" *Union Signal*, 28 April
1898, 262.

57   Larkin Baker Coles, *The Beauties and Deformities of Tobacco-Using:
or its Ludicrous and its Solemn Realities* (Boston: Ticknor, Reed, and
Fields, 1851), 83–7.

58   Gluttons fill "ther sowles with dedely synnes and flesshly lustes,"
"[I]ntemperancy begets incontinency, and after rioting and drunken-
ness, follows chambling and wantonness," and so on. Quotations from
William O. Ross, ed., *Middle English Sermons Edited from the British
Museum Royal 18 B. XXIII*, vol. 209, *Early English Text Society*
(London: Oxford, 1940), 101; and John Hart, *The Dreadful Character
of a Drunkard* (London: A.P. & T.H., 1678), no pagination.

59   *Permanent Temperance Documents of the American Temperance Society*,
vol. 1 (Boston: Seth Bliss and Perkins, Marvin, and Co., 1835),
ninth report, 7.

60   *Permanent Temperance Documents of the American Temperance Society*,
vol. 1 (Boston: Seth Bliss and Perkins, Marvin, and Co., 1835), annual
report for 1835, 7–17. It is also revealing that Justin Edwards, one of
the American Temperance Society's founders and easily its most
respected member, felt the need to codify these principles in "Hints for
Myself, and for Every Man who Engages in the Promotion of
Temperance" (1831). "Abstain entirely from tobacco, snuff, and all
needless things," he advised, adding that members should also be
"temperate in the use of tea, coffee, and every kind of food and of
drink." In William Allen Hallock, *"Light and Love": a Sketch of the Life
and Labors of the Rev. Justin Edwards, D.D.* (New York: American
Tract Society, 1855), 321–3.

61   A quality they shared with their English counterparts, as dryly
documented in Ian C. Bradley, *The Call to Seriousness: the Evangelical
Impact on the Victorians* (London: Jonathan Cape, 1976), 24–6.

62 Hiram Mattison, *Popular Amusements: an Appeal to Methodists, in Regard to the Evils of Card-Playing, Billiards, Dancing, Theatre-Going, etc.* (New York: Carlton & Porter, 1867), 4.

63 William Andrus Alcott, *The Young Wife, or Duties of Woman in the Marriage Relation* (New York: Arno Press, 1972), 110 (1st ed. 1837); *The Young Husband, or Duties of Man in the Marriage Relation* (New York: Arno Press, 1972), 110, 135 (1st ed. 1838).

64 Carolyn De Swarte Gifford, ed., *Writing Out My Heart: Selections from the Journal of Frances E. Willard, 1855–96* (Urbana: University of Illinois Press, 1995), 72.

65 Frances E. Willard, *Glimpses of Fifty Years: the Autobiography of an American Woman* (New York: Source Book Press, 1970), 634 (1st ed. 1889).

66 Anna A. Gordon, *The Beautiful Life of Frances Willard* (Chicago: Woman's Temperance Publishing Association, 1898), 338.

67 Phoebe Worrall Palmer, *The Way of Holiness, with Notes by the Way; Being a Narrative of Religious Experience Resulting from a Determination to be a Bible Christian* (New York: Lane & Scott, 1851), 123.

68 Michel Chevalier, *Society, Manners, and Politics in the United States: Letters on North America*, ed. John William Ward (Garden City: Doubleday & Company, Inc., 1961), 268 (1st ed. 1839).

69 Clarence Cook, *The House Beautiful: Essays on Beds and Tables, Stools and Candlesticks* (New York: Scribner, Armstrong and Company, 1878), 211.

70 David Lawton, "Life's Purpose," in *Readings and Recitations. No. 5. A New and Choice Collection of Articles in Prose and Verse, Embracing Argument and Appeal, Pathos and Humor, by the Foremost Temperance Advocates and Writers*, ed. L. Penney (New York: National Temperance Society and Publication House, 1886), 60.

71 A source of endless invidious comparisons. Francis Grund (1805–1863), a native of Bohemia, was clearly impressed, so much so that he ended up immigrating to America. The "great prosperity of the country enables much beyond the reach of superior orders in Europe," he reported in 1837. In *The Americans in their Moral, Social and Political Relations*, vol. 1 (New York: Augustus M. Kelley, 1971), 47 (1st ed. 1837). Edward Hitchcock, a man of austere habits and an active member of the American Temperance Society, was considerably less sanguine. "How immense is the intemperance in food and the gluttony of our land!" he exclaimed in 1830. "In other countries, you will undoubtedly find examples of greater excess of this kind among the higher classes of society: but probably in no other part of the world,

have the great mass of the people the means of furnishing their tables with so great a variety as among us." In *Dyspepsy Forestalled & Resisted: or Lectures on Diet, Regimen, & Employment; Delivered to the Students of Amherst College; Spring Term, 1830* (Amherst, Massachusetts: J.S. & C. Adams and Co., 1830), 65.

72   William J. Rorabaugh, "Estimated U.S. Alcoholic Beverage Consumption, 1790–1850," *Journal of Studies on Alcohol* 37, no. 3 (1976), 361.

73   Jack S. Blocker, *American Temperance Movements: Cycles of Reform* (Boston: Twayne Publishers, 1989), 10.

74   Detailed in William J. Rorabaugh, *The Alcoholic Republic: an American Tradition* (New York: Oxford University Press, 1979).

75   Charles L. Wallis, ed., *Autobiography of Peter Cartwright* (New York: Abingdon Press, 1956), 146 (1st ed. 1856).

76   William Peter Stickland, ed., *Autobiography of Rev. James B. Finley; or, Pioneer Life in the West* (Cincinnati: Cranston and Curts, 1853), 248.

77   Frances Trollope, *Domestic Manners of the Americans*, ed. Donald Smalley (New York: Alfred A. Knopf, 1949), 241 (1st ed. 1832).

78   Thomas Trotter, *An Essay, Medical, Philosophical, and Chemical on Drunkenness and its Effects on the Human Body*, ed. Roy Porter (London: Routledge, 1988), 158–9 (1st ed. 1804).

79   Ronald L. Numbers, *Prophetess of Health: a Study of Ellen G. White* (New York: Harper & Row, 1976), 61. By 1880, European countries were starting to catch up, but per capita consumption was still highest in America, at 3.87 pounds, followed by Germany at 3.6, and Austria at 3.15. Calculated by Jan Rogozinski, *Smokeless Tobacco in the Western World 1550–1950* (New York: Praeger, 1990), 110.

80   Frederick Marryat, *Diary in America*, ed. Juless Zanger (Bloomington: Indiana University Press, 1960), 191 (1st ed. 1839).

81   Charles Dickens, *American Notes* (London: Macmillan and Co., 1893), 98–9 (1st ed. 1843).

82   Larkin Baker Coles, *The Beauties and Deformities of Tobacco-Using: or its Ludicrous and its Solemn Realities* (Boston: Ticknor, Reed, and Fields, 1851), 129.

83   Frances E. Willard, *Glimpses of Fifty Years: the Autobiography of an American Woman* (New York: Source Book Press, 1970), 600 (1st ed. 1889).

84   Harvey A. Levenstein, *Revolution at the Table: the Transformation of the American Diet* (Berkeley: University of California Press, 2003), 7.

85   Kennth L. Sokoloff and Georgia C. Villaflor, "The Early Achievement
     of Modern Stature in America," *Social Science History* 14 (1982),
     453–81; Robert W. Fogel, et al., "Secular Changes in American and
     British Stature and Nutrition," in *Hunger and History. The Impact of
     Changing Food Production and Consumption Patterns on Society*, eds.
     Robert I. Rotberg and Theodore K. Rabb (Cambridge: Cambridge
     University Press, 1986), 247–83; Hillel Schwartz, *Never Satisfied: a
     Cultural History of Diets, Fantasies and Fat* (New York: Free Press, 1986),
     41. The typical European, by contrast, subsisted almost entirely on
     starches. Examples in Paolo Sorcinelli, "Identification Process at Work:
     Virtues of Italian Working-Class Diet in the First Half of the Twentieth
     Century," in *Food, Drink and Identity: Cooking, Eating and Drinking in
     Europe since the Middle Ages*, ed. Peter Scholliers (Oxford: Berg, 2001),
     83; A.E. Dingle, "Drink and Working-Class Living Standards in
     Britain, 1870–1914," *Economic History Review* 25, no. 4 (1972), 608;
     Eric Hopkins, *Childhood Transformed: Working-Class Children in
     Nineteenth-Century England* (Manchester: Manchester University Press,
     1994), 109–10. "The better-paid workers – particularly when the whole
     family works in the factories – enjoy good food as long as they are in
     employment. They have meat every day and bacon and cheese for
     the evening meal. The lower-paid workers have meat only two or three
     times a week, and sometimes only on Sundays. The less meat they can
     afford, the more potatoes and bread they eat . . . The poorer workers
     can afford no meat at all and they eat cheese, bread, porridge, and pota-
     toes," Friedrich Engels, *The Condition of the Working Class in England*,
     trans. W.O. Henderson and W.H. Chaloner (Oxford: Basil Blackwell,
     1958), 85 (1st ed. 1844). From the same year there is this claim by
     William Andrus Alcott: "The people of the United States are believed
     to eat, upon the average, an amount of animal food equal at least to
     one whole meal once a day, and those of Great Britain one in two
     days," *Vegetable Diet Defended* (London: John Chapman, 1844), 12.

86   Frances Trollope, *Domestic Manners of the Americans*, ed. Donald
     Smalley (New York: Alfred A. Knopf, 1949), 297 (1st ed. 1832).

87   William Cobbett, *A Year's Residence in the United States of America in
     Three Parts* (New York: Augustus M. Kelley, 1969), 347–8 (1st ed.
     1818–19).

88   Larkin Baker Coles, *Philosophy of Health: Natural Principles of Health and
     Cure; or, Health and Cure without Drugs. Also, the Moral Bearings of
     Erroneous Appetites*, 26th ed. (Boston: Ticknor, Reed, and Fields,
     1851), 136.

89   Benjamin Rush, *An Inquiry into the Effects of Ardent Spirits upon the Human Body and Mind. With an Account of the Means of Preventing, and of the Remedies for Curing Them*, 8th ed. (Boston: James Loring, 1823), 27 (1st ed. 1784).

90   William Andrus Alcott, "Gluttony," *Library of Health* 6 (1842), 293.

91   *Moral Reformer* 1 (1835), 198.

92   Richly documented in William J. Rorabaugh, *The Alcoholic Republic: an American Tradition* (New York: Oxford University Press, 1979).

93   From *The Danger of Increasing Riches* (1740?), in Albert C. Outler, ed., *The Works of John Wesley*, vol. 4 (Nashville: Abingdon Press, 1987), 183.

94   Charles Grandison Finney, *Views of Sanctification* (Toronto: Toronto Willard Tract Depository, 1877), 202 (1st ed. 1840).

95   *Permanent Temperance Documents of the American Temperance Society*, vol. 1 (Boston: Seth Bliss and Perkins, Marvin, and Co., 1835), Annual Report for 1834, 1–2.

96   John Wolfe, "Anti-Catholicism and Evangelical Identity in Britain and the United States, 1830–1860," in *Evangelicalism: Comparative Studies of Popular Protestantism in North America, the British Isles, and Beyond, 1700–1990*, eds. Mark A. Noll, David William Bebbington, and George A. Rawlyk (New York: Oxford University Press, 1994), 179–97.

97   Thomas H. O'Connor, *Boston Catholics: a History of the Church and its People* (Boston: Northeastern University Press, 1998), 64–6.

98   Lyman Beecher, *A Plea for the West*, 2nd ed. (Cincinnati: Truman & Smith, 1835), 69.

99   Harriet Martineau, *Society in America*, vol. 3 (New York: AMS Press, Inc., 1966), 236 (1st ed. 1837). Further examples in Richard Carwardine, "Evangelicals, Politics, and the Coming of the American Civil War: a Transatlantic Perspective," in *Evangelicalism: Comparative Studies of Popular Protestantism in North America, the British Isles, and Beyond, 1700–1990*, eds. Mark A. Noll, David William Bebbington, and George A. Rawlyk (New York: Oxford University Press, 1994), 201.

100   Even Frances Willard, as good a Methodist as any, could find herself deeply moved by the example of Saint Francis of Assisi, so much so that "Thinking of him, my small privations seemed so ridiculously trivial that I was eager to suffer something really worthy of a disciple for humanity's sweet sake." *Glimpses of Fifty Years: the Autobiography of an American Woman* (New York: Source Book Press, 1970), 344 (1st ed. 1889).

TWO

1   Anna A. Gordon, *The Beautiful Life of Frances Willard* (Chicago: Woman's Temperance Publishing Association, 1898), 188.

2   Most notably in John Allen Krout, *The Origins of Prohibition* (New York: Alfred A. Knopf, 1925); Ian R. Tyrrell, *Sobering Up: from Temperance to Prohibition in Antebellum America, 1800–1860* (Westport: Greenwood Press, 1979); William J. Rorabaugh, *The Alcoholic Republic: an American Tradition* (New York: Oxford University Press, 1979); and the first two chapters in Jack S. Blocker, *American Temperance Movements: Cycles of Reform* (Boston: Twayne Publishers, 1989).

3   *Contra* Brian S. Katcher, "Benjamin Rush's Educational Campaign against Hard Drinking," *American Journal of Public Health* 83, no. 2 (1993), 273–81.

4   Most notably from George Cheyne, *An Essay of Health and Long Life*, 4th ed. (London: George Strahan, 1725), 43, 50. If Rush was guilty of parroting Cheyne, so were a good many other people – the Royal College of Physicians in 1726, the physiologist Stephen Hales in 1733, Bishop Thomas Wilson in 1736. Background in Roy Porter, "The Drinking Man's Disease: the 'Pre-History' of Alcoholism in Georgian Britain," *British Journal of Addiction* 80, no. 4 (1985), 385–96; and Jessica Warner, *Craze: Gin and Debauchery in an Age of Reason* (New York: Random House Trade Paperbacks, 2003). Cheyne's essay went through several editions in nineteenth-century America, as noted by R. Marie Griffith in *Born Again Bodies: Flesh and Spirit in American Christianity* (Berkeley: University of California Press, 2004), 44.

5   Benjamin Rush, *An Inquiry into the Effects of Ardent Spirits upon the Human Body and Mind. With an Account of the Means of Preventing, and of the Remedies for Curing Them*, 8th ed. (Boston: James Loring, 1823), 5, 16–17, 22 (1st ed. 1784). Rush's remarks about beer – "many of the poor people in Great Britain endure hard labor with no other food than a quart or three pints of beer, with a few pounds of bread a day" – are even more baldly derivative, appearing (among others) in Josiah Tucker's *Impartial Enquiry*, published in 1751, and Henry Fielding's *Dissertation on Mr. Hogarth's Six Prints*, also published in 1751.

6   William J. Rorabaugh, "Estimated U.S. Alcoholic Beverage Consumption, 1790–1850," *Journal of Studies on Alcohol* 37, no. 3 (1976), 361.

7   Hunter Dickinson Farish, *The Circuit Rider Dismounts: a Social History of Southern Methodism, 1865–1900* (New York: Da Capo Press, 1969), 307–8 (1st ed. 1938). The same events are given a more positive spin

in William J. Rorabaugh, *The Alcoholic Republic: an American Tradition* (New York: Oxford University Press, 1979), 207.

8   Thomas Coke and Francis Asbury, *The Doctrines and Discipline of the Methodist Episcopal Church, in America*, 10th ed. (Philadelphia: Henry Tuckniss, 1798), 133.

9   Charles Roy Keller, *The Second Great Awakening in Connecticut* (New Haven: Yale University Press, 1942), 136–7.

10   Leonard Woods, *History of the Andover Theological Seminary* (Boston: J.R. Osgood and Company, 1885), 199; William J. Rorabaugh, *The Alcoholic Republic: an American Tradition* (New York: Oxford University Press, 1979), 191.

11   Lebbeus Armstrong, *The Temperance Reformation: its History, from the Organization of the First Temperance Society to the Adoption of the Liquor Law of Maine, 1851; and the Consequent Influence of the Promulgation of that Law on the Political Interest of the State of New York, 1852*, 2nd ed. (New York: Fowlers and Wells, 1853), 18–26, 136.

12   Ronald G. Walters, *American Reformers, 1815–1860* (New York: Hill and Wang, 1978), 125–6. The first independent mention of this society dates from 1814, the year Heman Humphrey was invited to lecture its members on the "fatal effects of too frequent a use of ardent spirits." In *Intemperance: an Address, to the Churches and Congregations of the Western District of Fairfield County, Connecticut* (Ballston Spa: James Comstock, 1814).

13   Alexis de Tocqueville, *Democracy in America*, trans. Harvey C. Mansfield and Delba Winthrop (Chicago: University of Chicago Press, 2000), 489–92, from vol. 2 (1st ed. 1840). There is no shortage of examples. Sarah Connell Ayer, newly moved to the tiny Maine village of Eastport, proceeded to join six voluntary societies: a donation society, a maternal association, an education society for her church's children, a female missionary society, a female charitable society, and a female benevolent society. Mary Ryan, writing about Utica in 1828, found no fewer than forty-one voluntary associations – twenty-one religious or charitable societies, three reform societies, five benefit associations, six fraternal orders, and six self-improvement associations. Drawn from Martha Tomhave Blauvelt, "The Work of the Heart: Emotion in the 1805–35 Diary of Sarah Connell Ayer," *Journal of Social History* 35, no. 3 (2002), 585; and *Cradle of the Middle Class: the Family in Oneida County, New York, 1790–1865* (Cambridge: Cambridge University Press, 1981), 105–44.

14   The original name was the American Society for the Promotion of Temperance.

15   Barbara M. Cross, ed., *The Autobiography of Lyman Beecher*, vol. 1
     (Cambridge, Massachusetts: Belknap Press, 1961), 183.

16   Those attempts are detailed in Ford K. Brown, *Fathers of the Victorians:
     the Age of Wilberforce* (Cambridge: Cambridge University Press, 1961);
     and M.J.D. Roberts, "The Society for the Suppression of Vice and its
     Early Critics, 1802–1812," *Historical Journal* 26, no. 1 (1983), 159–76.
     Wilberforce has more recently emerged as the darling of the religious
     right, as noted in Adam Hochschild, "English Abolition: the Movie,"
     New York Review of Books, 14 June 2007, 75.

17   Joel Bernard, "Original Themes of Voluntary Moralism: the Anglo-
     American Reformation of Manners," in *Moral Problems in American
     Life. New Perspectives on Cultural History*, eds. Karen Halttunen and
     Lewis Perry (Ithaca: Cornell University Press, 1998), 15–39. Their
     English counterparts are discussed in Timothy C. Curtis and William
     A. Speck, "The Societies for the Reformation of Manners: a Case Study
     in the Theory and Practice of Moral Reform," *Literature and History* 3
     (1976), 45–64, Robert B. Shoemaker, "Reforming the City: the
     Reformation of Manners Campaign in London, 1690–1738," in *Stilling
     the Grumbling Hive. The Response to Social and Economic Problems in
     England, 1689–1750*, eds. Lee Davison, et al. (New York: St. Martin's
     Press, 1992), 99–120. The Yale Moral Society, which Beecher belonged
     to when he was an undergraduate, was almost certainly another
     influence. Noted by Charles Roy Keller, *The Second Great Awakening
     in Connecticut* (New Haven: Yale University Press, 1942), 146.

18   Lyman Beecher, *The Practicability of Suppressing Vice, by Means of
     Societies Instituted for that Purpose. A Sermon, Delivered before the
     Moral Society, in East-Hampton, (Long Island) September 21, 1803*
     (New London: Samuel Green, 1804), 4, 13.

19   Barbara M. Cross, ed., *The Autobiography of Lyman Beecher*, vol. 1
     (Cambridge, Massachusetts: Belknap Press, 1961), 125–6, 179–84.

20   Ian R. Tyrrell, *Sobering Up: from Temperance to Prohibition in Antebellum
     America, 1800–1860* (Westport: Greenwood Press, 1979), 37.

21   Detailed in Robert L. Hampel, *Temperance and Prohibition in
     Massachusetts, 1813–1852* (Ann Arbor: UMI Research Press, 1982),
     chapter 2.

22   Daniel Feller, *The Jacksonian Promise: America, 1815–1840* (Baltimore:
     Johns Hopkins University Press, 1995), 98–9.

23   Barbara M. Cross, ed., *The Autobiography of Lyman Beecher*, vol. 2
     (Cambridge, Massachusetts: Belknap Press, 1961), 22.

24   Lyman Beecher, *Six Sermons on the Nature, Occasions, Signs, Evils, and
     Remedy of Intemperance*, 10th ed. (New York: American Tract Society,

1833), 58–63 (1st ed. 1826). Theodore Sedgwick (1781–1839), the
Federalist turned Jacksonian Democrat, similarly claimed that the rural
poor were "beyond all others the drinking people of the United States."
Quoted in Marvin Meyers, *The Jacksonian Persuasion: Politics and Belief*
(Stanford: Stanford University Press, 1957), 128.

25 *Permanent Temperance Documents of the American Temperance Society*,
vol. 1 (Boston: Seth Bliss and Perkins, Marvin, and Co., 1835), report
for 1831, 14–15; Charles Roy Keller, *The Second Great Awakening in
Connecticut* (New Haven: Yale University Press, 1942), 156. By 1827,
Chapin had joined the American Temperance Society, as recorded in
the *First Annual Report of the American Society for the Promotion of
Temperance* (Andover: Flatt and Gould, 1827).

26 Justin Edwards, *The Well-Conducted Farm: a Narrative of Facts* (New
York: American Tract Society, 1835?), 11 (1st ed. 1825).

27 Edward Hitchcock, *Dyspepsy Forestalled & Resisted: or Lectures on Diet,
Regimen, & Employment; Delivered to the Students of Amherst College;
Spring Term, 1830* (Amherst, Massachusetts: J.S. & C. Adams and Co.,
1830), 157, 182.

28 *Diary of Sarah Connell Ayer* (Portland: Lefavor-Tower Co., 1910), 307.
Biographical details in Martha Tomhave Blauvelt, "The Work of the
Heart: Emotion in the 1805–35 Diary of Sarah Connell Ayer," *Journal
of Social History* 35, no. 3 (2002), 577–92.

29 Background in Thomas A. Horrocks, "'The Poor Man's Riches, The
Rich Man's Bliss': Regimen, Reform, and the 'Journal of Health,'
1829–1833," *Proceedings of the American Philosophical Society* 139, no. 2
(1995), 115–34.

30 *Permanent Temperance Documents of the American Temperance Society*,
vol. 1 (Boston: Seth Bliss and Perkins, Marvin, and Co., 1835), 5,
13–14, 21.

31 William Andrus Alcott, *Vegetable Diet: as Sanctioned by Medical Men,
and by Experience in All Ages* (New York: Fowlers and Wells, 1853), 21
(1st ed. 1838).

32 "Massachusetts Society for the Suppression of Intemperance," *Salem
Gazette*, 5 June 1829, 1.

33 Lorenzo Dow, *The Life, Travels, Labors, and Writings of Lorenzo Dow;
Including his Singular and Erratic Wanderings in Europe and America* (New
York: R. Worthington, 1881), 19 (1st ed. 1857); Charles L. Wallis, ed.,
Autobiography of Peter Cartwright (New York: Abingdon Press, 1956), 36
(1st ed. 1856); Frances E. Willard, *Glimpses of Fifty Years: the
Autobiography of an American Woman* (New York: Source Book Press,
1970), 624 (1st ed. 1889); Timothy Merritt, *The Christian's Manual, a*

Treatise on Christian Perfection; with Directions for Obtaining that State. Compiled Principally from the Works of Rev. John Wesley (New York: Carlton & Porter, no date), 82 (1st ed. 1824). Further youthful examples in William James, *The Varieties of Religious Experience: a Study in Human Nature* (New York: Modern Library, 1929) (1st ed. 1901–02).

34   Clifford Stephen Griffin, *Their Brothers' Keepers: Moral Stewardship in the United States, 1800–1865* (New Brunswick: Rutgers University Press, 1960), 70; Robert L. Hampel, *Temperance and Prohibition in Massachusetts, 1813–1852* (Ann Arbor: UMI Research Press, 1982), 49.

35   William J. Rorabaugh, *The Alcoholic Republic: an American Tradition* (New York: Oxford University Press, 1979), 232.

36   Ian R. Tyrrell, *Sobering Up: from Temperance to Prohibition in Antebellum America, 1800–1860* (Westport: Greenwood Press, 1979), 136–8.

37   L. Penny, ed., *The National Temperance Orator* (New York: National Temperance Society and Publication House, 1877), 148.

38   Timothy Shay Arthur, *Ten Nights in a Bar-Room, and What I Saw There*, ed. Donald A. Koch (Cambridge, Massachusetts: Belknap Press, 1964), 94 (1st ed. 1854).

39   "American Society for the Promotion of Temperance," *Christian Observer*, July 1826, 441. The early British temperance movement had reached the same conclusion, as noted by Lilian Lewis Shiman, *Crusade against Drink in Victorian England* (New York: St. Martin's Press, 1988), 10.

40   "Communication: Origin and Progress of the Temperance Reformation in the State of Maryland," *Baltimore Patriot*, 24 March 1831, 2.

41   L. Penny, ed., *The National Temperance Orator* (New York: National Temperance Society and Publication House, 1874), 34.

42   Discussed in Ian R. Tyrrell, *Sobering Up: from Temperance to Prohibition in Antebellum America, 1800–1860* (Westport: Greenwood Press, 1979), 149–51.

43   "Temperance in Maine," *New Hampshire Patriot and State Gazette*, 20 February 1837, 2.

44   "Temperance Convention," *Farmers' Cabinet*, 14 June 1839, 3.

45   "An Interesting Anecdote," *Farmers' Cabinet*, 9 May 1844, 3. Nineteenth-century dictionaries would also continue to cling to the old definition of temperance, equating it with moderation. The definition in the 1828 edition of Webster's *American Dictionary of the English Language* is typical. Here temperance is defined as "Moderation; particularly, habitual moderation in regard to the indulgence of the natural appetites and passion; restrained or moderate indulgence; as temperance in eating and drinking . . ." Only much later in the century does one

start to find reluctant concessions to popular usage, as in this wonderfully equivocal entry in *The Imperial Dictionary, English, Technological, and Scientific* (Glasgow: W.A. Blackie & Co., 1884): "Belonging to temperance, or moderation in the use of strong drinks, almost or quite to the extent of abstinence; as the *temperance* movement."

46 Lebbeus Armstrong, *The Temperance Reformation: its History, from the Organization of the First Temperance Society to the Adoption of the Liquor Law of Maine, 1851; and the Consequent Influence of the Promulgation of that Law on the Political Interest of the State of New York, 1852,* 2nd ed. (New York: Fowlers and Wells, 1853), 31.

47 As wryly documented in Catherine Gilbert Murdock, *Domesticating Drink: Women, Men, and Alcohol in America, 1870–1940* (Baltimore: Johns Hopkins University Press, 1998).

48 The subject of Elaine Frantz Parsons, *Manhood Lost: Fallen Drunkards and Redeeming Women in the Nineteenth-Century United States* (Baltimore: Johns Hopkins University Press, 2003).

49 "Why Don't He Come," in *The Sons of Temperance Offering: for 1850,* edited by Timothy Shay Arthur (New York: Nafis & Cornish, 1849), 297.

50 Frances E. Willard, *Glimpses of Fifty Years: the Autobiography of an American Woman* (New York: Source Book Press, 1970), 332 (1st ed. 1889).

51 Ruth Bordin, *Women and Temperance: the Quest for Power and Liberty, 1873–1900* (Philadelphia: Temple University Press, 1981), 160–1.

52 William Andrus Alcott, *Forty Years in the Wilderness of Pills and Powders; or, the Cogitations and Confessions of an Aged Physician* (Boston: John P. Jewett and Company, 1859), 85.

53 John Granville Woolley, "Neal Dow at Ninety," in *Civic Sermons* (Westerville, Ohio: American Issue Publishing Company, 1911), 76.

54 Discussed in R. Marie Griffith, *Born Again Bodies: Flesh and Spirit in American Christianity* (Berkeley: University of California Press, 2004), 35–6.

55 *Permanent Temperance Documents of the American Temperance Society,* vol. 1 (Boston: Seth Bliss and Perkins, Marvin, and Co., 1835), report for 1834, 10, 33, 87.

56 Charles Grandison Finney, *Lectures on Revivals of Religion,* revised ed. (Oberlin: E.J. Goodrich, 1868), 288–9 (1st ed. 1835).

57 C.E. Sargent, *Our Home or, the Key to a Nobler Life* (Springfield, Massachusetts: W.C. King & Co., 1884), 262.

58 L. Penny, ed., *The National Temperance Orator* (New York: National Temperance Society and Publication House, 1877), 174–5.

59 Terrence V. Powderly, *Thirty Years of Labor. 1859–1889. In which the History of the Attempts to Form Organizations of Workingmen for the Discussion of Political, Social, and Economic Questions Is Traced* (Columbus: Excelsior Publishing House, 1890), 610; James Timberlake, *Prohibition and the Progressive Movement 1900–1920* (Cambridge, Massachusetts: Harvard University Press, 1963), 84–6; Samuel Walker, "Terrence V. Powderly, the Knights of Labor and the Temperance Issue," *Societas* 5, no. 4 (1975), 279–93.

60 Milton A. Maxwell, "The Washingtonian Movement," *Quarterly Journal of Studies on Alcohol* 11, no. 3 (1950), 410–51; Ronald G. Walters, *American Reformers, 1815–1860* (New York: Hill and Wang, 1978), 131–4; Ian R. Tyrrell, *Sobering Up: from Temperance to Prohibition in Antebellum America, 1800–1860* (Westport: Greenwood Press, 1979), 161–9; Leonard U. Blumberg and Bill Pittman, *Beware the First Drink! The Washingtonian Temperance Movement and Alcoholics Anonymous* (Seattle: Glen Abbey Books, 1991).

61 Daniel Dorchester, *The Liquor Problem in All Ages* (New York: Phillips & Hunt, 1884), 271. Reference courtesy of Professor William Rorabaugh.

62 "A Washingtonian Lecturer," *Farmers' Cabinet*, 12 September 1844, 3.

63 John Bartholomew Gough, *Sunlight and Shadow or, Gleanings from My Life Work. Comprising Personal Experiences and Opinions, Anecdotes, Incidents, and Reminiscences, Gathered from Thirty-Seven Years' Experience on the Platform and Among the People, at Home and Abroad* (Hartford: A.D. Worthington and Company, 1881), 498.

64 Mark Edward Lender, *Dictionary of American Temperance Biography* (Westport: Greenwood Press, 1984), 199.

65 Frances E. Willard, *Glimpses of Fifty Years: the Autobiography of an American Woman* (New York: Source Book Press, 1970), 550 (1st ed. 1889).

66 John Bartholomew Gough, *Sunlight and Shadow or, Gleanings from my Life Work. Comprising Personal Experiences and Opinions, Anecdotes, Incidents, and Reminiscences, Gathered from Thirty-Seven Years' Experience on the Platform and Among the People, at Home and Abroad* (Hartford: A.D. Worthington and Company, 1881), 31, 348, 365.

67 John Bartholomew Gough, *Autobiography and Personal Recollections* (Toronto: A.H. Hovey, 1870), 352–6.

68 "From the Correspondence of the N.Y. Observer. Mr. Gough's Speech at Washington," *Farmers' Cabinet*, 27 March 1845, 1.

69 A friend, but not an equal. Gough acknowledged as much in his *Autobiography*, describing Beecher as "almost fatherly in his friendship towards me."

70 John Bartholomew Gough, *Sunlight and Shadow or, Gleanings from my Life Work. Comprising Personal Experiences and Opinions, Anecdotes, Incidents, and Reminiscences, Gathered from Thirty-Seven Years' Experience on the Platform and Among the People, at Home and Abroad* (Hartford: A.D. Worthington and Company, 1881), 28.

71 Quoted in *The Reminiscences of Neal Dow: Recollections of Eighty Years* (Portland, Maine: Evening Express Publishing Company, 1898), 572.

72 Frank Loyola Byrne, *Prophet of Prohibition: Neal Dow and his Crusade* (Gloucester, Massachusetts: Peter Smith, 1969); Ian R. Tyrrell, *Sobering Up: from Temperance to Prohibition in Antebellum America, 1800–1860* (Westport: Greenwood Press, 1979), 252–3.

73 *The Reminiscences of Neal Dow: Recollections of Eighty Years* (Portland, Maine: Evening Express Publishing Company, 1898), 197, 206.

74 Clifford Stephen Griffin, *Their Brothers' Keepers: Moral Stewardship in the United States, 1800–1865* (New Brunswick: Rutgers University Press, 1960), 148.

75 "Gov. Boutwell and Neal Dow Hung in Effigy," *Barre Patriot*, 4 June 1852, 2.

76 "The Portland Riot," *Farmers' Cabinet*, 14 June 1855, 2.

77 Neal Dow, "Neal Dow and Cider," *Barre Patriot*, 2 April 1852, 1.

78 Douglas Carlson makes a strong prima facie case for the existence of a viable temperance movement in the antebellum South. This, however, did not translate into support for statewide prohibition, and one is left to wonder whether the Southern movement was acting out of weakness – or out of a more pietistic understanding of what temperance entailed. See "'Drinks he to his Own Undoing': Temperance Ideology in the Deep South," *Journal of the Early Republic* 18, no. 4 (1998), 659–91.

79 Henry A. Scomp, *King Alcohol in the Realm of King Cotton: or, a History of the Liquor Traffic and of the Temperance Movement in Georgia from 1733 to 1887* (Chicago: Blakely Printing Company, 1888), 525.

80 Hunter Dickinson Farish, *The Circuit Rider Dismounts: a Social History of Southern Methodism, 1865–1900* (New York: Da Capo Press, 1969), 1–8 (1st ed. 1938).

81 Bertram Wyatt-Brown, *Southern Honor: Ethics and Behavior in the Old South* (New York: Oxford University Press, 1982), 129, 210, 293; Ian R. Tyrrell, "Drink and Temperance in the Antebellum South: an Overview and Interpretation," *Journal of Southern History* 48, no. 4 (1982), 485–510.

82 John Leland Peters, *Christian Perfection and American Methodism* (New York: Abingdon Press, 1956), 131; Vinson Synan, *The Holiness-Pentecostal*

Tradition: Charismatic Movements in the Twentieth Century, 2nd ed. (Grand Rapids, Michigan: William B. Eerdmans Publishing Company, 1997), 20; John B. Boles, The Great Revival, 1787–1805: the Origins of the Southern Evangelical Mind (Lexington: University of Kentucky Press, 1972), 125, 139–40, 172–82, 193. Reference courtesy of Professor William Rorabaugh.

83 Frances E. Willard, Glimpses of Fifty Years: the Autobiography of an American Woman (New York: Source Book Press, 1970), 487, 492 (1st ed. 1889).

THREE

1 Persuasively argued in James C. Whorton, "'Christian Physiology': William Alcott's Prescription for the Millennium," Bulletin of the History of Medicine 49 (1975), 466–81.

2 Ellen Gould White, Counsels on Diet and Foods (Hagerstown, Maryland: Review and Herald Publishing Association, 1976), 450.

3 Mary Tyler Peabody Mann, Christianity in the Kitchen: a Physiological Cook Book (Boston: Ticknor and Fields, 1857), 5. Background in Sidonia C. Taupin, "Christianity in the Kitchen," American Quarterly 15, no. 1 (1963), 85–9.

4 Catharine E. Beecher, Letters to the People on Health and Happiness (New York: Arno Press, 1972), 172 (1st ed. 1855).

5 Dio Lewis, Chastity or, our Secret Sins (New York: Arno Press, 1974), 283 (1st ed. 1874).

6 Ellen Gould White, Counsels on Diet and Foods (Hagerstown, Maryland: Review and Herald Publishing Association, 1976), 385; Ronald L. Numbers, Prophetess of Health: a Study of Ellen G. White (New York: Harper & Row, 1976), 161, 172.

7 Odell Shepard, ed., The Journals of Bronson Alcott (Boston: Little, Brown and Company, 1938), 115.

8 James C. Whorton, Crusaders for Fitness: the History of American Health Reformers (Princeton: Princeton University Press, 1982), 5, 31.

9 Howard M. Leichter, "Lifestyle Correctness and the New Secular Morality," in Morality and Health, eds. Allan M. Brandt and Paul Rozin (New York: Routledge, 1997), 359–78.

10 New Hampshire Patriot and State Gazette, 20 April 1835, 2.

11 William Andrus Alcott, The Physiology of Marriage (Boston: Dinsmoor and Company, 1866), 116–17 (1st ed. 1855); Vegetable Diet: as Sanctioned by Medical Men, and by Experience in All Ages. Including a System of Vegetable Cookery (New York: Fowlers and Wells, 1853), 154 (1st ed. 1838).

12   Gilbert H. Barnes and Dwight L. Dumond, eds., *Letters of Theodore Dwight Weld, Angelina Grimké Weld and Sarah Grimké 1822–1844*, vol. 2 (Gloucester, Massachusetts: Peter Smith, 1965), 531.

13   Jayme A. Sokolow, *Eros and Modernization: Sylvester Graham, Health Reform, and the Origins of Victorian Sexuality in America* (London: Associated University Presses, 1983), 57.

14   Helen Graham Carpenter, *The Reverend John Graham of Woodbury, Connecticut and his Descendants* (Chicago: Monastery Hill Press, 1942), 188–9.

15   William L. Clements Library, *Testimonials Concerning the Character of Sylvester Graham, Relative to his Entering the Christian Ministry, 1822–1828.*

16   William L. Clements Library, *Remonstrance by the Members of the Session of the Presbyterian Church of Bound Brook*, 15 October 1829.

17   James C. Whorton, *Crusaders for Fitness: the History of American Health Reformers* (Princeton: Princeton University Press, 1982), 40–2; Hillel Schwartz, *Never Satisfied: a Cultural History of Diets, Fantasies and Fat* (New York: Free Press, 1986), 30.

18   Heman Humphrey, *Intemperance: an Address, to the Churches and Congregations of the Western District of Fairfield County, Connecticut* (Ballston Spa: James Comstock, 1814); Richard C. Garvey, "Dr. Sylvester Graham," in *The Northampton Book: Chapters from 300 Years in the Life of a New England Town 1654–1954*, eds. Lawrence E. Wikander, et al. (Northampton, Massachusetts: The Tercentenary Committee, 1954), 103.

19   Listed in the First Annual Report of the American Society for the Promotion of Temperance (Andover: Flatt and Gould, 1827).

20   Sylvester Graham, *A Lecture on Epidemic Diseases Generally, and Particularly the Spasmodic Cholera*, revised ed. (Boston: David Cambell, 1838), 81 (1st ed. 1833).

21   Graphically documented by Hillel Schwartz, *Never Satisfied: a Cultural History of Diets, Fantasies and Fat* (New York: Free Press, 1986), 23–4.

22   One is reminded of Richard Hofstadter's characterization: "These spokesmen are in the main neither the uneducated nor the unintellectual, but rather the marginal intellectuals, would-be intellectuals, unfrocked or embittered intellectuals, and the literate leaders of the semi-literate, full of seriousness and high purpose about the causes that bring them to the attention of the world." In *Anti-Intellectualism in American Life* (New York: Alfred A. Knopf, 1966), 21 (1st ed. 1962).

23   Sylvester Graham, *Lectures on the Science of Human Life* (London: Horsell, 1849), i–ii (1st ed. 1839).

24   Lamar Riley Murphy, *Enter the Physician: the Transformation of Domestic Medicine, 1760–1860* (Tuscaloosa: University of Alabama Press, 1991), 70–1, 81–8; John S. Haller, *The People's Doctors: Samuel Thomson and the American Botanical Movement, 1790–1860* (Carbondale: Southern Illinois University Press, 2000), 37, 52.

25   John B. Blake, "Health Reform," in *The Rise of Adventism: Religion and Society in Mid-Nineteenth Century America*, ed. Edwin S. Gaustad (New York: Harper & Row, 1974), 37. Graham, acting on this logic, published a public apology when he himself succumbed to illness in 1841. Noted (and gently mocked) in one of Horace Mann's letters to George Combe. In Mary Tyler Peabody Mann, *Life of Horace Mann*, revised ed. (Boston: Willard Small, 1888), 154.

26   James C. Whorton, *Crusaders for Fitness: the History of American Health Reformers* (Princeton: Princeton University Press, 1982), 7, 114–15.

27   Sylvester Graham, *Graham's Lectures on Chastity Specially Intended for the Serious Consideration of Young Men and Parents* (Glasgow: Royalty Buildings, no date), 1 (1st ed. 1834). Further developed in *Aesculapian Tablets of the Nineteenth Century* (Providence: Weeden and Cory, 1834), vi–vii; and *Lectures on the Science of Human Life* (London: Horsell, 1849), 117 (1st ed. 1839).

28   Sylvester Graham, *Graham's Lectures on Chastity Specially Intended for the Serious Consideration of Young Men and Parents* (Glasgow: Royalty Buildings, no date), 14 (1st ed. 1834); John S. Haller and Robin M. Haller, *The Physician and Sexuality in Victorian America* (Urbana: University of Illinois Press, 1974), 96–7.

29   E.H. Hare, "Masturbatory Insanity: the History of an Idea," *Journal of Mental Science* 108 (1962), 1–25; Robert H. MacDonald, "The Frightful Consequences of Onanism: Notes on the History of Delusion," *Journal of the History of Ideas* 28, no. 3 (1967), 423–31; Jean Stengers and Anne Van Neck, *Masturbation: the History of a Great Terror* (New York: Palgrave, 2001), 67–107; Elizabeth Abbott, *A History of Celibacy* (Toronto: HarperCollins, 1999), 219–22; Thomas W. Laqueur, *Solitary Sex: a Cultural History of Masturbation* (New York: Zone Books, 2003), 32.

30   Stephen Wilner Nissenbaum, *Sex, Diet, and Debility in Jacksonian America: Sylvester Graham and Health Reform* (Westport: Greenwood Press, 1980), 35–6.

31   William L. Clements Library, Marriage Certificate for Sylvester Graham and Sarah M. Earl, Graham Family Papers, 19 September 1824; Sylvester

Graham, *Graham's Lectures on Chastity Specially Intended for the Serious Consideration of Young Men and Parents* (Glasgow: Royalty Buildings, no date), 11 (1st ed. 1834). An illustration of a point Peter Gay makes in *The Education of the Senses*, vol. 1, *The Bourgeois Experience: Victoria to Freud* (New York: Oxford University Press, 1984), 58: "Respectable nineteenth-century culture found the imagination a dangerous companion, and instead celebrated delay, modulation, control."

32 Erik R. Seeman, "'It Is Better to Marry than to Burn': Anglo-American Attitudes toward Celibacy, 1600–1800," *Journal of Family History* 24 (1999), 399–401; Thomas A. Foster, "Deficient Husbands: Manhood, Sexual Incapacity, and Male Marital Sexuality in Seventeenth-Century New England," *William and Mary Quarterly* 56, no. 4 (1999), 724.

33 Sylvester Graham, *Graham's Lectures on Chastity Specially Intended for the Serious Consideration of Young Men and Parents* (Glasgow: Royalty Buildings, no date), 9–10, 15 (1st ed. 1834).

34 Jean Stengers and Anne Van Neck, *Masturbation: the History of a Great Terror* (New York: Palgrave, 2001), 154.

35 Examples in Carl N. Degler, "What Ought to Be and What Was: Women's Sexuality in the Nineteenth Century," *American Historical Review* 79, no. 5 (1974), 1467–90; Peter Gay, *The Education of the Senses*, vol. 1, *The Bourgeois Experience: Victoria to Freud* (New York: Oxford University Press, 1984); and John D'Emilio and Estelle B. Freedman, *Intimate Matters: a History of Sexuality in America* (New York: Harper & Row, 1988).

36 Dio Lewis, *Chastity or, our Secret Sins* (New York: Arno Press, 1974), 21 (1st ed. 1874).

37 Orson Squire Fowler, *Sexual Science; Including Manhood, Womanhood, and their Mutual Interrelations; Love its Laws, Power etc.* (Philadelphia: National Publishing Company, 1870), 239.

38 Andrew J. Ingersoll, *In Health*, 4th ed. (Boston: Lee and Shepard Publishers, 1899), from the preface; Peter Gardella, *Innocent Ecstasy: How Christianity Gave America an Ethic of Sexual Pleasure* (New York: Oxford University Press, 1985), 68–73.

39 Sylvester Graham, *A Lecture on Epidemic Diseases Generally, and Particularly the Spasmodic Cholera*, revised ed. (Boston: David Cambell, 1838), 81 (1st ed. 1833).

40 William Andrus Alcott, *Vegetable Diet: as Sanctioned by Medical Men, and by Experience in All Ages* (New York: Fowlers and Wells, 1853), 39–40, 75 (1st ed. 1838).

41 Ellen Gould White, *Counsels on Diet and Foods* (Hagerstown, Maryland: Review and Herald Publishing Association, 1976), 494.

42   James C. Whorton, *Crusaders for Fitness: the History of American Health Reformers* (Princeton: Princeton University Press, 1982), 57.

43   William Andrus Alcott, *Forty Years in the Wilderness of Pills and Powders; or, the Cogitations and Confessions of an Aged Physician* (Boston: John P. Jewett and Company, 1859), 380–4.

44   Sylvester Graham, *Aesculapian Tablets of the Nineteenth Century* (Providence: Weeden and Cory, 1834), 17, 23, 57.

45   William L. Clements Library, "Poetry. For the Woodstock Age. Oh! Who Would Be a Grahamite?" Graham Family Papers.

46   An analogy Theodore Weld was quick to pick up on: "Of course, like all other reformers, he is everywhere spoken against, and by the medical profession jeered nearly as much as we abolitionists are by those who claim to sit in Moses' seat." In Gilbert H. Barnes and Dwight L. Dumond, eds., *Letters of Theodore Dwight Weld, Angelina Grimké Weld and Sarah Grimké 1822–1844*, vol. 2 (Gloucester, Massachusetts: Peter Smith, 1965), 531.

47   Robert H. Abzug, *Cosmos Crumbling: American Reform and the Religious Imagination* (New York: Oxford University Press, 1994), 177. Additional examples in Thomas H. Le Duc, "Grahamites and Garrisonians," *New York History* 20 (1939), 189–91; Louis Ruchames, ed., *The Letters of William Lloyd Garrison*, vol. 2 (Cambridge, Massachusetts: Belknap Press, 1971), 260, 272, 367; and Charles Wilbanks, ed., *Walking by Faith: the Diary of Angelina Grimké* (Columbia: University of South Carolina Press, 2003), 36–7.

48   Van Wyck Brooks, *The Flowering of New England 1815–1865* (New York: The Modern Library, 1936), 276.

49   Alcott was a huge admirer of Graham. His own commitment to vegetarianism, made in 1835, presumably dates from when he heard Graham lecture in Boston, and in 1848, when Graham had already faded into obscurity, the two men exchanged letters and compliments. Alcott's letter is reprinted in Richard L. Herrnstadt, ed., *The Letters of A. Bronson Alcott* (Ames: Iowa State University Press, 1969), 134–5.

50   Louisa May Alcott, "Transcendental Wild Oats: a Chapter from an Unwritten Romance," *Independent*, 18 December 1873.

51   Edith Roelker Curtis, *A Season in Utopia: the Story of Brook Farm* (New York: Russell & Russell, 1961), 258.

52   Joel Myerson, "Rebecca Codman Butterfield's Reminiscences of Brook Farm," *New England Quarterly* 65, no. 4 (1992), 616–17.

53   Russell Hickman, "The Vegetarian and Octagon Settlement Companies," *Kansas Historical Quarterly* 2, no. 4 (1933), 377–85.

54   *Northampton Courier*, 12 August 1851, in Richard C. Garvey,
     "Dr. Sylvester Graham," in *The Northampton Book: Chapters from
     300 Years in the Life of a New England Town 1654–1954*, eds. Lawrence E.
     Wikander, et al. (Northampton, Massachusetts: The Tercentenary
     Committee, 1954), 107.

55   The profession had at first endorsed Graham's lectures, as noted
     in Lamar Riley Murphy, *Enter the Physician: the Transformation of
     Domestic Medicine, 1760–1860* (Tuscaloosa: University of Alabama
     Press, 1991), 117.

56   James C. Whorton, *Crusaders for Fitness: the History of American Health
     Reformers* (Princeton: Princeton University Press, 1982), 50.

57   "Rev. Sylvester Graham," *Harper's New Monthly Magazine*, October
     1851, 696; also printed in *Farmers' Cabinet*, 1 October 1851, 2.

58   William Andrus Alcott, *Forty Years in the Wilderness of Pills and Powders;
     or, the Cogitations and Confessions of an Aged Physician* (Boston: John P.
     Jewett and Company, 1859), 380–2.

59   William Andrus Alcott, *Vegetable Diet: as Sanctioned by Medical Men,
     and by Experience in All Ages* (New York: Fowlers and Wells, 1853), iii
     (1st ed. 1838).

60   Mary Wood-Allen, *What a Young Woman Ought to Know*, revised ed.
     (Philadelphia: Vir Publishing Company, 1913), 154.

61   Stephen Wilner Nissenbaum, *Sex, Diet, and Debility in Jacksonian
     America: Sylvester Graham and Health Reform* (Westport: Greenwood
     Press, 1980), 146.

62   Dio Lewis, *Chastity or, our Secret Sins* (New York: Arno Press, 1974),
     81, 229 (1st ed. 1874).

63   John Cowan, *Science of a New Life* (New York: J.S. Ogilvie &
     Company, 1869), 115–17, 122.

64   William Andrus Alcott, *The Physiology of Marriage* (Boston:
     Dinsmoor and Company, 1866), 227 (1st ed. 1855).

65   William Andrus Alcott, *Vegetable Diet Defended* (London:
     John Chapman, 1844), 11.

66   Larkin Baker Coles, *Philosophy of Health: Natural Principles of Health and
     Cure; or, Health and Cure without Drugs. Also, the Moral Bearings of
     Erroneous Appetites*, 26th ed. (Boston: Ticknor, Reed, and Fields, 1851),
     134, 172, 174.

67   Aaron M. Powell, ed., *The National Purity Congress: its Papers,
     Addresses, Portraits* (New York: Arno Press, 1976), 264 (1st ed. 1896).

68   From *How to Live* (1866), in Ellen Gould White, *Counsels on Diet and
     Foods* (Hagerstown, Maryland: Review and Herald Publishing
     Association, 1976), 121.

69 Ronald L. Numbers, *Prophetess of Health: a Study of Ellen G. White* (New York: Harper & Row, 1976), 33–5.

70 Frances E. Willard, *Glimpses of Fifty Years: the Autobiography of an American Woman* (New York: Source Book Press, 1970), 35 (1st ed. 1889).

71 James C. Whorton, *Crusaders for Fitness: the History of American Health Reformers* (Princeton: Princeton University Press, 1982), 120, 133.

72 Horace Greeley, *Recollections of a Busy Life* (New York: J.B. Ford & Co., 1869), 104. Reference courtesy of Professor William Rorabaugh.

73 William Andrus Alcott, *Vegetable Diet: as Sanctioned by Medical Men, and by Experience in All Ages* (New York: Fowlers and Wells, 1853), 69 (1st ed. 1838).

74 Robert Samuel Fletcher, *A History of Oberlin College from its Foundation through the Civil War*, vol. 1 (Oberlin: Oberlin College, 1943), 330.

75 Russell Thatcher Trall, "Biographical Sketch of Sylvester Graham," *Water-Cure Journal* 12 (1851), 110–11.

76 From *Special Testimonies*, series A, no. 9 (1896), in Ellen Gould White, *Counsels on Diet and Foods* (Hagerstown, Maryland: Review and Herald Publishing Association, 1976), 35.

77 William Andrus Alcott, *The Young Wife, or Duties of Woman in the Marriage Relation* (New York: Arno Press, 1972), 101 (1st ed. 1837). Paraphrased in his *Young Man's Guide*, 20th ed. (Boston: T.R. Marvin, 1849), 280 (1st ed. 1833): "by the word SOBRIETY in a young woman, I mean a great deal more than even a rigid abstinence from a love of drink, which I do not believe to exist to any considerable degree, in this country, even in the least refined parts of it. I mean a great deal *more* than this; I mean sobriety of conduct. The word *sober* and its derivatives mean *steadiness, seriousness, carefulness, scrupulous propriety of conduct*." But it is in *Teacher of Health* (1843) that Alcott shows his hand most clearly. Here we read that to "diffuse light on the structure, functions and relations of man" is a "*means* to an end," that to "make men more healthy and long-lived, without making them any wiser or better" would "do little if anything more than to make them the more gigantic, if not the more mischievous animals." Quoted in James C. Whorton, "'Christian Physiology': William Alcott's Prescription for the Millennium," *Bulletin of the History of Medicine* 49 (1975), 470.

FOUR

1 Jack S. Blocker, *Retreat from Reform: the Prohibition Movement in the United States 1890–1913* (Westport, Connecticut: Greenwood Press, 1976), 167.

2 Regina Markell Morantz, "Making Women Modern: Middle Class Women and Health Reform in 19th Century America," *Journal of Social History* 10, no. 4 (1977), 491; Stephen Wilner Nissenbaum, *Sex, Diet, and Debility in Jacksonian America: Sylvester Graham and Health Reform* (Westport: Greenwood Press, 1980), 143–4.

3 Examples in Douglas W. Carlson, "'Drinks he to his Own Undoing': Temperance Ideology in the Deep South," *Journal of the Early Republic* 18, no. 4 (1998), 659–91; and Joe Layton Coker, *Liquor in the Land of the Lost Cause: Southern White Evangelicals and the Prohibition Movement* (Lexington: University of Kentucky Press, 2007).

4 Scomp, Henry A., *King Alcohol in the Realm of King Cotton: or, a History of the Liquor Traffic and of the Temperance Movement in Georgia from 1733 to 1887* (Chicago: Blakely Printing Company, 1888), 517–19.

5 *Methodism and the Temperance Reformation* (Cincinnati: Walden and Stowe, 1882), 110.

6 Laurence Michalak, et al., "Religion and Alcohol in the U.S. National Alcohol Survey: How Important Is Religion for Abstention and Drinking?" *Drug and Alcohol Dependence* 87 (2007), 268–80.

7 Louisa Degenhardt, et al., "Epidemiological Patterns of Extra-Medical Drug Use in the United States: Evidence from the National Comorbidity Survey Replication, 2001–2003," *Drug and Alcohol Dependence* 90 (2007), 210–23. Reference courtesy of Dr. Edward Adlaf.

8 Jacqueline E. Darroch, David J. Landry, and Susheela Singh, "Changing Emphasis in Sexuality Education in U.S. Public Secondary Schools, 1988–99," *Family Planning Perspectives* 32, no. 5 (2000), 204–11.

9 Frances E. Willard, "Home Protection," in *"Do Everything" Reform: the Oratory of Frances E. Willard*, ed. Richard W. Leeman (New York: Greenwood Press, 1992), 135 (1st ed. 1879).

10 The subject of James H. Moorhead, *American Apocalypse: Yankee Protestants and the Civil War 1860–1869* (New Haven: Yale University Press, 1978).

11 William Sumner Jenkins, *Pro-Slavery Thought in the Old South* (Gloucester, Massachusetts: Peter Smith, 1960), 218–24 (1st ed. 1935); Timothy L. Smith, *Revivalism and Social Reform: American Protestantism on the Eve of the Civil War* (New York: Harper Torchbooks, 1965), 217–19. Observed first-hand in Agénor Étienne Gasparin, *The Uprising of a Great People. The United States in 1861. To which Is Added a Word of Peace on the Difference between England and the United States*, trans. Mary L. Booth (New York: Charles Scribner, 1862), 93.

12 Paul A. Carter, *The Spiritual Crisis of the Gilded Age* (DeKalb: Northern Illinois University Press, 1971), 4.

13 Louis Menand, *The Metaphysical Club: a Story of Ideas in America* (New York: Farrar, Straus and Giroux, 2002), 62, 68.

14 Paul F. Boller, *American Thought in Transition: the Impact of Evolutionary Naturalism, 1865–1900* (Chicago: Rand McNally & Company, 1973), 150.

15 William James, *The Principles of Psychology*, vol. 1 (Cambridge, Massachusetts: Harvard University Press, 1981), 224, 229 (1st ed. 1890).

16 Kathryn Teresa Long, *The Revival of 1857–58: Interpreting an American Religious Awakening* (New York: Oxford University Press, 1998), 96.

17 "Every man, from considerations of personal safety, from moral considerations, from consideration of his relations to his fellow-men in social life, and from considerations of patriotism or of state, ought to take sides in this matter, and let his position be known of all men," quoted in L. Penny, ed., *The National Temperance Orator* (New York: National Temperance Society and Publication House, 1874), 111.

18 Henry Ward Beecher, "Progress of Thought in the Church," *North American Review*, August 1882, 109.

19 Frances E. Willard, *Glimpses of Fifty Years: the Autobiography of an American Woman* (New York: Source Book Press, 1970), 532–4.

20 Anthony Trollope, *North America*, eds. Donald Smalley and Bradford Allen Booth (New York: Alfred A. Knopf, 1951), 235 (1st ed. 1862).

21 Josephine Butler, *Personal Reminiscences of a Great Crusade* (Westport: Hyperion Press, Inc., 1976), 129 (1st ed. 1911).

22 Examples in Van Wyck Brooks, *New England: Indian Summer 1865–1915* (New York: E.P. Dutton & Co. Inc., 1940), 140–8.

23 Thomas H. O'Connor, *Boston Catholics: a History of the Church and its People* (Boston: Northeastern University Press, 1998), 125.

24 Jack S. Blocker, *Give to the Winds thy Fears: the Women's Temperance Crusade, 1873–1874* (Westport, Connecticut: Greenwood Press, 1985), 25.

25 Frederic H. Wines and John Koren, *The Liquor Problem in its Legislative Aspects* (Boston: Houghton, Mifflin and Company, 1897), 181.

26 John Granville Woolley, "The Norwegian System," in *Civic Sermons* (Westerville, Ohio: American Issue Publishing Company, 1911), 57–76.

27 Woolley was referring, of course, to the Committee of Fifty, that New York-based group of academics and savants whose exhaustive fact-finding trips had led them to reject prohibition in favour of the Gothenburg system. See Frederic H. Wines and John Koren, *The Liquor Problem in its Legislative Aspects* (Boston: Houghton, Mifflin and Company, 1897); and Raymond Calkins, *Substitutes for the Saloon: an Investigation Made for the Committee of Fifty* (Boston: Houghton, Mifflin

and Company, 1901). Background in Harry Gene Levine, "The Committee of Fifty and the Origins of Alcohol Control," *Journal of Drug Issues* 13, no. 1 (1983), 95–116.

28   Thomas C. Oden, ed., *Phoebe Palmer: Selected Writings* (New York: Paulist Press, 1988), 57, 66.

29   Peter Gardella, *Innocent Ecstasy: How Christianity Gave America an Ethic of Sexual Pleasure* (New York: Oxford University Press, 1985), 88.

30   John Leland Peters, *Christian Perfection and American Methodism* (New York: Abingdon Press, 1956), 33–4.

31   Harold E. Raser, *Phoebe Palmer: Her Life and Thought* (Lewiston, New York: Edwin Mellen Press, 1987), 293.

32   Tobias Spicer, "Self-Deception," *Christian Advocate and Journal*, 2 August 1855.

33   Phoebe Worrall Palmer, *The Way of Holiness, with Notes by the Way; Being a Narrative of Religious Experience Resulting from a Determination to be a Bible Christian* (New York: Lane & Scott, 1851), 100–1 (1st ed. 1843).

34   Donald W. Dayton, *The Theological Roots of Pentecostalism* (Metuchen, New Jersey: Scarecrow Press, 1987), 65.

35   J. Lawrence Brasher, *The Sanctified South: John Lakin Brasher and the Holiness Movement* (Urbana: University of Illinois Press, 1994), 29.

36   Thomas C. Oden, ed., *Phoebe Palmer: Selected Writings* (New York: Paulist Press, 1988), 297.

37   Richard Carwardine, "Evangelicals, Politics, and the Coming of the American Civil War: a Transatlantic Perspective," in *Evangelicalism: Comparative Studies of Popular Protestantism in North America, the British Isles, and Beyond, 1700–1990*, eds. Mark A. Noll, David William Bebbington, and George A. Rawlyk (New York: Oxford University Press, 1994), 210.

38   Donald W. Dayton, *The Theological Roots of Pentecostalism* (Metuchen, New Jersey: Scarecrow Press, 1987), 76.

39   Melvin Easterday Dieter, *The Holiness Revival of the Nineteenth Century* (Metuchen, New Jersey: Scarecrow Press, 1996), 102–3.

40   Kathryn Teresa Long, *The Revival of 1857–58: Interpreting an American Religious Awakening* (New York: Oxford University Press, 1998), 124.

41   Carolyn De Swarte Gifford, ed., *Writing Out My Heart: Selections from the Journal of Frances E. Willard, 1855–96* (Urbana: University of Illinois Press, 1995), 200; Charles Edwin Jones, *Perfectionist Persuasion: the Holiness Movement and American Methodism, 1867–1936* (Metuchen, New Jersey: Scarecrow Press, 1974), 12. Palmer's influence on Willard is detailed in Patricia Bizzell, "Frances Willard, Phoebe Palmer, and the

Ethos of the Methodist Woman Preacher," *Rhetoric Society Quarterly* 36, no. 4 (2006), 377–98.

42 Robert Samuel Fletcher, *A History of Oberlin College from its Foundation through the Civil War*, vol. 1 (Oberlin: Oberlin College, 1943), 519.

43 Frances E. Willard, *Glimpses of Fifty Years: the Autobiography of an American Woman* (New York: Source Book Press, 1970), 10, 36 (1st ed. 1889).

44 Barbara Leslie Epstein, *The Politics of Domesticity: Women, Evangelism, and Temperance in Nineteenth-Century America* (Middletown, Connecticut: Wesleyan University Press, 1981), 143–7; Ian R. Tyrrell, *Woman's World/Woman's Empire: the Woman's Christian Temperance Union in International Perspective, 1880–1930* (Chapel Hill: University of North Carolina Press, 1991), 243–5; Carolyn De Swarte Gifford, "'The Woman's Cause Is Man's?' Frances Willard and the Social Gospel," in *Gender and the Social Gospel*, eds. Wendy J. Deichmann Edwards and Carolyn De Swarte Gifford (Urbana: University of Illinois Press, 2003), 21–34.

45 *A Theology for the Social Gospel*, ed. Donald W. Shriver (Louisville: Westminster John Knox Press, 1997), 5, 104 (1st ed. 1917). Background in Paul A. Carter, *The Decline and Revival of the Social Gospel: Social and Political Liberalism in American Protestant Churches, 1920–1940* (Ithaca: Cornell University Press, 1954).

46 Anna A. Gordon, *The Beautiful Life of Frances Willard* (Chicago: Woman's Temperance Publishing Association, 1898), 391.

47 Disputed by Alison M. Parker, *Purifying America: Women, Cultural Reform, and Pro-Censorship Activism, 1873–1933* (Urbana: University of Illinois Press, 1997), 27.

48 Ruth Bordin, *Women and Temperance: the Quest for Power and Liberty, 1873–1900* (Philadelphia: Temple University Press, 1981), 151–2.

49 Joseph R. Gusfield, "Social Structure and Moral Reform: a Study of the WCTU," in *Drinking and Intoxication: Selected Readings in Social Attitudes and Controls*, ed. Raymond G. McCarthy (Glencoe, Illinois: Free Press, 1959), 401–2.

50 Leonard J. Moore, *Citizen Klansmen: the Ku Klux Klan in Indiana, 1921–1928* (Chapel Hill: University of North Carolina Press, 1991), 79.

51 Ruth Bordin, *Women and Temperance: the Quest for Power and Liberty, 1873–1900* (Philadelphia: Temple University Press, 1981), 150–1; Carolyn De Swarte Gifford, ed., *Writing Out My Heart: Selections from the Journal of Frances E. Willard, 1855–96* (Urbana: University of Illinois Press, 1995), 409.

52   Michael McGerr, *A Fierce Discontent: the Rise and Fall of the Progressive Movement in America, 1870–1920* (New York: Free Press, 2003), 215.

53   Detailed in Ruth Bordin, *Women and Temperance: the Quest for Power and Liberty, 1873–1900* (Philadelphia: Temple University Press, 1981), 141–5.

54   Paul A. Carter, *The Decline and Revival of the Social Gospel: Social and Political Liberalism in American Protestant Churches, 1920–1940* (Ithaca: Cornell University Press, 1954), 16; William G. McLoughlin, *Revivals, Awakenings, and Reform: an Essay on Religion and Social Change in America, 1607–1977* (Chicago: University of Chicago Press, 1978), 172.

55   "Enthusiasm High as Sunday Opens Great Campaign," *Des Moines Register and Leader*, 2 November 1914.

56   Billy Sunday, "A Plain Talk to Men," in *Billy Sunday Speaks*, ed. Karen Gullen (New York: Chelsea House Publishers, 1970), 91.

57   "Heaven," in Lyle W. Dorsett, *Billy Sunday and the Redemption of Urban America* (Grand Rapids: William B. Eerdmans Publishing Company, 1991), 171–2.

58   The dislike was mutual. That same year, when Sunday came to Columbus, Washington Gladden pointedly refused to offer any assistance. Noted in William G. McLoughlin, *Revivals, Awakenings, and Reform: an Essay on Religion and Social Change in America, 1607–1977* (Chicago: University of Chicago Press, 1978), 173.

59   David O. Moberg, *The Great Reversal: Evangelism versus Social Concern* (Philadelphia: J.B. Lippincott, 1972), 33; William G. McLoughlin, *Revivals, Awakenings, and Reform: an Essay on Religion and Social Change in America, 1607–1977* (Chicago: University of Chicago Press, 1978), 148–9.

60   "Sunday Hits New Deal Set-Up," *New York Times*, 23 May 1935, 23.

61   Billy Sunday, *Sundayisms*, in *Billy Sunday Speaks*, ed. Karen Gullen (New York: Chelsea House Publishers, 1970), 202.

62   Billy Sunday, "A Plain Talk to Women," in *Billy Sunday Speaks*, ed. Karen Gullen (New York: Chelsea House Publishers, 1970), 109, 111.

63   William G. McLoughlin, *Revivals, Awakenings, and Reform: an Essay on Religion and Social Change in America, 1607–1977* (Chicago: University of Chicago Press, 1978), 149; Robert Francis Martin, *Hero of the Heartland: Billy Sunday and the Transformation of American Society, 1862–1935* (Bloomington: Indiana University Press, 2002), 116.

64   William Curtis Martin, *With God on our Side: the Rise of the Religious Right in America* (New York: Broadway Books, 1996), 9.

65 Robert Francis Martin, *Hero of the Heartland: Billy Sunday and the Transformation of American Society, 1862–1935* (Bloomington: Indiana University Press, 2002), 108.

66 Billy Sunday, "The Sawdust Trail," *Ladies' Home Journal*, February 1933, 63, 89.

67 Billy Sunday, "The Sawdust Trail," *Ladies' Home Journal*, September 1932, 102.

68 Billy Sunday, "The Sawdust Trail," *Ladies' Home Journal*, February 1933, 89.

69 Robert Francis Martin, *Hero of the Heartland: Billy Sunday and the Transformation of American Society, 1862–1935* (Bloomington: Indiana University Press, 2002), 92.

70 "Billy Sunday Dies; Evangelist Was 71," *New York Times*, 7 November 1935, 1.

71 "Get on the Water Wagon," in Lyle W. Dorsett, *Billy Sunday and the Redemption of Urban America* (Grand Rapids: William B. Eerdmans Publishing Company, 1991), 199.

72 John Granville Woolley, "Abstinence from Evil," in *Civic Sermons* (Westerville, Ohio: American Issue Publishing Company, 1911), 96.

73 "Bringing in the Millennium: Reflections on Blue Laws," *Churchman*, 13 November 1920, 12, quoted in Paul A. Carter, *The Decline and Revival of the Social Gospel: Social and Political Liberalism in American Protestant Churches, 1920–1940* (Ithaca: Cornell University Press, 1954), 42.

74 Jack S. Blocker, *Retreat from Reform: the Prohibition Movement in the United States 1890–1913* (Westport: Greenwood Press, 1976), 91, 190.

75 "The Negro Problem and the Liquor Problem," in *The Passing of the Saloon: an Authentic and Official Presentation of the Anti-Liquor Crusade in America*, ed. George M. Hammell (Cincinnati: Tower Press, 1908), 340–1.

76 Peter H. Odegard, *Pressure Politics: the Story of the Anti-Saloon League* (New York: Columbia University Press, 1928), 62.

77 Leonard J. Moore, *Citizen Klansmen: the Ku Klux Klan in Indiana, 1921–1928* (Chapel Hill: University of North Carolina Press, 1991), 34. Also discussed in Thomas R. Pegram, "Kluxing the Eighteenth Amendment: the Anti-Saloon League, the Ku Klux Klan, and the Fate of Prohibition in the 1920s," in *American Public Life and the Historical Imagination*, eds. Wendy Gamber, Michael Gossberg, and Hendrik Hartog (Notre Dame: University of Notre Dame Press, 2003), 240–61.

78   Thomas C. Oden, ed., *Phoebe Palmer: Selected Writings* (New York: Paulist Press, 1988), 297.

79   Timothy L. Smith, *Called unto Holiness: the Story of the Nazarenes* (Kansas City: Nazarene Publishing House, 1962), 19.

80   J. Lawrence Brasher, *The Sanctified South: John Lakin Brasher and the Holiness Movement* (Urbana: University of Illinois Press, 1994), 35.

81   Melvin Easterday Dieter, *The Holiness Revival of the Nineteenth Century* (Metuchen, New Jersey: Scarecrow Press, 1996), 103.

82   Charles Edwin Jones, *Perfectionist Persuasion: the Holiness Movement and American Methodism, 1867–1936* (Metuchen, New Jersey: Scarecrow Press, 1974), 91; Vinson Synan, *The Holiness-Pentecostal Tradition: Charismatic Movements in the Twentieth Century*, 2nd ed. (Grand Rapids, Michigan: William B. Eerdmans Publishing Company, 1997), 62.

83   Timothy L. Smith, *Called unto Holiness: the Story of the Nazarenes* (Kansas City: Nazarene Publishing House, 1962), 125.

84   Robert Mapes Anderson, *Vision of the Disinherited: the Making of American Pentecostalism* (New York: Oxford University Press, 1979), 114; Vinson Synan, *The Holiness-Pentecostal Tradition: Charismatic Movements in the Twentieth Century*, 2nd ed. (Grand Rapids, Michigan: William B. Eerdmans Publishing Company, 1997), 129.

85   "We are emphatically a prohibition Church . . . We offer no compromise to and seek no terms for a sin of this heinous quality. We are opposed to all forms of license of this iniquity, whether the same be 'high' or 'low,'" Hunter Dickinson Farish, *The Circuit Rider Dismounts: a Social History of Southern Methodism, 1865–1900* (New York: Da Capo Press, 1969), 316–24 (1st ed. 1938). The Southern Churches' gradual warming to temperance is the subject of the dissertation Joe L. Coker wrote while a graduate student at the Princeton Theological Seminary, forthcoming as *Liquor in the Land of the Lost Cause: Southern White Evangelicals and the Prohibition Movement* (University of Kentucky Press).

86   Robert Mapes Anderson, *Vision of the Disinherited: the Making of American Pentecostalism* (New York: Oxford University Press, 1979), 36, 157.

87   Reprinted in Charles Edwin Jones, *Perfectionist Persuasion: the Holiness Movement and American Methodism, 1867–1936* (Metuchen, New Jersey: Scarecrow Press, 1974), 106.

88   *Book of Minutes: a Compiled History of the Work of the General Assemblies of the Church of God* (Cleveland, Tennessee: Church of God Publishing House, 1922), 16–17, 28, 46–7, 64, 125–8, 278–9.

89   From the Pentecostal magazine *Glad Tidings* 1, no. 4 (1916), 10, quoted in Grant Wacker, *Heaven Below: Early Pentecostals and American Culture* (Cambridge, Massachusetts: Harvard University Press, 2001), 127.

90 Robert Mapes Anderson, *Vision of the Disinherited: the Making of American Pentecostalism* (New York: Oxford University Press, 1979), 159.

91 Peter H. Odegard, *Pressure Politics: the Story of the Anti-Saloon League* (New York: Columbia University Press, 1928), 18; Jack S. Blocker, *Retreat from Reform: the Prohibition Movement in the United States 1890–1913* (Westport: Greenwood Press, 1976), 10; K. Austin Kerr, *Organized for Prohibition: a New History of the Anti-Saloon League* (New Haven: Yale University Press, 1985), 75, 132.

92 Timothy L. Smith, *Called unto Holiness: the Story of the Nazarenes* (Kansas City: Nazarene Publishing House, 1962), 125.

93 Hunter Dickinson Farish, *The Circuit Rider Dismounts: a Social History of Southern Methodism, 1865–1900* (New York: Da Capo Press, 1969), 356–7 (1st ed. 1938).

94 Detailed in Rufus B. Spain, *At Ease in Zion: Social History of Southern Baptists, 1865–1900* (Nashville: Vanderbilt University Press, 1967), 68–126 (1st ed. 1961). A more nuanced picture emerges from Walter Bronlow Posey, *The Baptist Church in the Lower Mississippi Valley 1776–1845* (Lexington: University of Kentucky Press, 1957), 89–98, who notes that there was considerable dissent on the subject before the formation of the Southern Baptist Convention in 1845.

95 E. Luther Copeland, *The Southern Baptist Convention and the Judgment of History: the Taint of an Original Sin* (Lanham, Maryland: University Press of America, 2002), 17–20.

96 Robert Mapes Anderson, *Vision of the Disinherited: the Making of American Pentecostalism* (New York: Oxford University Press, 1979), 195–201.

97 Timothy L. Smith, *Called unto Holiness: the Story of the Nazarenes* (Kansas City: Nazarene Publishing House, 1962), 309, 318; Vinson Synan, *The Holiness-Pentecostal Tradition: Charismatic Movements in the Twentieth Century*, 2nd ed. (Grand Rapids, Michigan: William B. Eerdmans Publishing Company, 1997), 42–3.

98 Walter Bronlow Posey, *The Baptist Church in the Lower Mississippi Valley 1776–1845* (Lexington: University of Kentucky Press, 1957), 42–3.

99 D. Leigh Colvin, *Prohibition in the United States: a History of the Prohibition Party and the Prohibition Movement* (New York: George H. Doran Company, 1926), 267–8; Rufus B. Spain, *At Ease in Zion: Social History of Southern Baptists, 1865–1900* (Nashville: Vanderbilt University Press, 1967), 178–9.

100 Joe Layton Coker, "Liquor in the Land of the Lost Cause: Southern White Evangelicals and the Prohibition Movement, 1880–1915"

(PhD Thesis, Princeton Theological Seminary, 2005), 350–1.
Forthcoming from the University of Kentucky Press.

101 From the Richmond *Religious Herald*, 6 June 1889, quoted in Rufus B.
Spain, *At Ease in Zion: Social History of Southern Baptists, 1865–1900*
(Nashville: Vanderbilt University Press, 1967), 194.

102 David Stricklin, *A Genealogy of Dissent: Southern Baptist Protest in
the Twentieth Century* (Lexington: University Press of Kentucky,
1999), 25.

103 Jack S. Blocker, *Give to the Winds thy Fears: the Women's Temperance
Crusade, 1873–1874* (Westport, Connecticut: Greenwood Press,
1985), 25.

104 Ruth Bordin, *Women and Temperance: the Quest for Power and Liberty,
1873–1900* (Philadelphia: Temple University Press, 1981), 143.

105 John Barnard, *From Evangelicalism to Progressivism at Oberlin College,
1866–1917* (Columbus: Ohio State University Press, 1969), 99–100;
K. Austin Kerr, *Organized for Prohibition: a New History of the Anti-
Saloon League* (New Haven: Yale University Press, 1985), 76–80.

106 David M. Fahey, *Temperance and Racism: John Bull, Johnny Reb, and the
Good Templars* (Lexington: University Press of Kentucky, 1996), 33.

107 *U.S. Census of Religious Bodies*, Part II (1916), 123–7.

108 Perry R. Duis, *The Saloon: Public Drinking in Chicago and Boston
1880–1920* (Urbana: University of Illinois Press, 1983), 211, 288.
Catholic antipathy to temperance was by no means monolithic. That
movement enjoyed considerable support among individual Catholics –
the Catholic Total Abstinence Union, founded in Baltimore in
1872, comes first to mind – but this group was always in a minority.
Theological differences, the antipathy of most bishops, the ill-disguised
nativism of groups like the Woman's Christian Temperance Union and
the Anti-Saloon League – all stood in the way of making the American
temperance movement a truly ecumenical cause. Discussion in Patrick
W. Carey, *Catholics in America: a History* (Westport: Praeger, 2004), 74;
and John F. Quinn, *Father Mathew's Crusade: Temperance in Nineteenth-
Century Ireland and Irish America* (Amherst: University of
Massachusetts Press, 2002), 154–69, 179–91.

109 Don Kirschner, *City and Country: Rural Responses to Urbanization in the
1920s* (Westport: Greenwood Publishing Corporation, 1970), 77.

110 Morton Keller, *Regulating a New Society: Public Policy and Social Change
in America, 1900–1933* (Cambridge, Massachusetts: Harvard University
Press, 1994), 142.

111 Don Kirschner, *City and Country: Rural Responses to Urbanization in the
1920s* (Westport: Greenwood Publishing Corporation, 1970), 41, 131;

David E. Kyvig, *Repealing National Prohibition* (Chicago: University of Chicago Press, 1979), 25.

112 Profiled in Jack S. Blocker, "The Modernity of Prohibitionists: an Analysis of Leadership Structure and Background," in *Alcohol, Reform and Society*, ed. Jack S. Blocker (Westport: Greenwood Press, 1979), 149–70.

113 Paul Boyer, *Urban Masses and Moral Order in America, 1820–1920* (Cambridge, Massachusetts: Harvard University Press, 1978), 205; K. Austin Kerr, *Organized for Prohibition: a New History of the Anti-Saloon League* (New Haven: Yale University Press, 1985), 142, 145.

114 As told in Don Kirschner, *City and Country: Rural Responses to Urbanization in the 1920s* (Westport: Greenwood Publishing Corporation, 1970).

115 "The Sahara of the Bozart," in *Prejudices: Second Series* (New York: Alfred A. Knopf, 1921), 136; "The Husbandman," in *Prejudices: a Selection*, ed. James T. Farrell (New York: Vintage Books, 1958), 167; and, from the latter volume, "The Triumph of Idealism," 136.

116 Clarence Darrow, *The Story of My Life* (New York: Charles Scribner's Sons, 1932), 299, 324.

117 The subject of Michael A. Lerner, *Dry Manhattan: Prohibition in New York City* (Cambridge, Massachusetts: Harvard University Press, 2007).

118 Catherine Gilbert Murdock, *Domesticating Drink: Women, Men, and Alcohol in America, 1870–1940* (Baltimore: Johns Hopkins University Press, 1998), 92.

119 "'Beer Parades' in New York. Big Processions Led by the Mayor," *Times*, 16 May 1932, 10.

120 Sean Dennis Cashman, *Prohibition: the Lie of the Land* (New York: Free Press, 1981), 156.

121 "Prohibition Enforcement in U.S. Law Repealed in Rhode Island," *Times*, 2 March 1932, 11.

122 Philip J. Pauly, "Is Drinking Intoxicating? Scientists, Prohibition, and the Normalization of Drinking," *American Journal of Public Health* 84 (1994), 310.

123 Kenneth T. Jackson, *The Ku Klux Klan in the City 1915–1930* (New York: Oxford University Press, 1967), 31.

124 Detailed in Leonard J. Moore, *Citizen Klansmen: the Ku Klux Klan in Indiana, 1921–1928* (Chapel Hill: University of North Carolina Press, 1991).

125 Morton Keller, *Regulating a New Society: Public Policy and Social Change in America, 1900–1933* (Cambridge, Massachusetts: Harvard University Press, 1994), 147.

126 "Demon Exorcized," *Time*, 14 March 1938; Ronald Roizen, "The American Discovery of Alcoholism, 1931–1939" (PhD Thesis, University of California, 1991), 180–97.

127 William G. McLoughlin, "Revivalism," in *The Rise of Adventism: Religion and Society in Mid-Nineteenth Century America*, ed. Edwin S. Gaustad (New York: Harper & Row, 1974), 74.

128 Nicely observed in Ronald G. Walters, *American Reformers, 1815–1860* (New York: Hill and Wang, 1978), 26–8.

129 Matthew Avery Sutton, *Aimee Semple McPherson and the Resurrection of Christian America* (Cambridge, Massachusetts: Harvard University Press, 2007), from the illustrations.

130 Drawn from H. Richard Niebuhr, *The Kingdom of God in America* (New York: Harper Torchbooks, 1959) (1st ed. 1937); Timothy L. Smith, *Revivalism and Social Reform: American Protestantism on the Eve of the Civil War* (New York: Harper Torchbooks, 1965), 149–61, 235; Ernest R. Sandeen, *The Roots of Fundamentalism: British and American Millenarianism, 1800–1930* (Chicago: University of Chicago Press, 1970); "Millennialism," in *The Rise of Adventism: Religion and Society in Mid-Nineteenth-Century America*, ed. Edwin S. Gaustad (New York, Harper & Row, 1974), 104–18; William Curtis Martin, *With God on Our Side: the Rise of the Religious Right in America* (New York: Broadway Books, 1996); and Randal Herbert Balmer, *Blessed Assurance: a History of Evangelicalism in America* (Boston: Beacon Press, 1999), 47–51.

131 Randal Herbert Balmer, *Mine Eyes Have Seen the Glory: a Journey into Evangelical Subculture in America*, 3rd ed. (Oxford: Oxford University Press, 2000), 173 (1st ed. 1989).

132 The subject of Jerome Himmelstein's *To the Right: the Transformation of American Conservatism* (Berkeley: University of California Press, 1990).

133 J. Lawrence Brasher, *The Sanctified South: John Lakin Brasher and the Holiness Movement* (Urbana: University of Illinois Press, 1994), 38.

134 Timothy L. Smith, *Called unto Holiness: the Story of the Nazarenes* (Kansas City: Nazarene Publishing House, 1962), 151–2.

135 C. Vann Woodward, *Origins of the New South, 1877–1913* (Baton Rouge: Louisiana State University Press, 1966), 65–6 (1st ed. 1951).

136 Walter Rauschenbusch, *A Theology for the Social Gospel*, ed. Donald W. Shriver (Louisville: Westminster John Knox Press, 1997), 108 (1st ed. 1917).

FIVE

1   Joseph Rowntree and Arthur Sherwell, *The Temperance Problem and Social Reform*, 7th ed. (London: Hodder and Stoughton, 1900), 604.

2   Kathleen Fitzpatrick, *Lady Henry Somerset* (Boston: Little, Brown and Company, 1923), 250.

3   Patricia E. Prestwich, *Drink and the Politics of Social Reform: Antialcoholism in France since 1870* (Palo Alto: Society for the Promotion of Science and Scholarship, 1988), 186.

4   Brian Harrison, *Drink and the Victorians: the Temperance Question in England 1815–1872* (London: Faber and Faber, 1971), 183–4.

5   A.E. Dingle, *The Campaign for Prohibition in Victorian England: the United Kingdom Alliance, 1872–1895* (London: Croom Helm, 1980), 14.

6   Frederic William Farrar, *Talks on Temperance* (New York: National Temperance Society and Publication House, 1881), 31–2, 182.

7   As in Josephine Butler, *Personal Reminiscences of a Great Crusade* (Westport: Hyperion Press, Inc., 1976), 35 (1st ed. 1911); and *The New Abolitionists: a Narrative of a Year's Work* (London: Dyer Brothers, 1876).

8   Clearly a sore point for Mary Clement Leavitt (1830–1912), a member of the Woman's Christian Temperance Union since 1882: "in England there are persons doing earnest work for purity, who are unwilling to investigate even the effects of alcoholic drinks upon chastity," Aaron M. Powell, ed., *The National Purity Congress: its Papers, Addresses, Portraits* (New York: Arno Press, 1976), 166 (1st ed. 1896).

9   Alan Hunt, *Governing Morals: a Social History of Moral Regulation* (Cambridge: Cambridge University Press, 1999), 176.

10 Women's Library of the London Metropolitan University, Josephine Butler to Fanny Forsaith, 8 April 1894; Josephine Butler to Frances Willard, 29 November 1897; Ian R. Tyrrell, *Woman's World/Woman's Empire: the Woman's Christian Temperance Union in International Perspective, 1880–1930* (Chapel Hill: University of North Carolina Press, 1991), 202–3; Jane Jordan, *Josephine Butler* (London: John Murray, 2001), 278–81.

11 Margaret Barrow, "Teetotal Feminists: Temperance Leadership and the Campaign for Women's Suffrage," in *A Suffrage Reader: Charting Directions in British Suffrage History*, eds. Claire Eustance, Joan Ryan, and Laura Ugolini (London: Leicester University Press, 2000), 73–5.

12 Edward J. Bristow, *Vice and Vigilance: Purity Movements in Britain since 1700* (Dublin: Gill and Macmillan, 1977), 49.

13 Jean Stengers and Anne Van Neck, *Masturbation: the History of a Great
    Terror* (New York: Palgrave, 2001), 124.

14 Brian Harrison, *Drink and the Victorians: the Temperance Question in
    England 1815–1872* (London: Faber and Faber, 1971), 173–5; Margaret
    Barrow, "Teetotal Feminists: Temperance Leadership and the Campaign
    for Women's Suffrage," in *A Suffrage Reader: Charting Directions in
    British Suffrage History*, eds. Claire Eustance, Joan Ryan, and Laura
    Ugolini (London: Leicester University Press, 2000), 70.

15 "American Society for the Promotion of Temperance," *Christian
    Observer*, July 1826, 441; August 1827, 497; May 1828, 340;
    June 1829, 387.

16 *Permanent Temperance Documents of the American Temperance Society*,
    vol. 1 (Boston: Seth Bliss and Perkins, Marvin, and Co., 1835), report
    for 1835, 36–7.

17 Lilian Lewis Shiman, *Crusade against Drink in Victorian England*
    (New York: St. Martin's Press, 1988), 83.

18 Most notably in Brian Harrison, *Drink and the Victorians: the Temperance
    Question in England 1815–1872* (London: Faber and Faber, 1971); Lilian
    Lewis Shiman, *Crusade against Drink in Victorian England* (New York:
    St. Martin's Press, 1988); Ian R. Tyrrell, *Woman's World/Woman's
    Empire: the Woman's Christian Temperance Union in International
    Perspective, 1880–1930* (Chapel Hill: University of North Carolina
    Press, 1991); David M. Fahey, "The Politics of Drink in Britain: Anglo-
    American Perspectives," *Proceedings of the Ohio Academy of History* 2
    (2000); and John R. Greenaway, *Drink and British Politics Since 1830: a
    Study in Policy-Making* (Basingstoke: Palgrave Macmillan, 2003).

19 William Lloyd Garrison, who dabbled in the Graham regimen, was an
    interesting exception. Elizabeth Cady Stanton had fond memories of
    the "impromptu tea parties" Garrison and his wife liked to host in their
    Boston home in the early 1840s. In Elizabeth Cady Stanton, *Eighty
    Years and More: Reminiscences, 1815–1897* (Boston: Northeastern
    University Press, 1993), 128–9 (1st ed. 1898).

20 Charles Grandison Finney, *Views of Sanctification* (Toronto: Toronto
    Willard Tract Depository, 1877), 200 (1st ed. 1840). Or as Asa Mahan
    put it in an address to the American Physiological Society, "Total absti-
    nence from all intoxicating drinks" "was soon found to be not the real
    principle of temperance, but only a branch of it. The identical reasons
    which every one assigned as demanding total abstinence from intoxi-
    cating drinks as a beverage, demanded a similar abstinence from many
    other articles of drink, and of food also." In "Intimate Relation between

Moral, Mental and Physical Law," *Graham Journal of Health and Longevity*, 11 May 1839, 155.

21 Ellen Gould White, *Counsels on Diet and Foods* (Hagerstown, Maryland: Review and Herald Publishing Association, 1976), 421.

22 Edward Hitchcock, *Dyspepsy Forestalled & Resisted: or Lectures on Diet, Regimen, & Employment; Delivered to the Students of Amherst College; Spring Term, 1830* (Amherst, Massachusetts: J.S. & C. Adams and Co., 1830), 184.

23 William Andrus Alcott, *The Young Wife, or Duties of Woman in the Marriage Relation* (New York: Arno Press, 1972), 193 (1st ed. 1837). Expanded in *Tea and Coffee* (Boston: G.W. Light, 1839).

24 Quoted in Alan Macfarlane and Iris Macfarlane, *The Empire of Tea: the Remarkable History of the Plant that Took over the World* (Woodstock: Overlook Press, 2004), 89–90.

25 Friedrich Engels, *The Condition of the Working Class in England*, trans. W.O. Henderson and W.H. Chaloner (Oxford: Basil Blackwell, 1958), 85 (1st ed. 1844). Also documented in Eric Hopkins, *Childhood Transformed: Working-Class Children in Nineteenth-Century England* (Manchester: Manchester University Press, 1994), 109–10.

26 As in William Antliff, *A Book of Marvels: or, Incidents, Original and Selected, Illustrative of Primitive Methodism, Temperance, and Other Subjects* (London: G. Lamb, 1873), 386–7; and Holliday Bickerstaffe Kendall, *The Origin and History of the Primitive Methodist Church*, vol. 2 (London: Edwin Dalton, 1905), 129.

27 Roy Hattersley, *Blood and Fire: William and Catherine Booth and their Salvation Army* (London: Little, Brown and Co., 1999), 16–17, 39–43, 56, 59.

28 Holliday Bickerstaffe Kendall, *The Origin and History of the Primitive Methodist Church*, vol. 1 (London: Edwin Dalton, 1905), 471.

29 William R. Ward, *Religion and Society in England 1790–1850* (London: B.T. Batsford Ltd, 1972), 289.

30 William Antliff, *A Book of Marvels: or, Incidents, Original and Selected, Illustrative of Primitive Methodism, Temperance, and Other Subjects* (London: G. Lamb, 1873), 366.

31 Bernard Semmel, *The Methodist Revolution* (New York: Basic Books, 1973), 137–44; David Hempton, "Evangelicalism in English and Irish Society, 1780–1840," in *Evangelicalism: Comparative Studies of Popular Protestantism in North America, the British Isles, and Beyond, 1700–1990*, eds. Mark A. Noll, David William Bebbington, and George A. Rawlyk (New York: Oxford University Press, 1994), 158–9.

32   Harold E. Raser, *Phoebe Palmer: Her Life and Thought* (Lewiston, New York: Edwin Mellen Press, 1987), 138; Lilian Lewis Shiman, *Crusade against Drink in Victorian England* (New York: St. Martin's Press, 1988), 53–6.

33   Background in Richard Carwardine, *Transatlantic Revivalism: Popular Evangelicalism in Britain and America, 1790–1865* (Westport: Greenwood Press, 1978).

34   Norman H. Murdoch, *Origins of the Salvation Army* (Knoxville: University of Tennessee Press, 1994), 8, 16.

35   Harold E. Raser, *Phoebe Palmer: Her Life and Thought* (Lewiston, New York: Edwin Mellen Press, 1987), 138–40.

36   Harriet Beecher Stowe, *Sunny Memories of Foreign Lands*, vol. 1 (Boston: Phillips, Sampson, and Company, 1854), 169, 172; "Mrs. Stowe on Temperance and the New President," *Times*, 2 September 1856, 7; Frank J. Klingberg, "Harriet Beecher Stowe and Social Reform in England," *American Historical Review* 43, no. 3 (1938), 542–52.

37   The subject of Ian C. Bradley, *The Call to Seriousness: the Evangelical Impact on the Victorians* (London: Jonathan Cape, 1976).

38   William R. Ward, *The Protestant Evangelical Awakening* (Cambridge: Cambridge University Press, 1992), 354.

39   Justin Edwards, *The Well-Conducted Farm: a Narrative of Facts* (New York: American Tract Society, 1835?), 3 (1st ed. 1826).

40   Edward P. Thompson, *The Making of the English Working Class* (London: Victor Gollancz, 1964), 11.

41   Brian Harrison, "Sunday Trading Riots of 1855," *Historical Journal* 8, no. 2 (1965), 219–45; Alan Hunt, *Governing Morals: a Social History of Moral Regulation* (Cambridge: Cambridge University Press, 1999), 72.

42   Ford K. Brown, *Fathers of the Victorians: the Age of Wilberforce* (Cambridge: Cambridge University Press, 1961), 18.

43   Sydney Smith, *Edinburgh Review* 1809, 337.

44   Brilliantly argued in Nathan O. Hatch, *The Democratization of American Christianity* (New Haven: Yale University Press, 1989).

45   Brian Harrison, *Drink and the Victorians: the Temperance Question in England 1815–1872* (London: Faber and Faber, 1971), 26–9. Quote from William T. Stead, *The Americanization of the World: the Trend of the Twentieth Century* (New York: Horace Markley, 1902), 263.

46   Brian Harrison, *Drink and the Victorians: the Temperance Question in England 1815–1872* (London: Faber and Faber, 1971), 101–2.

47   John Redwood, *Reason, Ridicule and Religion: the Age of Enlightenment in England, 1660–1750* (London: Thames and Hudson, 1976).

48 Ian C. Bradley, *The Call to Seriousness: the Evangelical Impact on the Victorians* (London: Jonathan Cape, 1976), 14; George Eliot, "Evangelical Teaching: Dr. Cumming," in *Essays of George Eliot*, ed. Thomas Pinney (London: Routledge and Kegan Paul, 1963), 158–89 (1st ed. 1855).

49 "Total Abstinence and Moderation," *Punch*, November 1851, 92–3.

50 "The Tea-Total Movement," *Punch*, April 1853, 62. Further anecdotes in Lilian Lewis Shiman, "John B. Gough: Trans-Atlantic Temperance Orator," *Social History of Alcohol and Drugs* 15, no. 1–4 (2001), 20–9.

51 "Temperance out of Temper," *Punch*, May 1854, 199.

52 "Jokes. From 'Punch,' of Yesterday," *News of the World*, 20 January 1856, 1.

53 "American Politics. By an Englishman Abroad," *Blackwood's Edinburgh Magazine*, July 1852, 45.

54 *Manchester Guardian*, 21 January 1856, 3; Thomas H. Barker, "The Maine Liquor Law," *Manchester Guardian*, 25 January 1856, 4.

55 "The Englishman in America. Second Notice," *News of the World*, 2 March 1856, 6.

56 *Times*, 28 December 1853, 6; "Temperance by Act of Parliament Impossible," 13 October 1856, 7.

57 "The Maine Law Movement," *Times*, 26 November 1856, 10.

58 *Times*, 18 October 1856, 6–7.

59 "Failure of the Maine Law in America," *Times*, 23 May 1857, 6.

60 William Andrus Alcott, *The Young Husband, or Duties of Man in the Marriage Relation* (New York: Arno Press, 1972), 108, 318–20.

61 Alexander Slidell Mackenzie, *The American in England*, vol. 1 (London: Richard Bentley, 1836), 264–5. Mackenzie would later oversee the trial and execution of the mutineers of the USS *Somers*, as graciously pointed out to me by Professor William Rorabaugh.

62 Joseph Ballard, *England in 1815 as Seen by a Young Boston Merchant* (Boston: Houghton Mifflin Company, 1913), 30–1.

63 "Popular Literature – Tracts," *Blackwood's Edinburgh Magazine*, May 1859, 526.

64 *Bailie*, 16 October 1878, quoted by Lilian Lewis Shiman, "John B. Gough: Trans-Atlantic Temperance Orator," *Social History of Alcohol and Drugs* 15, no. 3–4 (2001), 21–2.

65 John Bartholomew Gough, *Autobiography and Personal Recollections* (Toronto: A.H. Hovey, 1870), 281.

66 Mathew Arnold, *Culture and Anarchy*, ed. Stefan Collini (Cambridge: Cambridge University Press, 1993), 193, 199 (1st ed. 1867–68).

67 Isaiah Berlin, "John Stuart Mill and the Ends of Life," in *J.S. Mill's On Liberty in Focus*, eds. John Grey and G.W. Smith (London: Routledge, 1991), 131–61.

68 John Stuart Mill, *On Liberty*, eds. John Grey and G.W. Smith (London: Routledge, 1991), 30, 33, 65–8.

69 Lilian Lewis Shiman, *Crusade against Drink in Victorian England* (New York: St. Martin's Press, 1988), 81.

70 "Mr Mill upon the Permissive Bill," *Times*, 10 November 1868, 4.

71 William J. Rorabaugh, *The Alcoholic Republic: an American Tradition* (New York: Oxford University Press, 1979), 201.

72 Timothy Shay Arthur, *Ten Nights in a Bar-Room, and What I Saw There*, ed. Donald A. Koch (Cambridge, Massachusetts: Belknap Press, 1964), 238 (1st ed. 1854).

73 Kathleen Fitzpatrick, *Lady Henry Somerset* (Boston: Little, Brown, and Company, 1923), 71, 129–31; Carolyn De Swarte Gifford, ed., *Writing Out My Heart: Selections from the Journal of Frances E. Willard, 1855–96* (Urbana: University of Illinois Press, 1995), 411.

74 Lady Isabella's testimony was whitewashed by the Woman's Christian Temperance Union as "a most powerful prohibition argument which had wide influence," "Our World's Leader," *Union Signal*, 29 March 1900, 200.

75 "Obituary. Lady Henry Somerset," *Times*, 14 March 1921, 16.

76 Carolyn De Swarte Gifford, ed., *Writing Out My Heart: Selections from the Journal of Frances E. Willard, 1855–96* (Urbana: University of Illinois Press, 1995), 377. Background in Barbara Leslie Epstein, *The Politics of Domesticity: Women, Evangelism, and Temperance in Nineteenth-Century America* (Middletown, Connecticut: Wesleyan University Press, 1981), 143–7; Ian R. Tyrrell, *Woman's World/Woman's Empire: the Woman's Christian Temperance Union in International Perspective, 1880–1930* (Chapel Hill: University of North Carolina Press, 1991), 243–5; and Carolyn De Swarte Gifford, "'The Woman's Cause Is Man's?' Frances Willard and the Social Gospel," in *Gender and the Social Gospel*, eds. Wendy J. Deichmann Edwards and Carolyn De Swarte Gifford (Urbana: University of Illinois Press, 2003), 21–34.

77 A quality much admired by Sidney Webb: "Unlike so many temperance workers, Miss Willard threw herself with equal zeal into the abolition of the sweating system or the rehousing of the poor of our great cities, for she saw that in the absence of decent homes and living wages, no amount of preaching or prohibition would put down drunkenness," Anna A. Gordon, *The Beautiful Life of Frances Willard* (Chicago: Woman's Temperance Publishing Association, 1898), 408–9.

78 Ian R. Tyrrell, *Woman's World/Woman's Empire: the Woman's Christian Temperance Union in International Perspective, 1880–1930* (Chapel Hill: University of North Carolina Press, 1991), 264.

79 Paul A. Carter, *The Decline and Revival of the Social Gospel: Social and Political Liberalism in American Protestant Churches, 1920–1940* (Ithaca: Cornell University Press, 1954), 32, 228; James Timberlake, *Prohibition and the Progressive Movement 1900–1920* (Cambridge, Massachusetts: Harvard University Press, 1963), 26–7.

80 From *Tools and Men* (1893), quoted in Vinson Synan, *The Holiness-Pentecostal Tradition: Charismatic Movements in the Twentieth Century*, 2nd ed. (Grand Rapids, Michigan: William B. Eerdmans Publishing Company, 1997), 47.

81 Edward Reynolds Pease, *Liquor Licensing at Home and Abroad*, 2nd ed., Fabian Tract 85 (London: Fabian Society, 1899), 5.

82 Robin Room, "Alcohol and Harm Reduction, Then and Now," *Critical Public Health* 14, no. 4 (2004), 334.

83 Frederic H. Wines and John Koren, *The Liquor Problem in its Legislative Aspects* (Boston: Houghton, Mifflin and Company, 1897); Raymond Calkins, *Substitutes for the Saloon: an Investigation Made for the Committee of Fifty* (Boston: Houghton, Mifflin and Company, 1901). The subject of Harry Gene Levine, "The Committee of Fifty and the Origins of Alcohol Control," *Journal of Drug Issues* 13, no. 1 (1983), 95–116.

84 A.M. McBriar, *Fabian Socialism and English Politics 1884–1918* (Cambridge: Cambridge University Press, 1962), 223, 336.

85 David M. Fahey, "Temperance and the Liberal Party – Lord Peel's Report, 1899," *Journal of British Studies* 10, no. 2 (1971), 132–59; A.E. Dingle, *The Campaign for Prohibition in Victorian England: the United Kingdom Alliance, 1872–1895* (London: Croom Helm, 1980), 174–5.

86 Detailed in John R. Greenaway, *Drink and British Politics Since 1830: a Study in Policy-Making* (Basingstoke: Palgrave Macmillan, 2003).

87 Brian Harrison, *Drink and the Victorians: the Temperance Question in England 1815–1872* (London: Faber and Faber, 1971), 32, 287.

88 "Brewing Ban in America. Food and Fuel before Beer," *Daily News*, 9 October 1918, 5.

89 "Drink Reform Plans. Duties of Proposed Commissions. Mr. Lloyd George and the Churches," *Times*, 27 November 1921, 16.

90 Lawrence Spinelli, *Dry Diplomacy: the United States, Great Britain, and Prohibition* (Wilmington, Delaware: Scholarly Resources, Inc., 1989), xiv.

91 "Drink Reform Plans. Duties of Proposed Commissions. Mr. Lloyd George and the Churches," *Times*, 27 November 1921, 16.

92   Norman H. Clark, *Deliver us from Evil: an Interpretation of American
      Prohibition* (New York: W.W. Norton & Company, Inc., 1976), 138;
      Craig Heron, *Booze: a Distilled History* (Toronto: Between the Lines,
      2003), 179–83, 269–70.

93   Nick Heather and Ian Robertson, *Controlled Drinking* (London:
      Methuen, 1981), 214; Philip M. Boffey, "Controlled Drinking Gains as
      a Treatment in Europe," *New York Times*, 22 November 1983, C7.

94   Betsy Thom, "Drug Services in London" (paper presented at the
      Thirty-Third Annual Alcohol Epidemiology Symposium of the Kettil
      Bruun Society, Budapest, 5 June 2007).

95   Charles Edward Terry and Mildred Pellens, *The Opium Problem*
      (Montclair, New Jersey: Patterson Smith, 1970), 917 (1st ed. 1928);
      Virginia Berridge, "The 'British System' and its History: Myth and
      Reality," in *Heroin Addiction and Drug Policy: the British System*,
      eds. John Strang and Michael Gossop (London: Routledge, 2005).

96   Griffith Edwards, *Matters of Substance: Drugs – and Why Everyone's a
      User* (London: Allen Lane, 2004),121.

97   Melissa Coulthard, et al., *Tobacco, Alcohol and Drug Use and Mental
      Health* (Newport, South Wales: Office for National Statistics, 2002),
      23; Bridget F. Grant, et al., "The 12–Month Prevalence and Trends in
      DSM–IV Alcohol Abuse and Dependence: United States, 1991–1992
      and 2001–2002," *Drug and Alcohol Dependence* 74, no. 3 (2004),
      223–34; Peter Anderson and Ben Baumberg, *Alcohol in Europe: a Public
      Health Perspective* (London: Institute of Alcohol Studies, 2006), 81;
      Laurence Michalak, Karen Trocki, and Jason Bond, "Religion and
      Alcohol in the U.S. National Alcohol Survey: How Important Is
      Religion for Abstention and Drinking?" *Drug and Alcohol Dependence*
      87 (2007), 270.

98   For an especially gloomy assessment, see Martin Plant and Moira Plant,
      Binge Britain: Alcohol and the National Response (Oxford: Oxford
      University Press, 2006).

99   National Institute on Alcohol Abuse and Alcoholism,
      "Patient-Treatment Matching," *Alcohol Alert* 36 (1997) (online at
      http://pubs.niaaa.nih.gov/publications/aa36.htm); William R. Miller
      and Richard Longabaugh, "Summary and Conclusions," in *Treatment
      Matching in Alcoholism*, eds. Thomas F. Babor and Frances K. Del Boca
      (Cambridge: Cambridge University Press, 2002), 207–21. References
      courtesy of Dr. Kathryn Graham of the Centre for Addiction and
      Mental Health.

EPILOGUE

1   John Granville Woolley, "The Norwegian System," in *Civic Sermons* (Westerville, Ohio: American Issue Publishing Company, 1911), 58.

2   Mark Edward Lender, *Dictionary of American Temperance Biography* (Westport: Greenwood Press, 1984).

3   James C. Whorton, *Crusaders for Fitness: the History of American Health Reformers* (Princeton: Princeton University Press, 1982), 347–8; Harvey A. Levenstein, *Paradox of Plenty: a Social History of Eating in Modern America*, revised ed. (Berkeley: University of California Press, 2003), 262–3.

4   Nathaniel Altman, "Can a Non-Meat Diet Enhance your Love Life?" *Vegetarian Life*, July–August 1979, 1–3.

5   Arthur J. Barsky, *Worried Sick: Our Troubled Quest for Wellness* (Boston: Little, Brown and Company, 1988), chapter 7. It is also revealing that a survey conducted in the United States, Japan, Flemish Belgium, and France showed Americans to be the most obsessed with healthy eating habits – and the least likely to associate food with pleasure. From Paul Rozin, et al., "Attitudes to Food and the Role of Food in Life in the U.S.A., Japan, Flemish Belgium and France: Possible Implications for the Diet-Health Debate," *Appetite* 33 (1999), 163–80.

6   James C. Whorton, *Crusaders for Fitness: the History of American Health Reformers* (Princeton: Princeton University Press, 1982), 335–6, 343; Warren Belasco, "Food, Morality, and Social Reform," in *Morality and Health*, eds. Allan M. Brandt and Paul Rozin (New York: Routledge, 1997), 192–5.

7   "Only Step One, where we made the 100 per cent admission we were powerless over alcohol, can be practiced with absolute perfection. The remaining eleven steps state perfect ideals." From Step Six, in *Twelve Steps and Twelve Traditions* (New York: Alcoholics Anonymous World Services, Inc., 1972), 69 (1st ed. 1953).

8   Francis Hartigan, *Bill W.: a Biography of Alcoholics Anonymous Cofounder Bill Wilson* (New York: St. Martin's Press, 2000), 1, 2, 9, 208; Susan Cheever, *My Name Is Bill: Bill Wilson: His Life and the Creation of Alcoholics Anonymous* (New York: Simon & Schuster, 2004), 216–17.

9   Step Four, in *Twelve Steps and Twelve Traditions* (New York: Alcoholics Anonymous World Services, Inc., 1972), 52 (1st ed. 1953); *Alcoholics Anonymous: the Story of how Many Thousands of Men and Women Have Recovered from Alcoholism*, 4th ed. (New York: Alcoholics Anonymous World Services, Inc., 2001), 68–71 (1st ed. 1939).

10 Mariana Valverde, *Diseases of the Will: Alcohol and the Dilemmas of Freedom* (Cambridge: Cambridge University Press, 1998), 123–4.

11 Ernest Kurtz, *Not-God: a History of Alcoholics Anonymous* (Center City, Minnesota: Hazelden, 1991), 123, 208.

12 *Alcoholics Anonymous: the Story of how Many Thousands of Men and Women Have Recovered from Alcoholism*, 4th ed. (New York: Alcoholics Anonymous World Services, Inc., 2001), 32 (1st ed. 1939).

13 Allan M. Brandt, "From Nicotine to Nicotrel: Addiction, Cigarettes, and American Culture," in *Altering American Consciousness: the History of Alcohol and Drug Use in the United States, 1800–2000*, eds. Sarah W. Tracy and Caroline Jean Acker (Amherst, Massachusetts: University of Massachusetts Press, 2004), 385–6. The "Y," it is only fair to add, has shown an uncanny talent for reinventing itself, as noted by Mayer N. Zald and Patricia Denton, "From Evangelism to General Services: the Transformation of the YMCA," in *Social Movements in an Organizational Society: Collected Essays*, eds. John D. McCarthy and Mayer N. Zald (New Brunswick: Transaction Books, 1987), 143–160.

14 The void left by the evangelical churches was not filled by their main-line counterparts. They had never been fully committed to temperance, and by the 1940s, they were no longer sure that drunkenness was even a sin. Or so one might infer from their endorsement of the disease concept of alcoholism. The General Assembly of the Northern Presbyterian Church was the first to endorse the concept (in 1946), followed by the Federal Council of Churches (1947), the National Council of Churches of Christ (1958), the General Assembly of the Protestant Episcopal Church (1958), and the General Board of the National Council of Churches (1958). Background in Jack S. Blocker, *American Temperance Movements: Cycles of Reform* (Boston: Twayne Publishers, 1989), 149; and Sarah W. Tracy, *Alcoholism in America: from Reconstruction to Prohibition* (Baltimore: Johns Hopkins University Press, 2005), 283–4.

15 Vinson Synan, *The Holiness-Pentecostal Tradition: Charismatic Movements in the Twentieth Century*, 2nd ed. (Grand Rapids, Michigan: William B. Eerdmans Publishing Company, 1997), 205, 221.

16 Ralph H. Orth and Alfred R. Ferguson, eds., *The Journals and Miscellaneous Notebooks of Ralph Waldo Emerson*, vol. 9 (Cambridge, Massachusetts: Belknap Press, 1971), 392.

17 Details in Ronald L. Numbers, *Prophetess of Health: a Study of Ellen G. White* (New York: Harper & Row, 1976), 171, 186–91; James C. Whorton, *Crusaders for Fitness: the History of American Health Reformers* (Princeton: Princeton University Press, 1982), 201–5.

18   Mark Leibovich, "Fire in the Belly. Arkansas Gov. Mike Huckabee, Dedicated to Fighting Obesity, Could Have a Meaty Opportunity Ahead," *Washington Post*, 17 January 2006, C01.

19   R. Marie Griffith, *Born Again Bodies: Flesh and Spirit in American Christianity* (Berkeley: University of California Press, 2004), 177, 214, 234.

20   Kenneth F. Ferraro, "Firm Believers? Religion, Body Weight, and Well-Being," *Review of Religious Research* 39, no. 3 (1998), 238; Daniel Sack, *Whitebread Protestants: Food and Religion in American Culture* (New York: St. Martin's Press, 2000).

21   Dannah Gresh, *And the Bride Wore White: Seven Secrets to Sexual Purity* (Chicago: Moody Press, 1999), 136–7.

22   Cheryl Wetzstein, "More Young Men Heeding Messages on Abstinence. Educators Heartened by Finding in Teen Sex Surveys," *Washington Times*, 8 August 2000, A2.

23   The subject of Peter Gardella, *Innocent Ecstasy: How Christianity Gave America an Ethic of Sexual Pleasure* (New York: Oxford University Press, 1985). Also discussed in Linda Kintz, *Between Jesus and the Market: the Emotions that Matter in Right-Wing America* (Durham, North Carolina: Duke University Press, 1997), 65–8.

24   Brian Alexander, "One Preacher's Message: Have Hotter Sex," MSNBC.com, 14 September 2006.

25   Cindy Crosby, "The Best Sex (Survey) Ever!" *Marriage Partnership*, March 2004. The respective percentages were 23, 26, and 83.

26   Tim F. LaHaye and Beverly LaHaye, *Practical Answers to Common Questions about Sex in Marriage* (Grand Rapids: Zondervan Publishing House, 1984), 79–80.

27   *Pornography: Men Possessing Women* (New York: G.P. Putnam's Sons, 1981), 224 (1st ed. 1979); *Intercourse* (New York: Free Press, 1987), 16.

28   Catharine A. MacKinnon, "The Roar on the Other Side," in *In Harm's Way: the Pornography Civil Rights Hearings*, eds. Catharine A. MacKinnon and Andrea Dworkin (Cambridge, Massachusetts: Harvard University Press, 1997), 10–11.

INDEX

abstinence (*see also* chastity;
New Virginity; teetotalism;
vegetarianism): all-encompassing
nature of the original doctrine,
25-26, 93; attractions of, 2-6;
compatibility with individualism,
3, 73, 78-79, 90-91, 160; con-
traction of taboos over time, xii,
91-92; correlation with evangelical Protestantism, xii; definition,
xi; early relationship to social
reform movements, 25-26, 165;
emergence as an illiberal ideal,
xiii, 1-2, 97, 106-22, 127-29;
extension to all problematic
behaviours, 48-52, 72, 90; from
Coca-Cola, 119; from coffee and
tea, 26, 71, 79, 114, 135-36, 163;
from conjugal excess, 81-82, 89,
119-20; from masturbation,
79-83, 88-89, 132; from meat
(*see* vegetarianism); from tobacco,
26, 71, 79, 119, 120, 162; logical
problems with the concept,
7-8; meaning in Alcoholics
Anonymous, 162-63; origins in
America, 9-36; particular appeal
to radicals, 2; popularity among
abolitionists, xii, 25, 65, 85, 89,
104; popularity among African-
Americans, 2, 6; popularity
among nineteenth-century

feminists, xii, xiii, 89; quarrel
with moderation, 8, 37-70; rates
of abstention in contemporary
America, xi
abstinence-only sex education, x,
xi, 97
Alcoholics Anonymous, 2, 6, 8, 158,
161-62
Alcott, Abby May, 85-86
Alcott, Amos Bronson, 73, 85-86
Alcott, Louisa May, 9, 73, 85-86
Alcott, William Andrus, 2, 57-58,
73, 78, 84, 87-88, 90-91, 93,
135, 142
America (*see also* American
Midwest; American South):
excesses in alcohol, food, and
tobacco, 30-34; per capita consumption of hard liquor, 31, 53
American Bible Society, 41
American Home Missionary
Society, 41
American Midwest, 67, 96, 103,
123-24, 127
American Society for the Promotion
of Temperance. *See* American
Temperance Society
American South: initial resistance
to the temperance movement,
67-68, 96; later embrace of abstinence, 97, 126-29; pietism of, 68;
political resurgence of, 123

A NOTE ABOUT THE TYPE

The text of *All or Nothing* has been set in Goudy (often referred to as Goudy Oldstyle), a face designed in 1915 for the American Type Founders by the prolific typographer Frederic W. Goudy. Used with equal success in both text and display sizes, Goudy remains one of the most popular typefaces ever produced. It is best recognized by the diamond-shaped dots on punctuation; the upturned "ear" of the g; and the elegant base curve of the caps E and L.